Algerian Diary

....

"This book offers a rare glimpse at a legendary journalist at work during the earliest days of TV. As if to make up for the lack of appreciation during Kearns's life, Davis offers a loving tribute to a fearless reporter."

—*Kirkus Reviews*

"Frank Kearns was a fearless foreign correspondent—but was he also a spy? Gerald Davis has researched his subject exhaustively and provides here a richly detailed portrait of a brilliant, complex man. But he also lets Kearns speak for himself in his Algerian diary, a searing, compelling example of war reportage at its best."

—Hugh Wilford, author of *The Mighty Wurlitzer* and *America's Great Game*

"In an era of journalism now where the model is more attuned to balderdash based on weak or invalid claims, Kearns's work stands as an honorable model of what good reporting is."

—Terry Wimmer, Pulitzer Prize-winning reporter and editor and professor of journalism at the University of Arizona

"A fine book about a fascinating individual doing cutting-edge work in the early years of television war reporting."

—Tom Herman, former field producer for CNN and correspondent for NPR

"Even though Kearns was technically a journalist, my father Miles Copeland Jr. and the rest of his CIA cronies were in awe of him, not just because of his derring-do, but because he looked the part."

—Stewart Copeland, son of Miles Copeland Jr., spent his youth in Egypt and Lebanon while his father was a CIA skulduggerist in the Levant

"Here is an exciting, important book on Cold War journalism, focusing on reporter Frank Kearns and CBS News—the drama and danger are all there, but so too is the crucial ethical question, raised and described so well by Jerry Davis: should a reporter have cooperated with the US government in the global struggle against communism?"

—Marvin Kalb, senior adviser of the Pulitzer Center, former CBS reporter, and author of *Imperial Gamble: Putin, Ukraine and the New Cold War*

ALGERIAN DIARY

ALGERIAN DIARY

FRANK KEARNS & THE "IMPOSSIBLE ASSIGNMENT" FOR CBS NEWS

Gerald Davis

WEST VIRGINIA UNIVERSITY PRESS
MORGANTOWN 2016

ISBN:

paper 978-1-933202-62-4
epub   978-1-940425-76-4
pdf   978-1-940425-75-7

Cataloging-in-Publication Data is available from the Library of Congress.

Book and cover design by Than Saffel
Cover image: Frank Kearns often served as his own audio man in the field. (Photo by
Yousef Masraff. Courtesy of Michael Kearns.)

Editor's note: Only English-language resources were used in this edition.

For my beloved Judy

For the strength of our economy, for the richness of our culture, and for the defense of free men everywhere, our national interests are deeply involved in the lives and fortunes of our neighbors around the world. It is therefore essential that our citizens be kept alert to the affairs of people outside our borders so that they may continue to grow in understanding and in appreciation of the interdependence of mankind. . . . This is the basic assignment of our reporters serving overseas, and I believe they are fulfilling it in the finest tradition of American journalism.

—*President Dwight D. Eisenhower*[1]

Contents

	A Note to the Reader	xiii
	Foreword by Tom Fenton	xv
	Preface	xxi
1	A Small Office in Cairo	1
2	La Guerre d'Algérie	7
3	A Reporter's Journey to Algeria	14
4	"The Unrealistic or Impossible Assignment"	24
5	Algerian Diary	31
6	"Evidence of Considerable Interest"	87
	Epilogue	101
	Acknowledgments	113
	Appendix: Sound on Film Scripts from Algeria	117
	Chronology	163
	Notes	167
	Glossary	181
	Bibliography	183
	Index	189
	About the Authors	199

A Note to the Reader

··

Rather than quote expansively from the diary that Frank Kearns kept while embedded with the Algerian rebels, I elected instead to present his typewritten notes in their entirety as the centerpiece of this book. I draw from it where necessary to provide context. After struggling to transcribe his six-week experience, the record of which was stored in a shoebox full of loosely organized, small, sweat-stained spiral notebooks that Kearns kept while embedded with the Algerian rebels, further digging uncovered a fully realized manuscript that he had assembled after leaving Algeria for his television and radio editors back in New York. The typed pages—on thin, onionskin paper— were in an unmarked box that also contained the location photographs used in this book, most taken by his cameraman, Archak Yousef "Joe" Masraff. When researching and assembling this story, I made a conscious decision to stay faithful in presenting Kearns's text and left in the punctuation, spelling, and syntax exactly as he wrote it. After all, it is his story. By today's standards, some of his words may seem misplaced, misguided, and mistaken. But it's what he thought and what he wrote down while under six weeks of duress, living among the freedom fighters in the eastern mountains of Algeria in the summer of 1957. This period style may seem awkward to readers nearly sixty years removed from the conflict that Kearns was covering, but it's what makes this story so compelling. The Algerian diary is real. It is the story exactly as he experienced it, one that ultimately served him well.

Foreword

....

Gerald Davis interviewed me in 2006 at my home in London for the PBS documentary he wrote and produced on Frank Kearns. He has now produced a definitive account—much of it in Kearns's own words—that shines a light on a forgotten adventure in what was once a very different world of American TV news.

This book deserves to be read by a wider audience than journalism students or academics. It is not only a tribute to a legendary American foreign correspondent who helped make CBS News great. It is also a reminder of how much our country has lost with the dumbing down, downsizing, and trivialization of most of our news today. The CBS News that Frank Kearns worked for was not "infotainment." It was real news. Most important, it was an early warning service that kept the public educated, informed, and alert to the opportunities and dangers in the world beyond our shores.

Kearns belonged to the post–World War II generation of foreign correspondents who preceded me. Our paths crossed in 1971—his final year and my first year at CBS News—when we were both based in the Rome bureau. Yes, CBS not only had a Rome bureau in those days, but as you will learn from this fascinating account by Gerald Davis, it had a worldwide corps of correspondents, cameramen, soundmen (almost all were men in those days), and the support staff needed to run what was in effect a national intelligence network. Indeed. As you will see, there was a thin line between working for a first-rate American news organization and working for the United States government. Frank Kearns was a classic example and was no less a great correspondent for cooperating and exchanging information with America's official intelligence services.

How much does the public learn today from watching the big network evening news programs or twenty-four-hour cable news? What coverage was given to Osama bin Laden before al-Qaeda began the terrorist campaign that culminated in the 9/11 attacks? The rot that has eaten into the infrastructure of our national news organizations is not limited to foreign news coverage. How much advance warning were we given before the financial and economic crash of 2008, which left most of the world mired in the worst recession since the Great Depression? With the downsizing and cheapening of the news, we have lost one of the essential underpinnings of a sound economy and a rational foreign policy.

So this is more than the story of a gutsy foreign correspondent, a type of professional journalist that is becoming an endangered species. It is a measure of how far our standards of news coverage have fallen since the days of the "Murrow Boys" and the great correspondents who followed in their footsteps.

And yet in Kearns's day, it was far more difficult to produce reports for television news, especially when the reporting had to be done in difficult and dangerous places. One of the most remarkable changes in TV news since the early days is the amount of gear a television news team had to carry into the field. Frank Kearns and cameraman Archak Joe Masraff were sent to report behind the lines in Algeria with hundreds of pounds of equipment. Today, a correspondent on his own can produce endless hours of high-quality video and audio with a smart phone and transmit it directly from the scene.

There is another big difference between TV news then and now that may not be obvious to today's audience. Foreign news was not just something that ambitious correspondents did for a while because it looked good on their CVs and could be a stepping-stone on the road to becoming a news anchor. Pursuing a career as a foreign correspondent was an end in itself. It was (and still is, in my opinion) far more exciting, challenging, and important than reading a teleprompter. It was more than just an adrenaline rush. As one of my former colleagues used to say, it beats working. I don't know how many potential Frank Kearnses there are in journalism schools today, but their chances of being given the freedom to travel and report that Kearns enjoyed are slim in the current business climate that incentivizes American news organizations to focus on the bottom line and forget their public service mission.

Gerald Davis has recaptured some of the excitement and even the romance of the life of an American foreign correspondent in the formative years of television news. Frank Kearns and his cameraman, Joe Masraff, were both charmers—large personalities, great raconteurs, and the best possible company you could have on the road in dodgy and dangerous situations.

Joe, a great big teddy bear of an Arab, by the way, was an excellent cook—another reason why he was such a good companion on the road.

Masraff was my mentor when I made the leap from newspaper to television reporting. He filmed my first screen test in the Paris bureau of CBS News. "Just relax, look at the camera and pretend you are talking to me," was the only instruction he gave me. I had never had media training, or even seen the inside of a school of journalism. Joe Masraff behind the camera was all a foreign correspondent needed. Joe could get you safely in and out of the most dangerous situations and produce marvelous film sequences while you were there. And, I might add (I hope this won't shock the reader), he knew where to put the $100 bill in your passport in place of a nonexistent visa. The legislators who crafted the American law against bribing foreign officials never had to face big men armed with big guns when trying to negotiate a roadblock in unfriendly foreign territory.

Kearns had another prerequisite for a great foreign correspondent, in addition to having a great cameraman. He was a great storyteller, both on and off the camera. Read the daily diary that CBS ordered him to write while he was covering the war in Algeria. Gerald Davis had the good sense to reproduce it in full in this book. It takes you along with Frank and Joe as they negotiate the minefield of what Davis calls an "impossible assignment." Although Kearns never got around to writing a memoir, this is the next best thing.

Davis became one of his students and assistants when Kearns left CBS News to teach journalism at West Virginia University. By all accounts, Kearns was one of the most popular professors on the campus. He could have gotten away with just telling war stories to his classes. But I hope his enthusiasm for the job of reporting from dangerous and faraway places taught some of his students that firsthand reporting is a higher calling than anchoring a broadcast, even though news salaries teach the opposite.

Much of the damage to the American model of international news coverage was done at the end of Cold War I, when the United States believed it no longer had anything to fear from Russia or the rest of the world. I say

Cold War I because our public lack of knowledge of what has been happening overseas since the collapse of the Soviet Union has brought the United States nearer to what is beginning to look like a Cold War II with a a Russia led by Vladimir Putin.

And if that were not enough to convince you that international news is as important now as it was then, you need only look at the tragic turmoil in the Middle East and Africa, the parts of the world that Frank Kearns and Joe Masraff covered.

I try to imagine how Kearns and Masraff, if they were alive and working today, would report the ghastly civil war in Syria, the dangerous chaos in Libya, or the atrocities committed by the so-called Islamic State. They would, of course, have the right contacts, or would know how to reach out and find them. They would have found a way to cover the events in conflicts where American journalists have become prime targets. Unlike news teams who are "parachuted" into foreign conflicts these days (if indeed they go there at all), they would be on their own turf, working their beat as only experienced journalists can do. They would know the dangers—how to face them and when to avoid unnecessary risks. And they would have produced reports that told the real story, which can only be learned when you have boots on the ground.

Could the Algerian story be done today? Yes, of course. But I doubt that the introverted, ratings-obsessed, cost-conscious American cable, TV, and Web news purveyors who decide what Americans will watch would choose to send a news team behind the lines for six weeks. Frank Kearns's "impossible assignment" to cover the Algerian nationalists' war against their French rulers would never be undertaken or broadcast today by a major American news organization. It would be considered too costly, too uninteresting, and certainly not a ratings winner.

For me, reading Frank Kearns's scripts and his Algerian diary has been a stark reminder of how much America has lost with the evolution of television news since the days when he was a foreign correspondent. Yes, the public has far more access to what we still call "news" on our broadcasts, cable systems, computers, and hand-held devices. There is an endless stream of words and pictures. But how much of it is what could be called hard news—the real thing—reliable information that gives the public and politicians the facts to enable them to reach wise decisions on matters of vital importance to our country and the world? The goal of news should be "We give you the facts, and you make up your mind." Unfortunately, it is not just Fox News that fails to meet its own standards. The American public is being shortchanged. It gets views instead of news. And what is even more insidious, the public does not know what it is missing. In the flood of "news you can use"—celebrity news and infotainment—there is very little room for foreign news, either short or long form. Even in Frank's days, documentaries were usually aired in off-peak hours. Network news produced them because they were required by law to broadcast programs that were in the public interest. Now that news broadcasting standards have been lowered, documentaries on issues of national security have all but disappeared from mainstream news.

In the quote at the beginning of this book, President Dwight D. Eisenhower stressed that it was "essential that our citizens be kept alert to the affairs of people outside our borders. . . . This is the basic assignment of our reporters serving overseas, and I believe they are fulfilling it in the finest tradition of American journalism."

Well, there are now too few American reporters serving overseas to provide more than token coverage of an increasingly complex and dangerous world, and the companies that employ them seem to feel no responsibility to do better.

This account of the in-depth, boots-on-the-ground, international reporting that Frank Kearns and Joe Masraff once did in Africa is a reminder of how much American news organizations have cheapened the news. In today's increasingly complex and dangerous world, ignorance is an economy our country can no longer afford.

Tom Fenton
London, April 10, 2015

Preface

....

On August 1, 1986, at twenty-two minutes and forty seconds into *The CBS Evening News*, anchorman Dan Rather announced in a forthright yet somber tone that his former colleague, Frank Kearns, had died. For the next thirty seconds, he described Kearns's career at the network, concluding that he was "[a legend] around here."[1] That is a term, like "hero," that is handed out without much thought these days. But nearly thirty years ago, it still had meaning, even in the hyperbolic language that Dan Rather was known to use in his newscasts. Frank Kearns was one of those reporters who through hard work and courage had earned the respect of his peers inside CBS and many of his competitors who encountered him in war zones and in the bush. It had been ten years since anyone at CBS mentioned him on the air. The last time they did, they announced to the world that he was a spy, and Kearns was furious. In fact, he was so angry that the mere suggestion of this relationship led, in part, to his death, according to his wife.[2] He denied the allegation to his grave. The day after that story broke, Kearns called his closest friend at CBS, Eric Severeid, who worked with him in London and then moved to the Washington, DC, news bureau. Over the years they remained close. Severeid even served as best man to Kearns when he remarried. Always immaculately dressed, the distinguished commentator was one of the few survivors from the early days of Edward R. Murrow still working regularly on air at CBS News in 1976. He provided thoughtful analysis and sharp commentary on the evening newscasts two nights each week and was highly regarded for choosing just the right words whenever he spoke. In anguish, Kearns turned to his old friend and pleaded, "What was the network's purpose in doing this? What good does it do anyone? Why me? Why now? Whose idea is this?" But for once, the opinionated pundit was speechless.

I mention the announcement of his death and the network revealing a possible dual role in this reporter's life because they serve as guides to considering the story about Frank Kearns in Algeria. There was no question that he was a gutsy and dauntless journalist. A close look at the stories he covered, often isolated and in explosive locations, expose a courageous reporter. Known for having what his wife described as "sharp elbows," he posed hard-hitting, pointed questions to world leaders during interviews and didn't back down when they were evasive. This wasn't grandstanding for the camera. After all, he worked in the days before the star system of television network news changed the way stories got reported and promoted. Frank Kearns was a storyteller alright. That's what he liked about his work and why he embraced it as he did. Having long ago abandoned the Catholicism in which he was raised, Kearns nevertheless was a spiritual man. He viewed life like a good story. There's a beginning, a middle, and an end. Along the way, the story is influenced by many people and in different ways. Always present, however, is luck and it pays to have lots of it in his line of work.

Frank Kearns covered the growing influences of communism in Egypt and other parts of the Middle East, as well as breaking news in Europe. He stood alongside men firing rifles at each other on the rooftops in Beirut and took a bullet in the tape recorder hanging around his neck while covering street fighting in Cypress. That act alone impressed his bosses back in New York. Kearns was a fixture on the streets and in the embassies while covering the bloody "African World War" in the Congo as his camera crews came and went to other assignments. He was threatened with death by the paramilitary groups on both sides of the fighting in Northern Ireland, and he finished up his career at CBS News being held captive at the end of the cruel civil war that divided Nigeria. But the story that he held dearest was his work in Algeria during that country's struggle for independence from the French.

Like many of his peers in the field of journalism in the 1950s, Frank Kearns was a product of World War II. He had seen Armageddon in the concentration camps. He believed the United States and its allies in the West were working to keep the world safe. So many of them—Kearns included—allowed their reporting to be heavily influenced by the specific points of view of Western governments fighting the growing influence of communism. But it was in Algeria where Frank Kearns came to realize that for the newly independent countries and those still fighting for their independence, it was about nationalism and not communism. They cared about their heritages, their cultures, their ancestries, their immediate security, not about the world views of the nuclear superpowers. Insomuch as the "American point of view" and its interests lined up with theirs, they leaned in that direction. They liked the ideals of democracy and not domination by another country, but when the interests did not line up, they tipped in the opposite direction. Then came Vietnam and after a while no in-country reporter was following the official line of government. As any good journalist knows, what carries the story is the search for its truth.

Frank Kearns supported the American government's point of view when he was asked to go into Algeria and report the other side of the war with the French whose claim on this land and its people went back over a century. As his conversation with Eric Severeid showed all those years later, his devastation at being accused on the evening news after spending seventeen years in hot spots trying to uncover the local truth didn't make sense. If he once worked with the US Central Intelligence Agency (CIA), as his former boss's sworn testimony to a US Senate panel would have us believe, then his past patriotism had caught up with him and potentially ruined a hard-earned, death-defying career as a foreign correspondent—a war correspondent. If he was not working with the CIA, then a great disservice was done as a way for CBS News to clear its corporate conscience and distance itself from a past where its chairman and some of his direct reports had very close ties to the Pentagon, the CIA, the White House, and other intelligence agencies within the US government. CBS was not alone in this closely held activity. It had plenty of company as time and evidence presented at the Church Committee hearings revealed.

I had three objectives in mind when I began this book. The first was to introduce readers to Frank Kearns. In the dozens—perhaps hundreds—of books written about CBS and its many notable anchormen, correspondents, and executives dating back before the "Murrow Boys," Frank Kearns is rarely mentioned. For nearly two decades, he was challenged by needing to file reports from locations that didn't capture the attention or imagination of audiences in the United States—Aleppo, Khartoum, Dar-es-Salaam, Algiers, and Nairobi. Today these places dominate the headlines. They also were difficult destinations to reach in order to get stories. In the era before satellites, it took additional time for unprocessed film to reach New York, to get developed and synched with Kearns's taped narration, and to finally make it on the air. But more than being difficult places from which to report, Kearns would tell you, they were tricky, even dicey. Connections to get from one country to another that were adjacent or only inches apart on a map usually required plane transfers back through Europe. Long-distance telephone service required making reservations in advance, which certainly did not make possible on-the-spot, real-time reporting. Satellite communications didn't exist until the final years before Kearns retired.

The only meaningful attention paid to his work prior to writing this book was an Emmy-winning documentary that Chip Hitchcock and I produced in 2012, *Frank Kearns: American Correspondent.* That work was limited by money, time, and distribution. Only so much information can be stuffed into a fifty-eight-minute program for public television stations where audience size is narrow and scheduling can be somewhat haphazard for independent biographical films. Nevertheless it's been screened by nearly every PBS station in the United States and mentioned favorably in history professor Hugh Wilford's fine book *America's Great Game: The CIA's Secret Arabists and the Shaping of the Modern Middle East.*

The second reason for writing this book is to share an example of what it took for Frank Kearns and cameraman Joe Masraff to capture for radio and television audiences the beat that they covered, in this case an entirely different look at the Algerian struggle for independence. Until they spent six weeks with rebels in the summer of 1957, most Americans saw this revolution almost entirely from the French side. It was not a war that directly concerned the United States, but it was one that involved our credibility and growing concern about Soviet influence in North Africa during the Cold War. It took some doing for the CBS news team to finally connect with the Algerian freedom fighters, as you will soon read. They were assisted by Kearns's wartime friend Miles Copeland, who worked for the CIA under the cover of the management consulting firm Booz Allen Hamilton. It also took courage on their part. They were going into a dangerous war zone where they knew they were putting their lives on the line, and they weren't always sure about the people with whom they were entrusting their lives. To a certain extent, they knew that they were being used by the Algerians. A good face on American television wouldn't hurt the pressure that they were exerting in the United Nations and in European capitals to remove the last vestiges of French rule. The independence movement was sweeping across the Maghreb and throughout Africa. The Algerians no longer wanted to be a part of metropolitan Paris. Leadership of the FLN (Front de Libération Nationale), Algeria's National Liberation Front, expertly manipulated public opinion, and here was an opportunity for them to reach Americans in prime time. Kearns and Masraff would prove to be useful tools so long as they returned home safely. But they weren't the only ones working this story. CBS assigned David Schoenbrun, its Paris bureau chief, to cover the French side of the war. Reports from one side would be balanced by reports from the other side. That's the way journalism worked in the 1950s.

Foreign reporting can be a dangerous occupation in some parts of the world, especially for those covering wars among nations, undeclared wars, civil wars, and rebellions of all types. But this was what the job entailed. President Dwight Eisenhower recognized it as "essential that our citizens be kept alert" and that they "grow in understanding and appreciation for the interdependence of mankind." However, to get to some of these stories, "you can't just parachute in," as retired CBS News Senior European Correspondent Tom Fenton told me when I interviewed him for the documentary film about Kearns. "When you do, you're there too late. You have to get to know [the people you're covering]." That's what Frank Kearns was doing in Algeria in the middle of what would prove to be a costly, violent, and nearly decade-long war. He was doing what great journalists do. They go to see for themselves. They talk to people. They probe. They park their biases at the border and search for truth. Then they form opinions and file reports.

Some stories can be reported from the halls of governments, but men and women, like Frank Kearns, also go into dangerous parts of the world where trust is a scarce commodity and danger is ever present. They rely on tenuous contacts and follow leads that aren't always reliable. They tremble with fear just like the rest of us. But they push onward with the high-intensity flow of adrenaline and the natural curiosity that called them into the profession. Sometimes they are successful; sometimes, extraordinarily so. Many times they are not. Their worth is measured in "air time," the precious commodity of minutes and seconds in a half-hour newscast or special report. Their work is often marked by changes in attitudes or policies by the governments and people they cover, even by the people for whom they work. When they become lazy or jaded, they lose their opportunities to write the first chapters of history.

Broadcast news as we know it found its birthplace in London and the capitals of Europe during World War II. Here was the stoic reporting of Edward R. Murrow and his "Boys." When the war ended and technology advanced, this team of radio correspondents (as well as those at rival NBC) morphed into television news. CBS was the "A" team, the "Tiffany Network" as it was called then, and the Murrow Boys were the ones who gave it gravitas. What started out as separate news and public affairs divisions, the significantly smaller television staff was built begrudgingly around radio, but quickly grew to dominate the news operations.

As events moved rapidly from World War to Cold War because of highly differentiated philosophies—communism versus capitalism—the need for more and more news bureaus arose. CBS grew from its bases in major European cities to outposts in Moscow, Bombay, Tokyo, Hong Kong, Seoul, and Cairo, to name a few. They were staffed with reporters like Frank Kearns. He held down the Cairo post, along with cameraman Yousef Masraff. More an office and less a bureau, it was set up in one of the sophisticated centers of Cold War propaganda where they raced against NBC and the smaller ABC news teams to report on the latest threats, real or perceived, that might lead to nuclear annihilation back home.

In the early days of television, the New York City–based networks expanded their financial and geographic reach through local market ownerships in other major cities. Besides the advertising revenues to be had, the driving force behind this expansion was the Fairness Doctrine, a policy established by the Federal Communications Commission that required broadcast licensees to devote airtime to public affairs programming and to treat the issues presented in an honest and equitable manner, "fair and balanced," you might say.

With limited staff to produce these programs, in the early 1950s the White House spoon-fed the networks with programming ideas and went so far as to write scripts to satisfy their own rule making. The obvious consequence of this was programming that tilted toward the perspectives of the American government. The networks played along with the messaging that Washington so carefully crafted. These messages were often shaped in the field—the so-called

"CIA perspective"—and then sent back by reporters working overseas, creating just the right echo chamber to rally the country against the Soviet Union and its Warsaw Pact allies.

CBS News was anchored by battle-tested correspondents: Edward R. Murrow, Eric Severeid, Charles Collingwood, Howard K. Smith, Winston Burdett, William L. Shirer, Larry LeSueur, and others. Their work was augmented by "reporters," many of whom were part-time and paid a small base salary or on a piecemeal basis, or both. The job of keeping this pipeline coordinated fell to the foreign editor. He barked orders from his command center desk in what has been called the "fishbowl" because of its surrounding wall of glass that looked across the news studio. His job was to initiate or sort through story ideas that flowed from overseas bureaus. At the time, there was no road map for producing a television news program. TV took whatever it could from radio and the rest was seat-of-the-pants work, maturing as time passed. Reporters who caught on could count on a career among the elite in the industry. Those who didn't fell to the sidelines and were replaced by others with steadfast ambitions and talent like Walter Cronkite, Marvin Kalb, Daniel Schorr, Robert Trout, Frank Kearns, and many others.

To make the transition from "stringer," or part-time reporter, to a full staff correspondent showed that the journalist had proven himself through his bravery, imagination, and hard work. Some managed through intellect; others, through tenaciousness and fearlessness. Once again, luck also played a role.

With this foundation of hard-working professionals, the networks delivered digests of news and information that influenced the attitudes and beliefs of the American people. They also informed politicians and bureaucrats alike, providing them with extra eyes and ears—boots on the ground, as it was. Some played it too close, as it later came out during hearings by the US Senate Select Committee on Intelligence that was investigating the US Central Intelligence Agency (CIA) in the 1970s. There, it was brought to the forefront that the agency had hundreds of reporters working for them in various capacities. Media owners also played important roles in facilitating the government's need for information by providing cover for agents or access to raw field reports ahead of the editor's cut for the evening news or for a byline in the morning papers and news weeklies. CBS was a leading player in this arena. Its chairman, William S. Paley, a former executive member of the Office of

War Information management team in World War II, said he "thought it was [his] duty to help." This aspect of cooperation was hidden from the public until the Church Committee drew it out.

This questionable relationship, however, had its advantages. In Cairo, for example, Frank Kearns spent a lot of time with two former wartime roommates who worked under cover for the CIA. This, in turn, led to Kearns being cited by a correspondent in Rome as having an affiliation with America's spies, specifically, he thought, the Office of Naval Intelligence (ONI). Kearns told his boss at the time, Sig Mickelson, that he had close contacts with the CIA, but denied working directly for the agency. Nevertheless and with or without his knowledge, the CIA arranged to show Mickelson Kearns's tendered resignation from the agency before later being named a staff correspondent.

As a boy, Kearns had one goal and that was to be a journalist, especially a foreign correspondent. For a young man from Morgantown, West Virginia, it was a romantic escape that led to the capitals of Europe, the Middle East, Africa, and the Eastern Bloc countries, including the Soviet Union. Kearns was a network reporter when radio news ruled the airwaves. He transitioned from radio to television. So did many other reporters, some like Kearns with roots in the military but none that stretched into intelligence—or so it seemed. As the technology of broadcasting changed, Frank Kearns changed with it. In his later years with the network, his reports no longer took days to reach the air. Instead, they arrived by satellite. So he bridged the old with the new, the proven with the future. Satellites enabled broadcasters to move quickly and broadly, leading to CNN and Headline News (in its former, useful days before it got caught up in chasing celebrities and scandalous "breaking news").

Finally, *Algerian Diary* is meant to be both the telling of a good, true story that may have helped to influence the way the United States government viewed the Algerian war for independence and that serves as a brief biographical introduction to the life of Frank Michael Kearns. It's a life that is fraught with conflicting information. Since Kearns died without ever drafting the memoir that he once considered writing, this book is the first attempt to document a specific time in his life and, to a lesser extent, a broader look at his life. It also serves to illustrate the risks he was willing to assume for his profession. This book arrives almost six decades after Kearns's dangerous trip across the border from Tunisia to join the Algerian rebels to see firsthand their resolve to take back their country and more than fifty years since Algeria finally won that hard-fought independence from France.

The challenge of telling this story—this *"unrealistic or impossible assignment,"* as his editor of the time called it—is that the key participants who were most intimately involved in its undertaking—Frank Kearns, Yousef Masraff, and Ralph Paskman—are no longer living. The details they might have added would have enriched this work. Instead, the book relies on the material available from various archives and other sources to support the story of how the *Algerian Diary* came to be written and how its content formed the basis for an award-winning CBS News documentary, *Algeria Aflame.*

Frank Kearns arrived at CBS through a door that was opened for him by wartime friend Edward Saxe, a direct report to Chairman Paley. Saxe did so once before in Kearns's formative years as a freelance writer, coming as it did at just the right time in his life. Thereafter, triumph or failure was based on Kearns's own resourcefulness, intellectual skills, and hard work, and each time he rose to the occasion.

In short, the *Algerian Diary* is the centerpiece for how Frank Kearns came to be known as "a legend" in the commentary on the night he died. His reporting from Algeria is the story that established that legend.

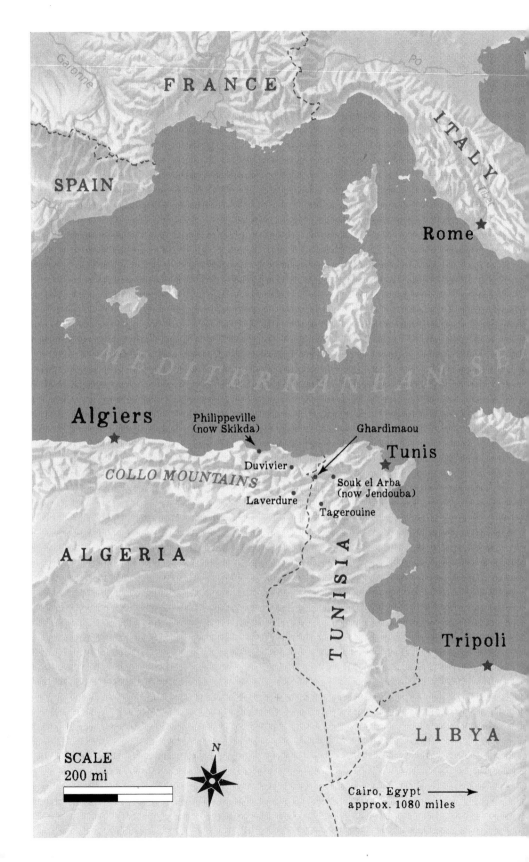

CHAPTER ONE

A Small Office in Cairo

....

A s the middle of the twentieth century rolled along, most of America was settling into a new suburban lifestyle. Demand for manufactured products and the good fortunes of an "Eisenhower economy" ushered in the age of consumerism. Safety and growing security at home allowed this to develop.

The first armed conflict in the Cold War era had ended in a stalemate at the 38th parallel on the Korean Peninsula, and Americans were feeling safe but cautious. They hadn't lost that war. They just hadn't won it. Vietnam wasn't yet the flame on the horizon that would burn into the American psyche. Politically the country had turned conservative.

The postwar surge of consumerism of the 1950s grew rapidly. By 1957, signs of it were everywhere. The Wham-O Company in Pasadena, California, produced the first Frisbee. Efficient and cost-effective mass-production houses—built on concrete slabs like those at Levittown, New York, or in a new style known as "mid-century modern"—were in high demand nation-wide, even in the growing towns of West Virginia, where Frank Kearns had grown up. The average cost of one of these new homes was around $12,000.

Map, opposite: Cairo-based CBS News stringers Frank Kearns and photographer Yousef Masraff were sent to northwestern Tunisia and northeastern Algeria in July 1957 to report on the conflict between Algeria and France.

Two-thirds of all new cars were purchased on credit, and the average car sold for almost $2,800. Marketers at the Ford Motor Company that year were finalizing plans for the second largest car launch ever. Their attention was focused on an unconventional and highly stylized new automobile debuting in the fall at more than 1,500 dealerships nationwide. It was named for the company founder's late son, Edsel. Ford's advertising medium of choice was television. It was a relatively new medium and worked like no other tool in the automobile manufacturer's marketing mix. Their message: Ford cars come from "'You Ideas'—developed, not just to arouse your curiosity, but to do something for you."[1] In an era of only 4 percent unemployment, many people would succumb to their enticing definition of who should drive an Edsel. Many would later regret it.

That year, forty-one million homes had television sets. Less than 1 percent received a signal in color; the rest watched grainy, rolling black and white. After dinner each evening, families settled down in their living rooms to watch television on a very small screen, eagerly anticipating the premier that fall of programs like the family sitcom *Leave It to Beaver* on CBS.

Actor Humphrey Bogart died in January, yet people still went to the movies. One of the trendy new films was based on a racy novel popularized the year before and then a decade later would be made into a television program for ABC. It was called *Peyton Place*. It grossed $16.1 million at the box office, not far behind David Lean's *The Bridge on the River Kwai*, which was named the Best Picture at the Academy Awards.

Some people, meanwhile, cheered that fall in 1957 as the Milwaukee Braves beat the New York Yankees in seven games of the World Series. The NBA Championship went to the Celtics in seven games, too, the first of many trophies to be displayed at the Boston Gardens. The Stanley Cup stayed in Montreal.

Although life at home was relatively protected, Americans were told to fear the growing influence of the Soviet Union in the "us-versus-them" thinking of the time. Every evening around dinnertime, families tuned in to watch the fifteen-minute newscast of *Douglas Edwards with the News* on CBS. John Cameron Swayze drew a larger audience over on NBC. Just as it does today, the *New York Times* influenced every facet of media—newspapers, radio, and television. The *Wall Street Journal* published the first of its still-running cartoon feature, "Pepper . . . and Salt."

In the United States, television was a local medium until AT&T finished linking the country with coaxial cables, which had enough bandwidth to not only carry the growing number of homes and businesses with telephones but to share the space with the more expansive needs of television signals. What began locally in the late 1940s now extended nationwide in the 1950s with what has been called "the Golden Age of Television." Despite technical limitations, the country was connected. Not only could people read about important stories of the day in newspapers or hear of them on radio, but now they could *see* events for the first time. Only five years before the launch of the Edsel and just as Frank Kearns was preparing to move his family to Egypt, television sets in American homes were establishing the groundwork for what later would become the world's largest advertising medium.

But TV didn't just mean news. It also meant variety shows, game shows, teleplays by noted writers of the day, and other creative productions. In fact, while financially lucrative, news helped the networks—ABC, CBS, NBC, and the DuMont Television Network. What these two categories of programs had in common in the early 1950s was the same thing: the networks that broadcast them didn't necessarily produce the programs that they were showing. Advertisers created entertainment programs, and for a period of time, the White House and other government agencies created public affairs programs, which helped to nudge public opinion in favor of America's Cold War policies. At the same time, it helped assure that the network-owned and operated stations were fulfilling their obligations as licensees by providing programs "in the public interest." This worked well in the early part of the decade when Sen. Joseph McCarthy claimed that communists were influencing governmental institutions. The final separation of government and the media really didn't end until Vietnam.

President Dwight Eisenhower alerted Congress to the growing global influence of the Russians who by the fall would flex their scientific muscles with that remarkable achievement, the first earth-orbiting satellite they called *Sputnik*. The two nations were locked in a competition to develop the now frightening Intercontinental Ballistic Missile (ICBM) systems.

The so-called Eisenhower Doctrine, announced in a special message to Congress in January, stood in for the faltering English and French in order to keep the shipping lanes open to commerce in the Suez Canal. America was going to balance the growing global influence of the Soviets and their politically aligned but "neutral" friend in the Middle East, Egypt's President Gamal Abdel Nasser.

Wherever the president of the United States focused his attention, the news media was there. CBS was well represented in Europe as tensions between East and West grew. Most of its correspondents there were part of the first generation of hand-picked reporters who covered World War II as part of Edward R. Murrow's "Boys"—Charles Collingwood, Bill Downs, Larry LeSueur, Richard C. Hottelet, Howard K. Smith, Eric Severeid, and William L. Shirer. But the spotlight now moved farther south, and CBS expanded its coverage area by recruiting second-generation members of Murrow's team—Walter Cronkite, Alexander Kendrick, Robert Pierpoint, and David Schoenbrun. In early 1953, the decision had been made by CBS in New York to open a small office at No. 8 Salah Ayoub Street in one of the British colonial–style villas on an island in the Nile River, called Zamalek, a fashionable residential suburb of Cairo.[2] The reporter they chose to be based there was Frank Kearns, a part-timer.

He brought into the Cairo office a stylish local photographer, Archak Yousef Masraff. "Joe," as he was known to the Americans, worked only part-time, too. He was a cosmopolitan, sophisticated, and talented professional of Armenian descent who spoke several languages fluently, among them Arabic, English, French, German, Italian, and Japanese. He was well known in Cairo for his work as chief picture editor of *Al' Ahram*, a weekly news magazine.[3] In fact, Masraff was among the favored photographers used by President Nasser for official portraiture and other government business. Years later, former CBS News President Van Gordon Sauter, who worked with Masraff in Paris, described him as "a marvelous raconteur."[4] While working in Egypt at the time, he was a good enough competitor to be invited regularly to join up-and-coming Egyptian actor Omar Sharif's contract bridge tournaments.

Frank Kearns and Joe Masraff formed a unique relationship from the very beginning as TV news grew in importance. They had professional respect for each other's talents as they moved from assignment to assignment in locations throughout the hostile and undeveloped Middle East and Africa. Theirs ultimately would become a lifelong friendship—a brotherhood—where they survived numerous attempts on their lives in hostile locations as well as attempts by the network to separate them. Their children often liked to refer to each man as father and stepfather, depending upon who was doing the speaking.[5]

In the summer of 1957, a cable from New York arrived for Kearns in Cairo. The sender was Ralph Paskman, the gruff and grumpy, street-toughened CBS foreign editor in New York who handed out assignments to the stringers. His correspondence was followed by a series of written directives to both Kearns and Masraff, advising them of the network's desire to cover the Algerian side of the war for independence and as precisely as possible how they should go about doing it.

Kearns was quickly earning a well-deserved reputation back in New York as a good, hard-nosed reporter unafraid of covering tough stories. He had recently reported on the violence at the Suez between the Egyptians and British, French and Israelis. From there, he moved over to Cyprus, where Greek and Turkish factions squared off and where he was nearly hit by a ricocheting bullet. Fortunately, the shell lodged deep in the tape recorder hanging from his neck instead of in his chest. That assignment earned him his first citation from the Overseas Press Club of America.

This time, however, the orders from Paskman were unusually detailed. The network planned "a very special story," he told his reporter. Since France did not consider this to be a war, he warned them, a news crew on the other side of the barrel from the French would certainly be working at great personal risk.

In 1957, several million French citizens called Algeria home. This southernmost outpost of the Fourth Republic had been occupied by France for over 120 years. This war or whatever it was called that Kearns and Masraff were going to cover had been underway for three years. Why an American news organization wanted to take such a risk with its employees wasn't completely clear since the United States thus far had shown only creative ambiguity toward Algeria. President Eisenhower and Secretary of State John Foster Dulles figured that France eventually would have to negotiate with the nationalists, but they didn't apply pressure on France "for fear of straining the Western alliance,"[6] which had been badly stressed because of the Suez crisis and France's unwavering relationship with Israel. Furthermore, policy makers back home were concerned about the growing tide of Arab unity in North Africa, but the audiences of nightly fifteen-minute television newscasts weren't following this story line. Americans were watching the Russians and not what was happening in Algeria.

As for Kearns, he needed the special pay that would come from an assignment like this. Not only was the network asking for footage for a planned documentary, but it also wanted filmed stories for nightly television news and audio reports for radio. So, of course, he'd go. He and Masraff wasted no time making the appropriate contacts in Cairo that would lead them across Tunisia and into Algeria with the nationalist rebels.

CHAPTER TWO

La Guerre d'Algérie

....

By the time Frank Kearns had picked up the cable from his editor in 1957, the histories of France and Algeria had been intertwined for over a century, going back to 1830 when France, under King Charles X, first occupied the country. At the time, Algeria was thought to be the least developed of all the North African countries that made up the Maghreb,[1] and therefore, the one with the greatest opportunity for French settlement. Abd al-Qadir al-Jazairi, an Islamic spiritual and military leader, was elected emir by fellow tribesmen and he set about unifying them in order to secure peace with the French. Later as his geographic influence spread, Abd al-Qadir planned to drive the French from Algeria, beginning near the border with Morocco, but the eastern tribes didn't give him their full support. It wasn't long before France's aggressive and determined policy of dealing with resistance soon overcame him and his followers. Al-Qadir surrendered in 1847 and was deported to France. He is widely recognized as the first hero of Algeria's war for independence. Over a hundred years later, his white-and-green flag was used as the symbol for the independence movement led by the nationalists in 1954.

During the Franco-Prussian war of 1871, France lost control of its agriculturally important border region known as Alsace-Lorraine. So it turned its attention to the fertile farmlands of Algeria as over 100,000 Alsatians chose to remain French citizens and relocated to Algeria, causing France to step up efforts to fully integrate the country within its metropolitan political structure. Bloody resistance was the norm, but by the turn of the century France was in firm control. It had successfully blended the productive natural resources of Algeria, dominated by enterprises run by the occupying European settlers, called *colons*, with the French economy. The primary industry was agriculture, led by development of its most productive properties for use as premium vineyards. The French regarded Algeria as its responsibility both administratively and constitutionally.

For the next sixty-five years, the biggest challenge that confronted France in colonizing this Muslim nation was how to allow the more educated and enlightened Algerians who wished to align themselves with France to do so without having to renounce Islam. What seemed a brilliant idea was met with intense political rejection by the *pied noirs* ("black feet" was the name given specifically to French settlers who grew up in Algeria), who forced the so-called Blum-Viollette proposal of 1936 off the table. Named for Popular Front leader Leon Blum and Maurice Viollette, the French premier and governor-general of Algeria, the bill would have extended citizenship rights to those Muslims—accountants, bankers, soldiers, lawyers, professors, and government administrators, known as *évolués*, the more "advanced" segments of Algerian society—who accepted it.

According to Columbia University historian Mathew Connelly, "French historians have long treated the defeat of the Blum-Viollette bill as a turning point—the point at which *pied noir* intransigence completely discredited loyal Muslim opposition."[2] Thus, a new and distinct social order in Algeria failed to develop.

The beginning of the latest Algerian uprising took place on November 1, 1954, All Saints Day. It was led by an inexperienced, ill-prepared faction of the newly formed Front de Libération Nationale (FLN), the National Liberation Front, concerned not so much with planning and execution as with their being discovered.[3] Their aim: Wage a military-style assault across the country and a diplomatic war from outside the borders of Algeria in order to bring an end to France's colonial rule. At that time, over three million French citizens lived and worked in Algeria with most settling in large cities along the coast. These *colons*, as they were called, were part of a growing movement of *Algérie française* who favored tighter integration by Algeria with metropolitan France.

The FLN's leadership group was made up of twenty-two young men who grew up in rural working-class families. These were "not ideologues" but nationalists "who modeled their movement on the French resistance against the Nazis."[4] It had worked for the French a decade earlier, but they failed to comprehend it when it was used against them by the FLN.

The revolt they planned was widespread and well coordinated. French intelligence failed to detect the coming insurrection. More than seventy locations were hit around the country, mostly in northwest Algeria. In Oran, one person was killed trying to protect a public service utility from a small group of terrorists. Elsewhere, shots were fired at a police station, killing a man. In Batna, an Arab Berber tribal town situated in a wide valley among the Aures Mountains and part of the Algerian Sahara Atlas range where Kearns and Masraff were headed, an ambush killed a rural chieftain and a passenger in his car. The passenger's wife was stabbed and raped, but she survived. Not far away, another group of rebels opened fire on an administrative center in Arris, near the Tunisian border, and an entire town was evacuated to protect its people from further threats.

While this new movement didn't lack volunteers, it was impoverished when it came to arming them. French war historian Yves Courriere suggested that "only half of those who took part in the All Saints uprising were armed."[5] It took the FLN months after the initial assault to organize shipments of armament from outside sympathizers. Its big break came only when France granted independence to neighboring Morocco and Tunisia in 1956. This completely opened the borders on both sides, allowing arms to flow.

Although a pragmatist who didn't think that France could continue its hold on Algeria without some fundamental changes in the way it governed, French Premier Pierre Mendes-France responded quickly. He sent sixteen hundred paratroopers and fourteen hundred security guards to reinforce the ten thousand French soldiers already encamped in Algeria. They used heavy artillery and American-built fighter planes, some of which were acquired from the United States through its North Atlantic Treaty Organization (NATO) alliance and meant to be used for national defensive purposes only. Instead, the French shipped the weapons to Algeria and used them to pursue the terrorists who were hiding in the mountains along the border with Tunisia. The US government looked the other way.

The official French position was that Algeria was a legitimate part of France. Therefore, any rebellion had to be considered treason. The French government would not negotiate on this point. It had already lost a lengthy and costly war in Indochina, so its leaders felt that there was no other option than to hold onto its increasingly fragile grip across this important coastal area of North Africa.

Terrorist acts weren't unique only to Algeria, however. The resident general of Morocco had been assassinated in Casablanca where the hired killers came from France. They formed the so-called "Le Main Blanche," the White Hand, a subterranean counterterrorism organization. Like a scene taken from the movie *Casablanca*, their group "committed more than 80 murders. In nine months the sympathetic local police have not made one arrest."[6] A European faction working to slow the flow of arms into Algeria was called "Le Main Rouge," the Red Hand.

In early 1955, Jacques Soustelle, a member of the French Assembly, was appointed by the premier to the position of governor general of Algeria. It was his job to broker a settlement and quiet the unrest. Soustelle was an imposing figure in France. Among the most gifted when he was a student, he joined the French *résistance* and led Charles de Gaulle's secret service in London during World War II. He was viewed as "a good liberal but at the same time tough, and not just a civil servant."[7] Experienced in setting up intelligence networks as well as managing antiterrorism forces, his appointment in Algeria was useful to the government in "establishing clandestine contacts in advance of negotiations"[8] when—and if—France prevailed against the rebellion. De Gaulle called him "this gifted man, this brilliant intellectual, this passionate politician."[9]

In making the appointment, Premier Mendes-France thought that if Soustelle could fix the unemployment problem in Algeria—"this Algerian scourge,"[10] he called it—then reform was possible. The rebels would be defeated. However, the French Assembly was not so encouraging and Soustelle's appointment was held up. A "whisper campaign" emerged from inside Algeria, suggesting that Soustelle "was, inter alia, a Soviet agent, a Jew like Mendes-France and his real name was 'Beni-Soussan.'"[11] Before the new governor general appointee could counter these rumors and get his sponsor's reform plan into operation, the government fell.

Soustelle was eventually approved, but not without considerable arm-twisting by Edgar Faure, who formed the new government. There was reluctant acceptance by Jacques Chevallier, the colonial mayor of Algiers, who was anxious for a peaceful settlement.

In April, the FLN gained its first diplomatic recognition when it was invited to Indonesia to attend the Bandung Conference, a meeting of twenty-nine Third World nations from Africa and Asia. Although its representatives went as unofficial delegates to the meeting, it marked the arrival of the radical group on the international stage and drove a wedge between the FLN and the new French leader in Algeria. Attendees at the conference adopted unanimously an Egyptian motion proclaiming Algeria's right to independence and called on France to liberate the country. With the spotlight now shining on the FLN, they turned their attention to New York and overdue recognition by the United Nations. The door was now open to wage an international strategy, just as they were coalescing support inside their country.

In the ensuing months leading up to the clandestine trip by Kearns and Masraff, the FLN's military arm, Armée de Libération Nationale—the National Liberation Army (ALN), massacred *pieds noirs* at Philippeville, a town of over twenty thousand located in the north Constantine region, where the resistance was well organized. Meanwhile, in France Guy Mollet succeeded Faure as prime minister, and Soustelle then was replaced by Robert Lacoste. After those moves, Algeria turned very bloody.

On September 30, 1956, the battle of Algiers began with the FLN's bombing of innocent civilians, mostly *pied noir*, at the Milk-Bar and Cafeteria in the infamous Casbah. The FLN hoped to scare the French back to France. The bombings continued unabated. Within weeks, Ahmed Ben Bella, one of the key FLN organizers, was imprisoned. Going on at the same time but nearly two thousand miles away, Anglo-French troops were embroiled in conflict at Suez. Frank Kearns was there to report that story. Between the Suez and Algeria, France had its hands full.

In January 1957, the FLN finally met with representatives of the United Nations. It argued that it was the legitimate diplomatic representative of Algeria since they had the support of most of the *indigènes*, the native Algerians. While they were in New York, a general strike across Algiers had been called to show the unilateral support that the FLN could muster. French paratroopers were sent to break it up. This move resulted in even more bombings. It was at this time that the French began to use torture as a central strategy to help them find the leaders of the rebellion.

A month later, the government of socialist Guy Mollet fell. France was in turmoil at home. The country went twenty-two days without a representative administration. By May, the FLN turned its attacks on local villages in the Kabylia region, like the one in Melouza, a mountain town not far from the coast, where "every male above the age of fifteen . . . [was] herded into houses and into the mosque and slaughtered . . . with rifles, pick-axes and knives."[12]

Over a seven-year period, more than a million Algerian Muslims, mostly Berbers, were sacrificed for the cause and another two million were displaced as the French tried to control nationalist fervor. As for the Frenchmen whose families had occupied Algerian soil for generations, many retreated to France, starting first as a trickle of expatriates but soon followed by an angry flood.

Support for the FLN came from Morocco in the west and Tunisia in the east. A major support group was started in Egypt, and sympathy for the Algerian endeavor spread across the Arab world. The Cold War superpowers—the United States and the Soviet Union—stayed out of open, direct support for either side.

Like America's recent decade-long war in Iraq, the conflict between two opposing, yet determined, forces was marked by guerrilla warfare, horrific terrorism against civilians to change or shape opinions, state-sponsored torture to find the leadership of the insurrections, and counterterrorism measures undertaken by the occupying army. On both sides in Algeria, careers as well as reputations were made and ruined.

Part of the FLN's strategy to win international support required the cooperation of Radio Cairo–based *Voice of the Arabs*, a radio service of the Egyptian State Broadcasting, which transmitted programming in several languages across North Africa, the Near and Middle East, the African continent, and even to parts of Latin America. Radio Cairo had stations in Cairo, Alexandria, and Assiout in the upper Nile. Often these broadcasts were picked up by other Arab stations and retransmitted to sympathetic listeners. Within the first two years of the conflict, the FLN had built a series of secret transmitters outside of Algerian borders to broadcast its own propaganda through the *Voice of Algeria*.[13]

The French were only partly successful in jamming these broadcasts, which tended to be highly inflammatory and lacking in any way a reasonable discussion about the homeland issues. However, the government did manage to close down independent Arab newspapers publishing in the metropolitan areas, banned the distribution of a number of foreign publications, and controlled the types of motion pictures reaching the movie houses in order to influence the content that could be viewed by the masses.

By and large, the American news media followed the story at a safe distance because that's how the US government played its hand . . . until July 2, 1957. In Washington, DC, an ocean away from the undeclared war in Algeria, Sen. John F. Kennedy, a member of the Senate Foreign Relations Committee, addressed his colleagues in the US Senate, telling them that things in North Africa were now "a matter of international, and consequently American, concern."[14] Further, he said it was up to the United States to "achieve a solution that will recognize the independent personality of Algeria and establish the basis for a settlement interdependent with France and the neighboring nations," and declaring that the US policy was "a retreat from the principles of independence and anti-colonialism" that "furnished powerful ammunition to anti-Western propagandists through Asia and the Middle East."[15]

The tide of world interest was beginning to turn, but not completely. President Dwight D. Eisenhower tried to stay neutral. France, after all, was a key NATO ally, so in his view this was still *their* problem.

CHAPTER THREE

A Reporter's Journey to Algeria

....

F rank Kearns was born on November 28, 1917, in Gary, Indiana. His father, Michael Joseph Kearns, was a civil engineer. A native of Wheeling, West Virginia, in the state's northern panhandle, he worked for years around the Appalachian coal mines before taking a management job in Chicago. Kearns's mother, Mary Ruth Semans, a divorcée, was born in Morgantown, West Virginia.[1] Both were twenty-two years old when they met in the southern part of the state and married on September 9, 1916. Shortly thereafter they moved to suburban Chicago for Michael's new job in the airline industry. Ruth, as his mother was known, was a direct descendant of Jonathan Cobun, one of the founding Revolutionary-era families who built Cobun's Fort near Dorsey's Knob, outside of Morgantown, and had a hard time breaking her ties back home.[2]

After young Frank was born, the family moved back to West Virginia, where he was fussed over by maternal grandparents, but more importantly by his aunts—Ruth's five sisters—who took turns caring for this only child, and they spoiled him rotten. His favorite was Aunt Georgia, Ruth's older sister. Throughout their lives, Georgia and her increasingly successful nephew would correspond regularly, and she followed and documented his career. While the aunts were busy taking care of the boy, his parents—without their only son in tow—settled in northern Virginia, where Frank's father took a new job helping to build the growing suburbs around the nation's capital.

Frank Kearns was raised by his extended family and graduated from Morgantown High School in 1934. A group of his closest friends, who referred to themselves as "the Chums," was made up of Ed Heiskell, Bob Shuman, Bob Burdett, Jack Blair, Gus Comuntzis, and a few others who moved in and out of their tight circle. Each boy was quite popular in school. Collectively, the Chums felt they had no social equal. Later, each man would excel in his chosen profession: physician, attorney, military general, entrepreneur, and network journalist.

After high school, Kearns and his friends stayed in town to attend college at West Virginia University. He rushed the Sigma Phi Epsilon fraternity where his best friend, Ed Heiskell, was the rush coordinator and who was devastated when Kearns told him that he might not want to join a fraternity that was struggling financially as the Sig Ep house was doing. As for the others, Shuman rushed Sigma Chi and Blair joined the Betas.

"That without a doubt knocked me flat," Heiskell wrote in his diary. "I'd die if I didn't have one swell guy to call a frat brother. At least *one* of the guys has to stick by me. If Kearns isn't initiated, I don't know what I'll do."[3]

Eventually Heiskell persuaded Frank Kearns to join him. They double-dated at dances, took long driving trips to Charleston and Pittsburgh, paid the pilot of a Ford tri-motor airplane, known in aviation circles as a "Tin Goose," to take them up and buzz over the campus, sneaked into Mountaineer football games, went swimming and boating at nearby Cheat Lake, and, more than anything, cemented their bonds of friendship that ultimately would bring Kearns back home.

The popular Kearns was elected president of his junior class and he joined the Reserve Officers Training Corps (ROTC). The following summer, he landed his first professional job on the copy desk of the *Tribune* in Miami, Florida, where he helped to produce five daily editions.[4] It was there that he got a taste of international life when he took a side trip to Cuba with money given to him by his father. This adventure ignited a passion that later in life would take him to over ninety countries around the world.

His parents were against him going into journalism. They preferred that he declare another profession—accountant, doctor, lawyer—but not a reporter.

But it didn't matter to young Frank. He'd made up his mind. As his grand-mother once said, "He had a will of his own and there wasn't anything you could tell him to do. If he didn't want to do it, he wouldn't do it." He wanted to be a journalist.

Kearns graduated in 1938 with a bachelor of arts degree in journalism and a minor in political science. When he returned to his alma mater as a celebrated correspondent decades later, he'd say that a major influence in the classroom was Perley Isaac Reed, PhD, who was the head of the journalism de-partment when Kearns attended there and for whom the School of Journalism at West Virginia University was named.

Described by some as a "stuffy, prissy, mild-mannered sort,"[5] Reed was the architect of the university's journalism program and founder of the school paper, the *Daily Athenaeum*, on which Kearns, like most other journalism students, was a reporter. Reed was highly disciplined and conservative in his outlook. He was remembered by a now-retired faculty member as being an innovator and visionary in the profession. He looked out for his students, and he impressed upon them his elevated standards. Like Kearns himself, Dr. Reed was never one to suffer fools gladly. He challenged his students in and out of the classroom, requiring them to keep a written record of what they learned from their readings as well as from his lectures. Kearns took it all in. He de-veloped his curiosity, learned to take good notes in order to make his stories accurate, and then layered it with his old professor's higher sense of journalistic ethics. He truly admired that old rascal.

After graduation, Frank Kearns worked as a reporter-photographer and copy editor for the *Morgantown (WV) Post*, an afternoon daily newspaper where he covered local stories and sharpened his skills as a writer. He also served as a correspondent for the *Post-Gazette* in nearby Pittsburgh, Pennsylvania, and the *Enquirer* in Cincinnati, Ohio.[6] But the lure of warmer weather and living near the ocean soon pulled him back to Florida, where he took a job as publicity director for the Miami Beach Chamber of Commerce. On the side, he served as a publicist for an unsuccessful gubernatorial candidate in south Florida and helped to develop a publicity campaign for unification of transportation facili-ties in greater Miami.[7] But the idea of being a publicist wasn't what he wanted to do. It wasn't fulfilling. So he returned to journalism, becoming the city ed-itor and a daily columnist for the *Sun-Tropics* in Miami Beach. He also wrote for *Rendezvous* magazine there and developed daily news scripts for WQAM-AM, a CBS affiliate.[8] That experience, however, was short-lived.

Like many young men in the late 1930s and early 1940s, Kearns was raised with a strong sense of nationalistic pride and willingness to serve his country. As the United States was entering World War II, he didn't wait to be drafted. On August 30, 1941, the twenty-three-year-old Kearns enlisted in the US Army.[9]

He didn't know how this new adventure would turn out, but he was sure that it would take him overseas, and if he was lucky enough, he might land a cushy role in a location like Australia, out of harm's way. Instead, he wound up in a motor pool in Chicago but soon was singled out and transferred to the nearby US Army Counterintelligence Corps (CIC) School. Upon graduation in January 1942, he was assigned to a newly formed detachment, where he worked as a "civilian-clothed Special Agent" in Washington, DC.[10]

One of the soldiers assigned to work with Kearns in Washington was Pvt. Miles Copeland, a native of Alabama. They became best buddies, and their lives would cross a number of times after the war. "When I first met him," Copeland wrote some forty years later, "he was the spitting image of my jazz band friend, Stan Kenton, except for circles under his eyes resulting from long evenings of mischief and merriment."[11]

The two men volunteered for duty overseas and shipped out with more than a dozen other CIC officers for the British Isles on July 1, 1942, crossing "the freezing cold, misty and grey North Atlantic on the Queen Mary's sister ship, the Queen Elizabeth."[12] Before leaving, he made sure that his mother received twenty-five dollars of his pay each month. Following orientation at the British Military Intelligence Training Centre in Matlock, England, the newly promoted Staff Sgt. Kearns and Copeland were assigned as plain-clothed special agents in a small CIC unit at the London field office.

Unlike most soldiers, Kearns and Copeland lived a very different life in the British capital. Their work consisted mostly of handling security violations. They weren't yet involved in catching spies or undertaking hazardous duties. Together with another CIC officer, they settled in a small flat in Ovington Square near Harrods, paying a hefty forty pounds, which included housekeeping and gardening services.

In November, Kearns was commissioned a second lieutenant and began investigative work in counter-sabotage as part of the CIC detachment at the headquarters of the European Theater of Operations, United States Army.[13] With his new rank, he was among the ninety or so soldiers invited regularly to visit the American Officers Club on Park Lane, where they frequently helped to "rescue a pregnant bottle in distress!"[14]

By May 1943, he was promoted to first lieutenant and assigned a six-week tour as base intelligence officer, Air Transport Command in Prestwick, Scotland.[15] His responsibility there was to assess the security of the base and recommend changes to keep the facility secure. When that assignment ended in mid-July, his commanding officer, Maj. Roy F. Atwood, reported that Kearns "discharged his duties in a superior manner in every case, and I cannot commend this officer too highly."[16] He returned to his former unit in London as its commanding officer and began preparing for his part in Operation Overlord, the Allied invasion of Normandy.

It was at that time he met a British fashion model, dancer, and actress, Gwendoline Ethel Shoring, who was twenty-six, a year older than Kearns. At the time, she was appearing at the Windmill Theatre in London, which was the basis for the 2005 British film *Mrs. Henderson Presents*. By all accounts, she was quite a catch, especially for an American soldier whose future was uncertain. Vivacious and beautiful, "Gwendy," as he called her, was every bit Kearns's equal in social settings. One West End theater owner thought her "the most beautiful show girl in London."[17] She later appeared fleetingly as one of the servant girls in the lavish 1946 British film, *Caesar and Cleopatra*, directed by Gabriel Pascal and starring Claude Rains, Vivien Leigh, and Stewart Granger.

On August 1, Lieutenant Kearns sent a memo to his commanding general. The subject line was brief and to the point. It read: "Permission to Marry."[18] The wedding took place at four o'clock on October 5, 1943. It was a typically rainy afternoon at St. Mary's, a large Anglican church in Bryanston Square in the Borough of Marylebone, London. Gwen's mother, Elizabeth Shoring, served as a witness. Her father, Harry Shoring, was part owner and manager of music halls throughout the city. Gwen detested him and couldn't forgive him for leaving her mother when she was born, so he was not invited. Because of the war, no member of Kearns's family nor any of his old Chums could attend.

The other legal witness and best man was Lt. Edward L. Saxe, Kearns's good friend and a member of Gen. Dwight D. Eisenhower's staff. A small group of military friends also attended the service. A reception followed "where surprisingly large stores of liquid rations have been cashed in preparation."[19]

As the war moved toward its most decisive moment in Europe, Kearns worked from an office across the street from Supreme Allied Command Headquarters. After the initial assault in June, he went ashore at Normandy in August 1944. Carrying with him two military-issue handguns—a .45 pistol and a .38 revolver—a fifteen-jewel pocket watch, a gas mask, and a portable Corona typewriter, he followed the advancing troops into Paris, where he was named commanding officer, CIC Detachment, Area "B," which covered half of the metropolitan area.[20]

When Paris was secure, Lieutenant Kearns briefly returned to London to "get as much information concerning sabotage as possible"[21] before going back to Europe and moving with the Allies into Germany. As cities fell, he quickly set up counterintelligence training programs to help secure the American troops now plunged deep into enemy territory and to apprehend named war criminals on the army's "Wanted List."[22] Throughout the rest of the war, Kearns and his troops pursued, arrested, and interrogated Nazi military officials, including members of the SS and Gestapo, as well as chased after common criminals and suspected politicians who associated with Nazi leader Adolph Hitler. For those detainee prisoners of war who were rounded up and deemed most important to the Allies, Kearns served as their escort back to London. On October 1, he was promoted to captain.

He also was one of the first American soldiers to see the horror inflicted on prisoners at Dachau, the second concentration camp to be liberated by British and American forces. This painful experience initiated the nightmares that haunted him for the rest of his life. He said the smell and sights were "just ghastly."

His separation from the army came on January 12, 1946.[23] For his service, the twenty-nine-year-old Captain Kearns was awarded the pre–Pearl Harbor service ribbon, European Theater of Operations service ribbon, a Bronze Star (Rhineland campaign), and five Overseas Stripes.[24] His time in the service also gave him language skills in German, French, Spanish, and Portuguese.

He and Gwen moved back to the United States, where Kearns picked up his career as a journalist once again. Over the next few years he moved from job to job, trying to find something that fulfilled his sense of adventure, allowed him to travel, and maintained his standing as a family man.

He returned to Miami Beach, this time taking the position of city editor and columnist for the *Star*, where he wrote about the area's attractive and fast-moving night life. But this lightweight assignment didn't satisfy him, so he signed on as an associate editor at *Digest & Review* magazine in New York. Yet for all of the prestige of an editorial job in the largest metropolitan media market, even it was too limiting. Looking to do more, he moved once again, taking his first step into what would later become the profession that defined his life: news editor at WMAL-AM in Washington, DC. But for all of the interesting work involved at a major broadcast outlet in the nation's capital, it still wasn't enough to satisfy the wanderlust in him that beckoned from his experiences during the war. Kearns wanted to go back to Europe.

Now confident in his own talent as a writer, he decided to become a freelancer. His long-term plan was to achieve enough success at home in order to take his wife back to Europe. So he and Gwendy settled temporarily in an apartment on West 80th Street in New York City, where he could get enough work that they could save up to move back to England.

Good writers need good agents, so Kearns signed a contract with Bertha Klausner, a leading New York and Hollywood literary agent who represented a broad range of established and promising writers. On her clientele list were social novelists Upton Sinclair and Anthony Burgess and actors Basil Rathbone, Joe E. Brown, Theda Bera, and Lionel Barrymore. Over her long career, she guided to the stage and movie screen such classics as *Yentl* and *Zorba the Greek*. Under the terms of their new relationship, she would market Kearns's manuscripts, challenge and nurture his creative abilities, and provide him with the muscle he needed to jump-start his career as a freelance writer.

Most of his successful output went to some of the leading magazines of the time—the *American Mercury*, *Salute*, *Coronet*, *Look*, *Cosmopolitan*, and *Esquire*. Then in 1948, his old wartime friend and best man, Edward Saxe, recommended to US WAC Capt. Kay Summersby and her publisher at Prentice-Hall that she let Kearns edit her postwar memoir, which was being developed under the working title, *Eisenhower's "Girl Friday."*[25]

For the attractive young Irish woman, widely recognized as the person who served as chauffeur of the then general and future president, it was to be a straightforward collaborative arrangement. Kearns was given a month to pull together her notes and create a workable, 110,000-word manuscript, of which *Editor & Publisher* later would describe him as "an able, experienced wordsmith."[26]

To launch their newfound partnership, Summersby paid Kearns one dollar in advance, and he agreed "to work diligently at the preparation of these memoirs."[27] Upon publication, he would get a byline—"Edited by Michael Kearns"—using his middle name instead of the name by which he would later be known, and 27 percent of the royalties paid by the publisher. From his portion of the receipts, Kearns paid Klausner a commission.

Anticipating a good launch, Prentice-Hall paid them an advance of $1,000, and Summersby split it evenly with Kearns. Her agent, George T. Bye, told him in a letter, "You would have been pleased to have heard the compliments for the writing in the book from the staff of Prentice-Hall."[28]

To nobody's surprise, the book was a sure bet. *Eisenhower Was My Boss*, the alternate title suggested by Kearns, became a runaway, international best seller.[29] The first and second hardcover printings of five thousand copies each sold out quickly and another fifteen thousand were hastily put on press. Kearns got his byline in the US edition, but he complained to his agent that the UK version, published by T. Werner Laurie Ltd., "makes me into a complete ghost—I have no sub-byline whatsoever!"[30] He already was aware that a friend of Summersby's had given an advance copy of the book to Academy Award–winning director William Wyler, whose most recent film, *The Best Years of Our Lives*, dramatized the problems of returning veterans. Kearns wanted to make sure that Hollywood didn't overlook his talents as a writer.

He voiced the same concern about recognition when several daily newspapers—the *Los Angeles Times*, the *Chicago Daily News*, the *Washington News*, and the *New York World Telegram*—picked up the story for serialization.[31] Although he ultimately got his byline when *Look* magazine picked it up for a three-part adaptation later that fall, he told Klausner that their version was "really appalling, the nuances they've inserted, the way they dug into the center of the book to get the lead, etc. I certainly feel no pride in the thing . . . all I'm interested in is the money from it," amounting to $1,500 more in income, the stake that he and Gwen needed to start their lives comfortably in England.

This success led to other proposed book deals at Prentice-Hall: ghosting another biography in the spring of 1949 for actress and model Anita Colby and even writing a cookbook. However, nothing ever became of these projects. As happens with publishers, they move on to stay ahead of their audiences. Then just as quickly the proposed topics no longer held any mass appeal.

In England, the reviews for the Summersby book were generally positive. The leading literary magazine there, *John O'London's Weekly*, said of Summersby (and by inference, Kearns), "She writes clearly, keeping the sentiment to a minimum, in unflagging spirits and generosity of tone. For a multitude of readers, *Eisenhower Was My Boss* can have no rival in freshness among books describing the personalities of the War."[32]

By October, Kearns and his wife had taken a six-month lease on a home in England at West Wittering, Sussex, where he set about writing article outlines that Klausner could pitch to magazine editors back home. He also started contacting publishers around London. The first major work he submitted was a sixteen-page manuscript, "Socialized Medicine Has Its Headaches," for the Toronto *Star Weekly*. He also agreed to go back to the United States in the spring to write a film based on Mooseheart, the headquarters of the Loyal Order of the Moose, today called Moose International. This project provided his family with some much-needed financial security. He told Klausner that "this is the first time in our married life we can look so far ahead with quiet nerves."[33] Gwendy, meanwhile, had taken up a new art form—sculpting.

While working on the Moose International script in Laguna Beach, California, Kearns wrote speeches for Robert Gross, president of Lockheed Corporation, and later accepted a position as assistant publicity director for incumbent California Gov. Earl Warren's successful 1950 reelection campaign.

Freelance writing, however, was hard work. Although he was becoming successful, Kearns started to look for a way to combine his talent with his daring spirit and desire to live full-time in Europe. As word of this started to make the rounds among his friends and colleagues, once again Edward Saxe was there to help.

Saxe, now an executive working directly for Columbia Broadcasting System chairman and CEO William S. Paley, challenged Kearns to accept an assignment to work for the network as a stringer, or part-time reporter, in Cairo, Egypt.[34] After successful interviews and auditions at the company's headquarters in New York, Kearns went home to pack.

CHAPTER FOUR

"The Unrealistic or Impossible Assignment"

....

F rank Kearns was thirty-five years old when he arrived in Cairo. A former colleague in London said it was like "having a film star walking into the office. He was so personable . . . so handsome, smiling."[1] He was six feet tall, weighed 185 pounds, and had blond hair and blue, piercing eyes. He exuded confidence and was ready for his new role as a network reporter.

Carrying with him two important contracts, they would sustain him and his family in their new life in the Middle East. The first and most important contract was with CBS News where, as a "Special Correspondent for the C.B.S. Radio Network," he would have responsibility for covering stories around Africa and the Middle East. His letter of introduction was written by Wells Church, director of news and public affairs for CBS Radio, who suggested that "Anything that may be done to facilitate his work will be greatly appreciated by the Columbia Broadcasting System."[2]

Working there as a stringer, he was paid a modest retainer and able to earn more on a piecework basis for contributions to commercial programs on the network. These included documentaries, television news reports, and stories for radio. It wouldn't be easy with a family. But this was the break he had been seeking. To pad his income, he had another contract. This one was with his old friends at Prentice-Hall. For them, he would write a book about modern Egypt. But reading through his signed contract, there was no mention of payment. Did he receive an advance to sustain his research in Egypt, or would payment come only at the end? What causes flags to be raised about this arrangement and the one with CBS is that it's hard to imagine that Kearns could sustain himself and his family on a stringer's salary. The only answer is that a subsidy would have to come from a third source. But where? A possible answer becomes much clearer later on.

At CBS Television, the News and Public Affairs departments in 1953 were separate operations and competed for airtime. News often found itself with more content available than it could fit into the nightly, fifteen-minute newscasts. Much of it was the result of on-the-spot coverage of breaking events shot by a global team of staff and freelance cameramen using a relatively portable, 16-millimeter format—mostly silent, black-and-white film, but some sound-with-film reports were available—rather than carefully crafted and staged productions, like those developed by Edward R. Murrow and Fred Friendly in bulky and more costly, Hollywood-style, 35-millimeter format.

As a result of their increasing productivity, more long-form programming was being recommended by the far-flung bureaus at CBS. Within three years, news managers knew that if they didn't fill the time that had been allocated to the recently canceled *See It Now*, they'd lose it to what an embittered Murrow later described as "evidence of decadence, escapism and insulation from the realities of the world in which we live."[3] A growing list of cameramen—Bill McClure, John Tiffin, and Johnny Peters in London, Gerhard Schwartzkopf in Frankfurt, George Markham in Paris, and Paul Bruck in Israel—delivered material that was growing in sophistication . . . and volume.

In his first two years in Cairo, Kearns worked mostly for CBS Radio. Then on July 21, 1955, he filed his first report for television where he and cameraman Yousef Masraff covered an "Underground Press Conference" in Cairo featuring Egyptian antiquities Professor Zakaria Ghonem, who discovered the Sakkara Step Pyramid.[4] It wasn't until November 11 before he submitted another report, which was his first of many on the Israeli-Egyptian war. A week later, he interviewed Egyptian President Nasser the first time for television. By year-end, he'd filed three more TV news reports.

The television work picked up considerably in 1956. Frank Kearns filed eighteen reports that year, starting with an interview with Maj. Gen. Ali Au

Nuwar of the Jordanian army and quickly moving to Nicosia, Cyprus, to deliver impressive reports on the street battles there between Greek and Turkish factions. Of this coverage, a wire from his boss in New York said it all: "Kearns from [John] Day want to express deepest appreciation for continuingly superb job during long crisis."

Two other international events took place in late 1956 that generated what CBS News President Sig Mickelson called "of sufficient public interest and adequate resources to deliver extended coverage"[5]: the anti-communist revolution in Hungary and the continuation of the Egyptian-Israeli war. These dramatic centers of ideological and economic conflicts along with an increasing public demand for more information about them allowed CBS "to exploit this new capability. It furnished an opening to use surplus camera footage for clarifying some of the murky issues that lurked in the background."[6] It also allowed the network to demonstrate the cohesion and value that rose out of the combined radio and television news operations, which had been formally merged back in August 1954. Over the next two years, CBS News employed 165 full-time staff for television, plus fifty-three correspondents, not including "the small army of domestic and foreign stringers who are available on call."[7] Kearns was among them.

At the start of 1957, four programs were ordered up for production. The first scheduled to run was *The Arab Tide* (broadcast date unknown), which focused on the growing Arab unity movement, led by Egyptian President Nasser; *Jordan, Key to the Middle East* (broadcast August 27, 1958), which highlighted the struggles of a newly formed country carved out next to Israel by agreements forged in World War II but without a unifying population; and *Kuwait: Middle East Oil Prize* (broadcast July 23, 1958), which focused attention on the key resource being fought over in the Middle East.[8] A fourth program, *Mid East Smoke Screen* (broadcast December 3, 1957), would be a special report on the overall situation in that volatile region of the world.[9]

Just as the business of news was changing, the television networks—especially CBS—began to exercise a new level of independence and deliver programming that didn't always toe the line being disseminated by politicians in Washington. Their reporting was no longer in lockstep with the views of the United States government. They were dance partners nonetheless. Case in point: The CBS Sunday public affairs program, *Face the Nation*, broadcast an hour-long interview with Soviet Premier Nikita Khrushchev, treating him with the same deference that was given other political leaders who sided with US views. Despite harsh backlash, CBS Network President Frank Stanton said that "Khrushchev and his views are of great importance to our world and the world of our children. The less this man . . . remains a myth or a dark legend or a mystery to the American people, the more certain they are to size him up correctly."[10] The movement toward news programming of broader, not always government-friendly, interest was underway.

Also on television's programming schedule, its darker, more cynical side was showing. The prime-time quiz show scandals had erupted. All of the major networks—ABC, CBS, and NBC—were affected. As licensees of the Federal Communications Commission, this forced them to counterbalance these scandalous program offerings by serving up prestigious documentary shows—*Close-Up* on ABC, *NBC White Paper*, and *CBS Reports*—even if most of these news programs were "generally relegated to late nights and the Sunday afternoon 'cultural ghetto.'"[11]

By late spring of 1957 at the CBS News headquarters' famed Graybar Building on Lexington Avenue and Forty-Second Street in New York, foreign editor Ralph Paskman and his team had a bold idea for yet another program—one that they described as "a special show"—which would get out ahead of all the others in production. Their plan was to devote a full hour to the Algerian situation. The first half of the program would show the French side—some of the hundreds of thousands of French troops fortifying towns around the countryside and patrolling in the notorious Casbah. It would be reported by their award-winning, Paris-based correspondent David Schoenbrun, who was close to the French government. The second half would be devoted to the nationalist rebels, showing how they recruit and train troops, supply them with arms, and fight in these extraordinary circumstances. For that part of the story, they turned to their Cairo-based stringers—Frank Kearns and Yousef Masraff—to go to work on what Paskman acknowledged "may be a bit unrealistic or impossible" but "should serve to stimulate your imagination."[12] Kearns reported back that he thought they could make the right contacts that would get them into Algeria.

For help, Kearns turned to his close friends Miles Copeland Jr. and James Eichelberger. Copeland lived with his family in a suburb of Cairo in a house where only a fence separated him from one of Nasser's closest associates. They exchanged information on almost a daily basis. As head of the CIA station in Egypt, Eichelberger would know exactly how to connect Kearns to the FLN. There's little question that they would help their friend because whatever he would find out would strengthen their reports back to officials in Washington.

As their departure date of July 11 grew closer, Paskman sent a three-page letter to Kearns, explaining what New York hoped to accomplish by their trip, but instructing him "to make the most of this opportunity and get everything you can this time because undoubtedly there'll be no chance to go back once you get out."[13]

The experienced foreign editor knew that with a news crew drawn from reliable stringers he still had to provide more guidance than usual in order to get professional—versus amateur—results if their part of the story was to be included in a major production.

"Masraff has done wonders with his camera work," Paskman acknowledged, "particularly when you consider that he receives so little real guidance from New York and has never seen how we use film. Even so, *we must emphasize the absolute need for shooting complete sequences instead of a series of unintegrated shots* [emphasis indicated by Kearns]. We know that you and Masraff want to turn out the best possible job and we want to make the most possible use of your work, therefore the special stress on this point.

"If Masraff has even the slightest feeling that something went wrong during one of his filmings please make every effort to do it over again," Paskman continued. "We would hate to lose any vital segments because of technical trouble."[14]

In a detailed instruction sheet from Jack Bush, manager of film production for CBS News, Masraff was specifically told that in shooting each sequence he should provide "enough detail to allow the television viewer time to identify himself as a spectator. Individual, quick shots create an emotional detachment which loses for us the opportunity to recreate the realism of the event."[15] The team in New York clearly understood the power of the medium.

Paskman specified what equipment his stringers should take with them, including some being shipped by CBS in New York and other components they would have to acquire in Cairo, amounting to some 400 pounds in total. This included 18,000 feet of raw film stock—40 100-foot rolls and 10 400-foot rolls of tropic-packed DuPont 930,[16] 80 rolls of 100-foot Tri-X and 10 200-foot rolls of Tri-X[17]—a tripod, and "more than one exposure meter in case one goes bad." They wouldn't, however, be getting a Zoomar lens[18] "because its use would be more of a risk than an advantage—you can't focus it through the lens."

Further, Paskman urged Kearns to keep a daily diary "to give us an even better knowledge of exactly what you have seen and experienced.... This would be an invaluable aid for scripting and film editing and could possibly even add up to a special radio show."

To get their story back to New York after they have gotten out of Algeria, the instructions were specific: "We do not want you to entrust your film and tape to anybody for shipment. Rather than take chances we want you to hold on to all of it for shipment at one time by Masraff when he himself can get to an airport and consign it properly. Carry it out yourselves instead of giving it to anybody to hold and deliver to you. One mishap here could wash the whole job down the drain."

Paskman knew that the story his team was about to pursue was dangerous. He told Kearns, "If we don't hear from you by a certain date we will make inquiries if necessary."

To drive home the point, he continued, "[W]e don't want you and Masraff to expose yourselves to danger any more than necessary. We don't expect either of you to risk getting shot or captured while trying to cover some real action with yourselves in the middle."

As if to lighten the moment, he continued, "We like you fellows too much and, besides, you aren't any good to us dead—we need you back in Cairo sooner or later!"

In closing, Paskman said that he simply wanted them to do their "usual thorough, honest, and objective reporting. We have no axe to grind and want nothing more or less than the truth of what is happening in Algeria. You will have a unique opportunity to make such a report—the first one by an experienced American newsman—so really lay it on the line."[19]

Rebellion with its sudden bloody street clashes, its explosive, murderous ambushes, and its cruel and persistent attacks against unarmed populations wasn't new to Frank Kearns. A year earlier, he had won an Overseas Press Club of America citation for his reporting from strife-torn Cyprus. He'd been

covering deadly fighting in the Middle East and Africa for four years. His
detailed reports from Sinai that same year were widely recognized as first-rate
back in New York.[19]

During World War II he was briefly stationed in Algiers, where he helped
to plan the security requirements for the Allied assault against the Germans
across the southern Mediterranean, starting in Sicily and advancing through
Italy. So he had a general idea of the landscape and what they'd be up against
on this trip.

Knowing the inherent danger in reporting a story like this, Kearns and
Masraff made the decision to go into Algeria without passports, visas, or the
credentials normally possessed by newsmen covering a war today. There was no
practice of *embedding* reporters, like the American's had done in Iraq. Kearns
was fully aware that, if caught pursuing this nearly impossible assignment, he
would probably be shot. Masraff could expect a similar fate. But, as good journalists and not as easily mobile because of the technology used in that time,
they went anyway, taking with them four hundred pounds of gear.

Frank Kearns often served as his own audio man in the field. (Photo by Yousef Masraff. Courtesy of Michael Kearns.)

In 1956, Frank Kearns worked as a stringer for CBS News in Cairo, Egypt. Here he interviews two members of the United Nations Emergency Force at the Suez Canal after British and French forces left the region. UN troops would remain there until May 1967.

Egyptian President Gamal Abdel Nasser patiently waits while CBS News's Frank Kearns and Yousef Masraff (behind the camera, under the tree branch) shoot a cutaway. This was Kearns's first interview with Nasser. Just before the interview started, Nasser told Masraff that his reporter was working with the CIA. (Photo by Yousef Masraff. Courtesy of Sara Kearns.)

In the days leading up to his investigation in Algeria, Frank Kearns conducts an interview in front of the Great Sphinx of Giza, near Cairo, Egypt. (Photographer unknown. Courtesy of Michael Kearns.)

Preparing for their arduous six-week trek into the mountains of eastern Algeria, Frank Kearns and Yousef Masraff took daily hikes around Tunis and Carthage. (Photo by Yousef Masraff. Courtesy of Sara Kearns.)

Yousef Masraff (fourth from the left) and Frank Kearns (plaid shirt) pose with a fighting unit of FLN soldiers, armed with automatic weapons brought over from Tunisia. (Photographer unknown. Courtesy of Michael Kearns).

Frank Kearns shoots a "stand upper" report for the documentary Algeria Aflame. Yousef Masraff is behind the camera. Kearns said that the Algerian army is "sustained by a singleness of purpose. Even the most neutral, objective reporter must report that the vast majority of these men are here for one reason only . . . to fight the French, to force the French to leave what they regard as their country."

Every day, patrols arrive and leave the camp. The wounded who make it back to the camp receive first-aid treatment and then return to their units. Frank Kearns watches as one of "the unlucky ones" is loaded into a truck and taken across the frontier to a hospital in Tunisia.

Under the watchful eye of an armed sentinel, Frank Kearns takes a break from the march, which covered up to 375 miles through rugged mountains. With every step they had to avoid the French army, which had learned that two journalists were among the FLN rebels.

Camp life often was routine. Here Frank Kearns (seated) gets his beard trimmed as Yousef Masraff (cup in hand) looks on.

In a report prepared especially for television, Kearns summarized what he had learned about the Algerians: "Put it all together . . . civilian resistance . . . organized terrorism . . . ambushes . . . sabotage . . . a tough army created especially for this war, this mountain country . . . and you begin to understand how the Algerians tie-up a great, modern army like that of the French here in Algeria."

Frank Kearns works on a news script. He noted that "in private conversations, these soldiers admit frankly they're oriented toward the West, want no part of the communist East. . . . They say they are not going through all this to replace what they describe as French colonialism and imperialism, for Russian colonialism and imperialism."

Frank Kearns takes a break with some of the young soldiers leading him through the mountains of Algeria. Along the way, he asked if there is a single leader for the army rather than a committee running it, as he has been told. His conclusion: The army is directed by "a mysterious, shadowy, secret figure—one of the most mysterious men in the world today."

Leaving behind the indelible words he saw scribbled across Europe during World War II, Frank Kearns posted a message for whomever followed behind him.

Lost for three days in the Sahara Desert in 1963 when the truck in which he was riding was ambushed by Moroccan soldiers, Frank Kearns waits to be transported back to Algiers. It was the safe guidance of shooting stars following prayers by Yousef Masraff that led both men and their loved ones to wear a gold-chain necklace of the Southern Cross. (Photo by Yousef Masraff. Courtesy of Michael Kearns.)

In October 1963, Frank Kearns interviewed former FLN rebel leader Hocine Ait Ahmed at his mountain stronghold. A month earlier he started the Socialist Forces Front (FFS), the historical political opposition in Algeria set up after the country won its independence from France.

CHAPTER FIVE

Algerian Diary

....

DIARY:

THURSDAY, JULY 11TH — This is the Big Day. By tomorrow
night, we'll be in Tunis.[1] Then, several days later, with
the Algerian rebels, deep inside Algeria. Feeling more and
more like a character in a spy movie, paid a last quick
visit to the Algerian offices here in Cairo.[2] The entrance
fits the mood — over the door is the sign of an Egyptian
stamp dealer, a scene straight from a Hitchcock thriller.
Our contact, one of 34 members of the central committee
which runs the Algerians' National Liberation Front, the
FLN, says he's sorry, but he can't go with us, as planned.[3]
Instead, we'll be met at Tunis airport, he says, by a short
man in dark glasses, a man who has seen us here in Cairo.
Just in case anything goes wrong, he gives us a letter of
identification, and an address in Tunis, in the Arab quarter, as an emergency contact. I ask about our mountainous luggage, 24 pieces of radio and TV equipment. Won't it
create a scene, focus attention on us, at Tunis airport?
No, he assures me; everything is arranged. "You'll have
100-percent safety," he adds, "sécurité totale." Masraff[4]
and I still have our doubts. But this is a story, a real
story; and we're reporters. At the same time, we're fathers
and husbands, and the parting from our families tonight is
going to be especially painful. The takeoff is scheduled
just after midnight.

FRIDAY, JULY 12TH — So far, so good. We're in Tunis. Took
off from Cairo just after 1 o'clock this morning, stopped
briefly in Athens, arrived in Rome in time for breakfast.

A wonderful Italian breakfast, too, with wonderful Brioche, at a sidewalk café with an impromptu floorshow. The show: A beautiful Italian blonde, strolling and jiggling by to the corner, waiting impatiently for the bus. Made Marilyn Monroe look like a skinny, awkward, frigid adolescent. After breakfast, made most of our six-hour stopover by strolling along the streets and shops of Rome, almost exciting after the Middle East. No beggars, no loafers, no dirt and dust, no galabayas;[5] it's good to be back in the West, even for a few hours. Got some travelers checks at American Express, attended to some final business details and sent a final cable to CBS news, in New York, at the Rome CBS Bureau.[6] Warmed by a waiting cable which wishes us best of luck in our adventure. Same time, went out and bought a vicious-looking dagger-knife, just in case. Also, some flashlights with extra batteries. Yet, at the airport bar, I find myself gulping 3 glasses of milk . . . delicious after the Gamoosa, or water buffalo, milk of Egypt. From Rome to Tunis, from Europe to Africa, takes just 1 1/2 hours.[7] Circling the beautiful Bay of Tunis, as blue as that of Naples, both of us admit to somewhat nervous stomachs. On the ground, in the modernistic El Aouina airport building, we look around frantically for a small man with dark glasses. Virtually every man there is small, and wearing dark glasses. Customs people question the cigarettes in our hand luggage, then pass us on to the police window, for passport inspection. Later, as the customs men stare with horror at our 24 pieces of luggage, one small man with dark glasses comes up and introduces himself, in French. We have made contact. He helps us through customs, introduces us to his friend, then escorts us outside the customs barrier to an entire committee of the FLN. We feel about as inconspicuous as two elephants in a tea shop. But everyone is warm and cordial, apparently perfectly at ease. No one speaks English, but their French is perfect, obviously more natural than Arabic, and Masraff speaks fluent French, as well as Arabic, plus Italian, Spanish, Greek, Armenian, and assorted other tongues. The committee steps aside for a whispered conference, then returns to tell us that, instead of putting us up at a secret house in the Arab quarter, they're taking us to an inconspicuous hotel. Two cars and a station wagon are waiting. Our equipment is whisked off to the secret house; we are taken to the hotel. Whispered

conversation in the lobby, over soft drinks, then a two-
hour siesta. Then, a drive out to the beach, at Gamiyart,
near ancient Carthage, for beer or ice cream, overlooking
the magnificent bay, under a full moon. Later, dinner with
one of the FLN leaders, and a long, long conversation,
Masraff translating on both sides, ranging over Algeria,
Tunisia, France, America, Egypt, Gamal Abdel Nasser,
Palestine, Israel, the Russians, Morocco, EVERYthing. And
now, to bed. Outside, on the patio just below my first-floor
window, is a Christian wedding party, complete with rock-
n-roll music amplified to deafness pitch by a very efficient
public address system. Even so, sleep will come easy tonight. Fatigue is the best sleeping-pill.

SATURDAY, JULY 13TH - Two FLN friends pick us up at 10 a.m.
One says our departure will be delayed several days - the
French army is deploying units all along the Tunisian-
Algerian border.[8] Downtown to unmarked fourth-floor office
and long chat about situation. One of the more military
types is horrified at our 374 pounds of luggage, reminds us
it all has to be hand-carried for our entire trip. What
about the horses and donkeys mentioned back in Cairo? I
ask. He laughs. This trip, he emphasizes, will all be made
on foot. We'll walk, he adds, about 10 or 12 days straight,
to get to an area of what he calls "sécurité totale." This,
we gather, is the FLN army's mountain headquarters, where
we can work in peace . . . unless, of course the French
mount a sudden attack, with up to 18-thousand troops.
What happens then? "Mobilité," he replies. "We just bury
the equipment and scatter, run and hide." Hide? Hide from
18,000 trained French soldiers? He laughs again, but makes
no comment. We decide to jettison as much of our equipment as possible, get down to bed-rock. Even WE will have
to carry up to 30 pounds of equipment apiece. There'll be
rest-period every 4 or 5 hours, we're told. But, altogether, we'll have to walk about 600 kilometers - 375 miles,
375 miles on foot. While we taxi-riding foreigners try to
digest this indigestible fact, the hike of 375 miles, one
of the leaders takes our measurements. We will have to wear
uniforms, it seems; otherwise, the Algerian rebel units, or
the Algerian villagers, might shoot us. This seems logical, and we agree. Then we're asked, what kind of arms do
you want? Rifle, revolver, sub-machine gune (sic), or what?

Here, we disagree. We're journalists, not soldiers; we're
foreigners, not Algerians; we're reporters, not partisans.
One of the men points out that the French don't acknowledge this as a war; therefore, there's no such thing as a
war correspondent. Besides, he adds, if they start shooting
close, you can hardly defend yourself with a press card. He
has a point. But we insist, no arms; uniforms, okay; but,
no arms. One leader explains we'll be delayed 4 or 5 days
in leaving; a special army section he says, is being sent
down from the mountain quarters to meet us at the border
crossing-point.[9] These men, he adds, will make in 4 or 5
days the same trip they expect us city-boys to take 10 or
12 days to complete. Impressed, and very, very thoughtful,
we go to lunch, a good French lunch, with one of the FLN
committee members, a former professional man from Algeirs
(sic). As we go downstairs from the office, one of the
toughest of the group cries out in alarm—one of my shoe
laces is untied. The same man who has just told us about
walking 375 miles through 18,000 French soldiers shakes his
head reprovingly, at my flapping shoelaces . . . "It's dangerous!" he says. After a short siesta back at the hotel,
Masraff and I start the first of a series of daily hikes
around Tunis, to toughen up, to get in training. After an
hour, it takes all our will power not to take a taxi back
to the hotel. Instead, however, we walk. And a short time
later, two FLN men pick us up for a wild, 70-miles-per-
hour ride to an Arab suburb where we're ushered into a low,
squat, whitewashed building which is one of their secret
hangouts. We shake hands silently with a group of comrades,
mostly teen-agers (sic). At our friends' request, one shows
us his scarred and atrophied arm, result of wounds in a
mountain battle with the French, plus the scars where a
bullet entered the center of his chest and came out, mirac-
ulously, under his armpit. Obviously, these boys know what
war is like. In a locked storeroom filled with rifles, shot-
guns, sub-machine guns and boxes of ammunition, we inspect
our radio and TV equipment, set it up and test every part.
Everything is okay. Then, after typical Arab hospitality,
dishes of sherbert (sic), we are taken back to the hotel. A
walk downtown, for dinner, then more walking, for exercise,
and back to sleep. Tonight, it's a Moslem wedding in the
patio, all women, with sweets and cakes, fruit juices and
soft drinks, the bride enthroned on the veranda, and wild,

ear-splitting Arabic music, plus belly-dancer and high-
voiced Arabic singers.

SUNDAY, JULY 14TH – Bastille Day, the French 4th of July.[10]
Walking and shopping around Tunis, you begin to understand
why the French are so reluctant to give up North Africa.
This place is completely French. The English, somehow, were
never so successful in Anglicizing Egypt, or Cyprus, or
even Jordan. Tunis, for example, has seen a lot of invaders
come and go, starting back in the 12th Century, B.C., when
Carthage was bustling and alive. It has been through the
pagan and Christian Roman epochs, the vandal and Byzantine
epochs, and the Moslem epoch which began in 647 A.D. Not
very long ago, this place was full of Germans and Italians,
then Americans and the British. But it is, above all, even
now, with its new independence from the French, predomi-
nantly French.[11] I've seen a lot of world capitals, but this
is the first place I couldn't find an English or American
book or magazine . . . not a single English newspaper.
Everyone from shoeshine boy to taxi driver speaks French.
Arabic papers have little circulation here in Tunis. A
pharmacist told us today that practically everything in
his shop comes from France; no drugs from Italy, America,
Germany or Britain; all French. Ditto for the shops,
all French merchandise, everything from radios and light
plugs to clothes and bijou. French cars in the streets,
French clothes on the people, the French language on their
tongues. Sidewalk cafes, broad, tree-fringed boulevards,
Gitane and Gaulois cigarettes . . . all French. Hollywood
cowboy movies, with cowboys speaking well-synchronized
French. Pushing such thoughts aside, spent most of today
studying pamphlets, leaflets and documents furnished by the
FLN, plus some background notes and material I brought from
Cairo, to balance with some French viewpoints and sta-
tistics. Masraff and I spent hours walking around Tunis
again, "in training." At 6:30 p.m., a brief meeting with
FLN leaders. Both of us notice they seem to have friends
and contacts all over Tunis . . . on the streets . . . in
the shops . . . in some of the hotels . . . and restau-
rants. A word here, a nod there. At one restaurant the
other day, the waiter silently indicated we should move to
the next room. "A friend of ours," the FLN man explained.
"He was worried about us talking, so close to the French

head-waiter." Back to the hotel to sleep, despite another
wedding party in the patio, the third straight . . . this
time, a Jewish wedding . . . a wonderful comment on Tunisia
is tolerant live-and-let-live attitude, refreshing after
the atmosphere these days in Cairo.

MONDAY, JULY 15TH — No one shows up for our clandestine
10 a.m. meeting. Masraff and I spend the shank[12] of the
day "hiking" around Tunis, especially the port area. At
4:30, our friends show up, bringing the English-speaking
friend I requested. He is a young student with good academic knowledge of English, but, unfortunately, absolutely
no practice. Conversation with him is painful; we end up in
part-English, part-French, part-Arabic baby-talk. No good
for American radio or TV, as a FLN spokesman. Later, at
their downtown offices, the leaders say our departure will
be delayed another 6 or 7 days, probably until next Monday.
The explanation is vague. But we gather that the French
are making it more and more difficult to travel through the
mountains. Whatever the reasons, the delay is definite, and
makes us still more restless and nervous. One man in the
office has just come back from what he describes as a regular trip to Tripoli, to bring arms in from Libya . . . pre-
sumably, altho (sic) there is no evidence, from Egypt.[13] We
learn, with straight faces, that there are some 80-thousand
French troops in the mountains we plan to enter . . . and
we will walk 375 miles there and back, sometimes right
through the camps of 80-thousand French soldiers. Our
professional ego is soothed somewhat, however, by assur-
ances that we'll be the first foreign journalists ever to
make this trip right in to the rebel headquarters, that CBS
news will have another beat, a scoop, another First. In the
evening, we take a tiny taxi to a suburban address, a big
and lush villa. There, in a beautiful garden, under a full
moon, we see a propaganda movie produced for the FLN by a
nervous young Frenchman. The film is intensely anti-colonial
and sincere on the surface, but dull and amateurishly
produced. Privately, Masraff and I fear the young producer is a French agent. He is much too curious about us, asks
far too many questions, and says he is leaving for France
soon . . . to show the film at so-called private meetings.
However, the FLN men accept him at face-value. And there's
nothing we can do about it. Also see a Tunisian newsreel;

the second, incidentally, we've seen here with smiling,
grinning propaganda films from Red China. Arab hospitality –
coffee, a steady procession of sweetmeats and cakes and
cookies, lemonade, and heavy rose syrup made from roses.
The FLN top brass leave early, before the newsreel, for an
important rendezvous somewhere. We finally get a ride downtown, about midnight. The patio below is silent for the
first time. And both of us find it impossible to sleep, after
the last three wedding parties, in this excrutiating (sic)
silence. First time we've had a chance to think . . . to
imagine what the trip is going to be like . . . that's the
trouble. A 375-mile hike through 80-thousand French troops
who have orders to shoot anything or anybody who moves, to
shoot on sight. . . . It's taking four sleeping pills to
smother these thoughts.[14] But, now, at 4:30 a.m., sleep is
coming.

TUESDAY, JULY 16TH – Another delay. This time, in our trip
South, to make radio and TV reports on a typical Algerian
refugee camp. All set for 5 o'clock this morning, then,
last night, postponed 24 hours. Meantime, we've been getting acquainted with "Mahmoud," who, it turns out, is to
be the leader of our expedition. We're both happy about
this, as Mahmoud is the one man we'd both choose to take
on this job. Tall, solidly built, like a fullback, with a
powerful jaw and bright, intense eyes, he is a born leader,
and radiates strength. Yet, unlike most men of this type,
Mahmoud is gentle, polite, and warmly friendly, never feels
called upon to flout his authority or his power. His men,
obviously, would follow him straight into Paris, if necessary. Young, about 25, he's absolutely frank about his
work and his cause, but has the guerrilla leader's natural
reticence about his personal background. We know only that
he comes from a good family in Algeria, a land-owning
family; that something unmentionable happened to his wife
and child; that his brother was killed by the French, the
same French who, searching for Mahmoud killed his father
for not "cooperating." So Mahmoud, not unnaturally, has
pretty strong feelings about the whole situation. His
is absolutely dedicated to his cause, yet, strangely, is
surprisingly objective and not fanatic. He speaks fluent
French, as well as Arabic, calls his companions "Frere" or
"Ikhwan" . . . brother . . . and means it. In any country,

he would be a born leader, and regardless of how you look
at the political scene, an absolutely sincere patriot. He
has been traveling back and forth into the Algerian mountains some 9 or 10 months now, knows every rock and crag
and bush and tree of the entire, vast area. And I imagine
he can be utterly ruthless, when necessary. At the same
time, when I asked about dogs in the mountains, he replied
with obvious pain, that most of the mountain dogs had to
be killed. Too noisy; unconscious traitors to their beloved
owners, was the way he put it. Do the French use dogs? I
asked. Yes, he replied, and they are formidable. Then he
grinned. "But we have a special technique for discourag-
ing bloodhounds. The last man in a mountain patrol simply
sprinkles a special powder for bloodhound noses: Hot red
pepper." Mahmoud, incidentally, just telephoned to tell us
to be ready at 8 o'clock tomorrow morning for our trip to
the Algerian refugee camp.

WEDNESDAY, JULY 17TH - Off to an unexplained late start,
10:30 a.m. Most of our equipment tucked away in a secret
compartment of Mahmoud's French car. Drove 125 miles south,
through broad, rolling Tunisian countryside sometimes remindful of parts of Southern California, cowboy country.
Good road, huge, neat, European-style farms. Mostly vineyards and orchards, plus wheat. Mahmoud drives as one would
expect, impatiently, but efficiently, about 70 miles-per-
hour, even over roads under repair. Finally arrive at a sunbaked little village called Tagerouine, near the Algerian
border. And, for the first time, we go to work. Three full
rolls of silent film, 300 feet, and 400 feet of sound-on-
film - a total of 700 feet for CBS News television. Later,
I tape an on-the-spot report for CBS news radio. Everything
is said in those TV and radio reports, so there's little to record here. Only that these are the most tragic of
all refugees I've seen since France and Germany, 1944 and
1945. So far, 100-thousand Algerian refugees have poured
into Morocco, 200-thousand into Tunisia.[15] Already, they're
creating a problem one-third as big as the sad Palestine
refugee problem. And more are arriving daily. Exactly
4,617 have arrived here at Tagerouine to date. And most
of them are women, women with babies and small children.
Plus grandmothers and grandfathers. We photographed one
old man of 87. And a baby whose gaunt little body reminded

me immediately of human skeletons seen years ago at a Naza
(sic) camp called Dachau. Really pitiful sights. Only the
rags on their backs, not even any rags left over for patch-
es. And almost everyone arrived here barefoot, coming as
far as 100 miles through the mountains, traveling at night
to avoid French patrols and control points. The old man of
87 was one of the few with shoes, and his were run-over
woman's shoes. We watched two refugee doctors at work,
shooting a priceless injection into one baby and an ancient
old woman, sparing a few eye-drops for eyes infected with
trachoma, treating the usual foot wounds. The doctors say
they can do little for the worst ailment of all . . . mal-
nutrition. The diet here is simple: One hunk of bread, one
tiny piece of Tunisian tuna-fish. By all laws of nutrition,
the doctor says, all these people should be dead. And, he
added, when winter comes, their first in this barren little
mud-hut camp, most of them probably will be dead . . .
unless something is done. No one is helping them, but the
Algerians are trying to take care of themselves. Most of
the food and medicine comes from the Algerian Red Crescent,
the Arab equivalent of our Red Cross. But it's very little.
Spirits are surprisingly high, though. We filmed, for TV,
live-sound, a group of youngsters who can't wait to grow up
and fight; armed with home-made guns, they train like the
grownup men, drill and march, and sing the nationalists'
liberation song. One especially moving line translates,
"O God, O God, why don't WE have the same liberty as people
in other countries?" Later we watch and film with live sound
a man teaching a group of refugee children. One of their
changes is the verse from the Koran which says, roughly,
that Believers who fight in the name of God will live forever in Paradise . . . this is the Jihad verse, the Koranic
verse usually quoted for a Holy War.[16] And these small, ragged, barefooted children, handsome and bright-eyed, all sat
there facing West, the mountains silhouetted against the
setting sun . . . the mountains of their homeland, Algeria.
There, the problem may be political. But here, and in the
other refugee camps all along the Tunisian and Moroccan
borders, the problem is strictly humanitarian. It's already
festering on the world's conscience . . . and becoming a
world problem. So far, however, these are the forgotten
people of the undeclared war in Algeria . . . the homeless,
the starving, the dying, the destitute, the widowed and

the orphaned. Later, on the way back, Mahmoud drives off
the main road to a secret nationalist hideaway unknown to
either the Tunisians or the French. It's near the border.
At his knock on a weathered old door, a smart, uniformed
soldier with a Thompson sub-machine-gun jumps out, challenging. Then, at the sight of Mahmoud, he salutes, and we
are admitted inside. An entire platoon of very smart and
tough-looking soldiers jumps to attention, presents arms.
They've been training on a machine-gun, British-made, and
another special British-made gun used against low-flying
French observation planes. The headquarters office is whitewashed, spotlessly neat and clean. We have a bite to eat
here, Cous-cous (sic), the Tunisian national dish, preceded by good potato salad, accompanied by good fresh milk,
fruits for dessert. In a storeroom we are shown piles of
uniforms, mostly camouflage material strikingly similar to
that of French paratroopers, plus new command-type tennis
shoes, and guns and ammunition. The guns are all types,
obviously collected from anywhere and everywhere, ranging
from modern Thompsons to old but still effective shotguns.
None is communist-made. Everything pigeon-holed in the
best army quartermaster style. Mahmoud served everyone at
the table, several soldiers helped out, and each man was
called brother. All in all, it is the most comradely spirit
I have ever seen anywhere, natural, not artificial, something deeper than the mere buddy-buddy atmosphere of small
army units. "This," Mahmoud said, "is our strongest weapon,
our secret weapon, something we have that the French don't
have. We," he added, "we know WHY we are fighting, and BE-
LIEVE in why we are fighting. And all the people of Algeria
are with us. The French," he concluded, "can never beat
this." On the long drive back to Tunis, through the dark,
Mahmoud carried a Thompson[17] on the seat beside him, with
two extra clips. "The French," he explains "sometimes stop
cars on the road at night . . . even here in Tunisia." We
arrived back in Tunis about 11 p.m., tired, but impressed,
really impressed, for the first time.

THURSDAY, JULY 18TH - Spent most of today typing up dopesheets[18] to accompany our TV film, retyping TV and radio
scripts, and so forth. Both of us are tired, dead tired,
after our 20-hour day yesterday. No word from Mahmoud. But

the newspapers here say the French are negotiating secretly, right here in Tunis, with FLN leaders.

FRIDAY, JULY 19TH — Still no further word from Mahmoud, or
his friends. This waiting and delay, this building up of
tension, is beginning to tell on both of us. With nothing
to do today, except wait, just wait, we can't help thinking
of the trip ahead. And both of us confess to rapid pulse,
flies in the stomach, a bad case of nerves and jitters.

SATURDAY, JULY 20TH — No word. No contact. Masraff hikes
around town, toughening up his legs, working off excess
energy and tense nerves. I spent most of the day in bed,
sick, with intestinal trouble which stems straight from
jumpy nerves.

SUNDAY, JULY 21ST — Another Moslem wedding in the hotel
patio here tonight. I had to close window and shutters to
stifle the noise and record this. Two meetings today, both
important. The first, with Mahmoud's friend, establish-
es, definitely, that we'll be leaving within a day or two
at most . . . although it's now known that the French are
setting up barbed-wire blockades in the mountains, plus,
perhaps, booby-traps, and talking about burying mines. We
plan to film and interview some Foreign Legion deserters,
Germans, hidden away in an apartment here in Tunis. Also,
to visit some of the FLN wounded in local hospitals, including some men allegedly suffering from French chemical
warfare . . . gas. Both plans are cancelled, however; might
focus too much attention on us, just before we're leaving.
At 10 p.m. tonight, four FLN men pick us up for a special, high-level meeting. Stopped by a policeman on the way
downtown, because the car has no tail-lights, and we have
a few anxious moments. As soon as the policeman learns the
driver is Algerian, however, he waves us on with a friendly warning. Our meeting is held over soft drinks at one of
the biggest and most public cafes in Tunis. We meet a top
FLN leader seen earlier in Cairo, an FLN "Colonel," and the
latter's young cousin, 17, at long last a man who can speak
English, and who will accompany us on our trip. The two
older men — I say "older," but they're both well under 35 —
apparently are part of the top brass. They say they are part

of the original group which started the fight for Algeria's
liberation from France, that they've been "wanted" by the
French ever since 1950. They've been on the run almost sev-
en years now. The Colonel, highly respected by the rest of
the group, will be in personal charge of our safari. He is
tall, boyish-faced, soft-speaking, uses cultivated French.
His friend, short, poker-faced and tough as steel, has all
the dignity and assurance of the natural underground leader. The best news they have for us is that everything is
ready. Three couriers have been sent to the mountain headquarters, to announce our coming; three, to make sure one
gets through all right. A section of 50 FLN soldiers will
start clearing the border area, ahead of us, starting tomorrow morning.[19] We'll have a squad in front of us, another
behind, and one with us, fanning out on the sides. So we'll
be well-protected. "Our honor is at stake," the short man
explains. "You are the first journalists to visit our headquarters, so we want to make sure you come back safe and
alive, to tell our story." Under pressure, he admits there
are several areas on our route, about 7 or 8 miles apiece,
where it'll be mostly a matter of pure luck whether we get
through. I ask if we won't create attention checking out of
our hotel. They tell us to give them our extra equipment
tomorrow, then walk out Tuesday morning as though we're
just going out for a few hours. "Leave your personal luggage behind," they say, "and we'll take care of your hotel
bill and pick up your things in two or three days. We'll
say," he adds, "that you decided to go on to Libya." I ask
about security, and censorship. Can we photograph faces,
for example? Are there landmarks en route which we should
not film? Immediately, they tell us . . . the French know
all FLN leaders, and they know all Algerians are suspect.
So feel free to photograph any of us. In fact, the short
man stresses, you have no restrictions whatsoever; you can
go anywhere, see everything, talk to anyone — we ask only
that you tell the truth. He grins. Ask your American journalist friends if the French let them do the same around
Algeria! We have nothing to hide, he repeats, seriously.
I explain that our final instructions from CBS News in New
York stress that we have no axe to grind, that our only
orders are for honest, objective reporting . . . and the
truth, nothing more, than the truth. These are good orders,
coming from the newest journalistic media, radio and TV,

but in the oldest and highest ideals of American journalism. They constitute one of the reasons all of us are proud
to report for CBS News. And I am especially proud of them
at this secret meeting. We return to the hotel about 12:30,
both excited, frankly a little scared, but happy this long,
nerve-wracking waiting period is over, anxious to get
started, the day after tomorrow.

MONDAY, JULY 22ND – Our last day in Tunis. We spend most
of it packing up. Masraff takes our camera batteries, now
fully charged, and other incidental equipment, out to the
FLN hideout in an Arab suburb. In the afternoon, we get
a haircut, make minor purchases of everything from toilet
paper to some candy drops to keep our throats from getting
dry during the long hike. The TV film we've already ex-
posed, and my radio tapes, and this portion of our diary,
are being left behind, just in case. If we don't come back,
at least CBS News will have this much of our report. Both
of us hope to get to sleep early; it's our last night in a
bed. Not much else to say tonight. Tomorrow morning, we're
off to war.

TUESDAY, JULY 23RD – Another delay. Returned to hotel
last night, after what we thought was our last dinner in
Tunisia, to find a message at the hotel, a message to telephone a certain number. While I engaged the curious hotel
clerk in conversation, Masraff telephoned, talked to
Mahmoud and his friend. Our departure, they said, was
postponed another 24 hours . . . until Wednesday morning.
Both of us disappointed, but the Algerians probably have
a good reason. Tried to calm our nerves and kill the day
by taking a 20-minute train trip out to ancient Carthage,[20]
prowling around the ruins dating back to 12 centuries,
before Christ. Usual reaction to such ruins: Invaders,
empires, come and go . . . nothing, nothing, is permanent . . . nothing is new, really new. Walked by the seaside palace of the Bay (sic) of Tunisia,[21] who is due to be
stripped of his titles and powers any day now, any hour.
Only several bored sentries in sight, all windows shut-
tered. This evening, had what we now hope, once more, is
our last dinner in Tunisia – beer, wine, lobster and sole,
a fitting farewell meal, shared with a German journalist
from Cairo. Tomorrow . . . Algeria . . . we hope.

WEDNESDAY, JULY 24TH – On our way, at last. Mohamed and
friend picked us up at 1 o'clock this afternoon, and we
left Tunis about 1:15 p.m. Paid our current bill at hotel
and left money with the Algerians to pay rest of our bill
in several days; we left our personal luggage behind, to be
picked up by the Algerians in about three days, so our departure wouldn't be so well-advertised. Cloak-and-dagger, to
the last. Masraff took various shots from car as we traveled
through rolling, European-like countryside of wheat fields,
vineyards, olive orchards and well-landscaped farms imitat-
ing French originals. This must be one reason the French
love North Africa, hate to leave it – all this beautiful
farmland, unknown in the Middle East, precious to land-
hungry and land-loving Frenchmen. Plenty of cattle, like
America's mid-West (sic), but cacti-fences and occasional mosques. At Souk el Arba,[22] a town some 60 miles from
Tunis, noticed same message on walls of houses and buildings . . . in French . . . "Evacuation of the French Army,
or Death!" The French Army is still here, but Tunisia now
has its independence. At tiny village called GHARDIMAOU[23]
(sic), Mohamed stops for a minute. Then, when we continue,
a small canvas-covered van, or truck, is just ahead of us,
obviously leading us. We turn onto dirt roads, criss-
crossing the fields, fields of green tobacco, with foothills
in the distance. A huge cloud of dust follow the truck
ahead, remindful of cowboy-and-Indian stories, only
this time we are the Indians, following a covered-wagon.
Finally, after a wild, dusty ride, we pull up near the
foothills. Algerian soldiers, apparently our bodyguard on
this last stage of the trip, jump out of the van. Among
those there to greet us is Rushdi, our English-speaking
friend from Tunis, a young student who has spent several months in London and speaks English surprisingly well.
At 17, he will be the youngest member of our entire party,
and is going by special dispensation of his cousin, a Major
in the Algerian army. The driver of the van looks sadly
at Rushdi, says, "You will never return; you will die in
Algeria!" Cheerful Charlie. We tote our equipment through
the inevitable olive orchard, come to our first real border
camp, with headquarters in a small thatched-roof hut. Two
dozen uniformed and well-armed Algerian soldiers are lined
up to receive us. Masraff films our arrival, the soldiers,
their stacked guns, and piles of ammunition boxes. The

ammo is French, captured from French forces; and there's
plenty of it. Ready to start out across the frontier at
sundown, we find an important item of equipment has been
left behind by our friends . . . a bag with our recorder
microphone, with radio recording tapes, and so forth. So
once again, another delay: 24 hours, again. Instead of the
promised uniforms - necessary, they said, if we didn't want
to be shot by villagers and guerrillas - we were presented
with civilian trousers, jackets and the thick-soled French
tennis shoes used by all Algerian soldiers. Several items
don't fit, so we ride back into the town of Souk el Arba to
find other clothes, and spent the night. Sometime tomorrow,
we return to the border camp, and, at sundown, take off.

THURSDAY, JULY 25TH - Up till 3 o'clock this morning, interviewing and talking with Algerians who were our hosts
last night. One, a 29-year-old 2nd Lieut(enant) . . .
another, 31, who used to run a bookshop and a café, now in
public relations for the Algerian army. . . . The third, a
former student, 27 now. . . . And a 22-year-old obviously
in intelligence work for the Algerians. All four are intelligent, extremely intelligent, and patriotic beyond question, absolutely devoted to their cause . . . but, unlike
Arabs of the Middle East, quietly and logically patriotic, without being emotionally fanatic. This is no place to
record hours upon hours of conversation, but both Masraff
and I are impressed. Impressed, for example, by the complete organization of the Algerians, their army, and their
civilian organization. Take voluminous notes on detailed
framework of FLN, starting with 5-man executive committee, 34-man national committee, and breakdown into divisions . . . villages, sectors, regions, zones and departments. Notes on base-pay of various army ranks, family
allowances, and so on. And interview each of the four on
his background, what members of his family have been killed
or are in prison, why, in his own words, he joined the
mountain army, his experiences, and what he hopes to do,
if and when the undeclared war is over. This morning, also
interviewed a 21-year-old nurse, who, when asked if she had
any trouble with the men, looked horrified and replied, "It
is forbidden; the penalty is death." Besides, she added, I
am known only as The Little One, in a uniform I look just
like a little boy . . . and we are all one family, brothers

and sisters. Some of this I know, for all these Algerians
call each other AAKH, or Brother, all the time, even soldiers to officers. I absolutely find no evidence of communism, or communist thinking, among these four young men,
despite continual verbal probing.[24] What about communist
arms? Not yet, they say, although the Russians have offered arms. But if the undeclared war goes on and on? The
Second Lieutenant replies for all. "If I am drowning and
the only man around hands me a red-hot poker," he says,
"what can I do?" "I have no choice." All insist, however,
they know of absolutely NO communist in the FLN, that they
consider communists as dangerous as the French, and want
no part of what they frankly describe as Russian imperialism, any more than they want what they call French imperialism . . . xxx.[25] After lunch, we are driven in a closed
truck back to the first border camp. And in a few minutes,
at sundown, we start the long hike, off to war.

SATURDAY, JULY 27TH - I used to laugh at calendar watches, but now I wish I had one. Already, days are melting
into nights, and it's difficult to know the exact date.
Thursday night, we set out at sundown, all afoot except
Masraff, who wisely accepted a ride on an extra mule.
Hiking at night was bad, but not as bad as I expected. Did
feel, however, that these parts have the greatest collection of stones in the world; found myself stumbling, stub-
bing toes, almost continually. Noticed a new awareness of
life, of being alive, as we hiked single-file through the
darkness, into black foothills, across open fields and over
dry creek beds. Felt alive, really alive . . . fright-
ened . . . but with all senses working overtime, full-
speed, all valves open. First hour was the worst, but by
end of second hour, when we came to a halt, found walking automatic, most nervousness gone. A second section of
soldiers was to follow us, but they failed to appear, so
we had to bed down here in a hut for the night. Yesterday,
Friday, I think, we loafed most of the day, shot some film
of soldier life by day. And heard on our portable radio
that Premier Boughiba (sic) had deposed the Bay (sic) of
Tunis, declared Tunisia a Republic. The organization of our
trip seems to be fouled up, somewhat. We were to go on from
here Thursday night, then, again, last night; now, we're
to leave tonight. Last night, part of our escort showed up

in the hut and announced they had to leave us . . . heading for FLN headquarters at Collo mountains,[26] to take arms
and ammunition in. Before leaving, I recorded them singing a song, a tune familiar to Western ears, but the words
in Arabic . . . Auld Lang Sine (sic).[27] They have to pass
through some 15,000 French troops to reach their destination. Only a dozen soldiers were left with us, here in
No-Man's-Land between Algeria and Tunisia; another section is due in. This afternoon, a new Lieutenant told us it
was impossible to take us through to Collo, as originally
planned; he said it would take a month or two longer,
time which we cannot afford. He also pointed out that any
French attack would mean we'd have to scatter, lose all
our equipment and film and tapes. So, we agreed to give up
the idea of Collo, to go inside Algeria in a vast circle,
come back within one month. Then, this afternoon, Mohamed
showed up, said that plan was cancelled, that we are going
in HIS (sic) department, not the Lieutenant's. Thoroughly
depressed and fed up, we had a long, show-down talk with
Mohamed, stressing all the continual, incessant delays and
changes of plans. This is war, Mohamed replied, and we can
only plan day to day, hour to hour. What seemed to us poor
organization and slipshod arrangements, he explained, was
due to French activities in the mountains. We had been
spotted by the French, he claimed, who had launched an
offensive along the border to prevent the entry of two
American journalists into Algeria. He said they got this
information through their intelligence, which, he said,
knows everything the French plan and do. There were similar reasons, he added, for all our delays. True or not,
I don't know. But at long last we're all set to start out
again at sundown. Meanwhile, we've been stuck at this
hut-camp, sleeping on the floor, ant-bitten, eating lamb
killed an hour before, drinking from the same well bucket as 45 other men . . . and the donkeys. And, of course,
no baths, no shaves. We ain't pretty, we don't smell pretty . . . but we're getting in the swing of things. This
was a quiet morning, they tell us. A French observation
plane buzzed us in this olive orchard, only 300 yards away,
about 80 yards above ground; gone before we could take
any film. There've been B-26's,[28] American B-26's, French
Air Force, overhead all day. And explosions on the other
side of the hills; the boys here say their commandoes have

been blowing up the railway track. Also, artillery fire
in the distance, from the direction in which we're headed; American 105's,[29] they tell us. A quiet morning. After
all, we still haven't crossed the actual, literal frontier.
We're close, but still in Tunisia, still in the no-man's-
land which separates Tunisia from Algeria. Tonight, IF our
plans aren't changed again at the last minute, we take off,
definitely. I won't be able to record anything for a day
or two . . . we'll be marching four or five hours a night,
always at night . . . then resting up during the day. And
it'll be a couple of days before we reach a point of com-
parative security, where we can work with TV camera, radio
recorder and typewriter. Now, in just one hour, about 5
p.m., we start the big march.

MONDAY, JULY 29TH — This weekend has been the low point of
our trip so far. Saturday afternoon as I finish recording
this diary, under an olive tree, French fighters and bombers
are attacking the other side of the hill — American planes,
P-38's[30] and B-29's.[31] Regardless, the order to take off
still stands and we finally start marching down a dirt road
toward Algeria. Several times we hit the dirt as a curious
plane flies overhead, till the Sergeant in command chooses
the hard way, up over the hills. Even at 6:15 and 6:30 at
night, it's hot — the North African Sirocco[32] (Seer-O-coe)
is blowing up from the Sahara, furnace-hot. Within minutes
our clothes are soaked with perspiration, faces dripping,
even our belts and wristwatch straps soaked through. But
it's bearable, and, after a time, not bad. In fact, it's
exhilarating, marching single-file through the sun setting
behind the Algerian mountains. We stop at a hillside rebel
camp, picturesque as a movie set, for a brief rest and some
dirty but wonderful water. Then, abruptly, the picturesque
vanishes — we've started over the mountains, real mountains. Rather, UP the mountains. And this is work, hard
work. Legs accustomed to elevators and taxis suddenly ache
and pain. The heart pounds harder and harder. But worst of
all is the breathing. With each step up the steep mountainside, each breath is agony, has to be pulled up from somewhere down around the ankles, rattles like that of a dying
person. Any fear of the French disappear(s) completely. In
fact, all thoughts and emotions are wiped out by the supreme effort to take another breath, another step. Above

all, I am afraid, horribly afraid, of collapsing, of losing
face. But, somehow, the feet and legs and lungs keep working. Up and up, as the going gets rougher, as dusk, then
darkness settles over the mountains. The air is cool, even
cold, but our clothes are still soaked, perspiration drips
from our faces. Then, just as collapse seems inevitable, we
come to a halt on a mountaintop. We all sink to the ground
without a word, without question. I spread like a man
staked-out, unable to move even if the whole French army
attacks. Later, a drink of water, tastier than the best
champagne, a cautious, careful cigarette . . . then, questions. It soon becomes apparent that we are lost, that the
Sergeant in charge is asking a civilian to lead us to the
next camp, one, two or three kilometres away, somewhere in
the mountain blackness. The reluctant civilian finally
agrees, and we start out again, in even blacker darkness,
up even higher mountains. It's almost impossible to see the
man only one yard in front, definitely impossible to see the
path, the stones, the logs. We stumble along, always up-
ward, following sound rather than figures. At one point, we
move slowly along the edge of an unseen cliff, where one
wrong step means Finish. At another point, we lose the path
completely, on a mountainside so steep we can barely walk,
one foot on a level with the knee of the other leg; we move
along on the sides of our shoes, digging in. Masraff, who
has been battered by hundreds of unseen tree branches,
while riding his mule, has to dismount and struggle with
us. Even the mule cannot travel here with a load. Then, in
a particularly black clearing, the civilian refuses to lead
us any farther . . . and disappears. The Sergeant starts
off again, but the going is so rough, so impossible in the
utter darkness, that our friend Rushdi insists we stop till
first daylight, then look for the camp. After he explains,
Masraff and I agree he was absolutely right. The Sergeant,
it seems, does NOT know the way exactly. Apparently he had
told his superiors this, before leaving; but they, well
aware of our increasing impatience at continual delays,
ordered him to start out anyhow, to keep on schedule. At
10:30 p.m., 4 hours after starting our night march up the
mountains, we are shown to a lean-to, given some gree(n),
leafy branches to cover the rocks on the ground, and told
goodnight. Strangely, not a soldier has a canteen, but one
finds a sulphur spring. We have no blankets. I have been

(to) a lot of places in a lot of countries, but I shall
always remember that night as one of the most miserable of
my life. Rocks in the earth make it impossible to be comfortable. The ground is alive with ants, spiders and various unknown insects. Above all, however, it is cold; not
cool, cold. We spend the entire night bitching, scratching,
turning, tossing, smoking cigarettes, and shivering, even
trembling, in the sudden cold. And looking at our watches . . . till the magic hour, 5 a.m., daylight. I mention
all this, not complainingly, but only to explain what the
average Algerian soldier goes through daily, weekly, monthly, yearly. The soldiers with us are so accustomed to this
life they fell asleep immediately, without dinner, without
water, without blankets. You have to believe pretty strongly in a cause to keep on living and fighting this kind of
life. Anyhow, at 5 a.m., we're underway again, tired,
sleepy and still frozen, but at least able to see in the
beginning of daylight. And a short distance away we come to
our destination, the first rebel camp in Algeria. It's a
permanent mountaintop camp, completely hidden under the
tall leafy tops of oak and cork trees. The "tents" are made
of tree branches, instead of canvas . . . Indian-like
lean-tos, with low log-cabin walls. There's a picnic table
of small oak logs, a first-aid infirmary, military policemen,
military latrine, chow-hut, even a small parade-ground with
flagpole and flag, the green-and-white Algerian flag with red
crescent and star. Above all, however, it has soldiers,
real soldiers, and a Captain, a real Captain. After a warm
welcome, and welcome water, soap, coffee and biscuits, we
sit down at the picnic table for a man-to-man chat. We
explain, in great detail, we are here to tell the nationalist side of the story; the truth, nothing more, nothing
less, than the truth. We explain we are willing to walk
till our feet are bloody, and literally, to risk injury or
death, to report this story to the American people. But, we
emphasize, we are fed up with delays and changes of plans.
And we are not prepared to hike all over the Algerian
mountains, through thousands of French soldiers, in the
dark, behind a Sergeant who couldn't even find his way the
first night, across the border. The Captain agrees whole-
heartedly, immediately send(s) a message to his superior
asking if he himself, the Captain, can accompany us. For
the first time, we are relieved, and confident. Especially as

we talk with the Captain, learn he is a professional soldier, a veteran of 14 years in the French army through
World War I and Indochina, including Dianbienphu[33] (sic),
and has won 12 Croix de Guerres.[34] Upon their return to
Algeria, his unit was used against Algerian civilians – and
the Captain walked out, deserted, taking his entire company
of 92 men and all their material, loaded on 80 mules. We
spend the rest of the day filming camp life here, and interviewing soldiers. Most of them, it's soon apparent, are
Algerians who deserted the French army in protest against
French action against Algeria; the majority of veterans of
World War II and Indochina, real soldiers. One, for example, a tall, lanky, hollow-cheeked man(,) is even called
"Indo-Chine," as a nickname. He spent 5 long years in
Indochina, fighting with and for the French, deserted in
Algeria for the usual reason. His entire family has been
killed by the French, he says grimly . . . Mother and
father, 4 sisters, a brother 4 uncles . . . 20 in all. I
ask him, immediately, a direct and pointed question: What
does he think should be done with the million or so French
and other Europeans in Algeria, if and when the war is won
by Algerians, he replies soberly: "We shall forget all the
past and work for the prese(n)t. All we ask," he adds, "is
that they leave us in liberty, so that everyone can live
and work in equal freedom." This, I might add parentheti-
cally, is no parroted propaganda, it is personal, straight
from the heart. Most of the men are in their 20's, between
18 and 35. There's one youngster of 16, though, who has
been working for the French major commanding this region,
until two years ago, when he quit and come (sic) to the
mountains, bringing the major's gun as his passport.
Another youngster of 14 showed up several days ago, a shy,
quiet boy with a heart-breakingly sad manner; his father,
the Captain says, has been killed by the French recently
and the boy is now all alone. Like the men, he headed for
the mountains. The Captain says he hopes to send this boy
to school. After long, detailed interviews with a number of
soldiers, we have dinner, a good dinner cooked by a man who
used to serve as chef for an American World War II unit in
Algiers. Then, a long, long talk, all politics. And to bed,
on branches laid over log poles, in the Captain's cabin.
The only woman in camp, an attractive brunette in khaki
trousers and shirt, a camouflage hat, and a viscious (sic)

knife in her belt, joined us at dinner. And, at bedtime she
crawled into our long joint bed, with the Captain, Rushdi,
Masraff and I. We've been around, but we're a little surprised. The others in the cabin, however, accept it as
normal, and somehow, it seems natural. The women here are
literally accepted as sisters, as comrades. Meanwhile, in
bed I make a mental note to record not only this, but the
fact that I've been making a big, horrible mistake up till
now – Masraff and our equipment have been riding, not on
donkeys, as I reported, but on mules. Incidentally, neither
Masraff nor I, nor Rushdi, slept last night . . . too cold,
freezing cold. Everyone else slept like the proverbial log.
Today, we hiked to this outfit's parade-ground, a clearing
on a mountaintop, to film and record for radio, a full flag-
raising ceremony. A complete company of 130 well-uniformed,
well-armed men. Impressive. In the distance, we could hear
the drone of B-26's, and the tharump of bombs. And we asked
what if a plane suddenly appeared overhead, the company
demonstrated – not a man in sight, in less than 7 seconds.
Also saw and filmed some beautiful camouflage, soldiers who,
one minute, looked like leafy bushes; the next, tough
soldiers charging at our camera. Took my recorder (Rushdi
carrying it) and marched along with the company on drill,
trying to describe the scene and their arms. Used the
sound-camera to film the Algerians marching behind their
flag, singing the national anthem forbidden by the French.
One amplifier battery is low, however, and it's doubtful if
the sound-track is okay. Masraff hiked back to camp to get
a spare sent from New York; to our disgust and horror, it
is the wrong type. Masraff spends the rest of the day
making an emergency connection; so far it works. But don't
know if it'll hold up for the long marches ahead, over more
mountains and possible flights from French ambushes, or
French stafings (sic) and bombings. Meantime, the sun is
sinking, light is growing thin and dim. Time for dinner and
prayers that tonight, out of sheer fatigue, we may sleep.

TUESDAY, JULY 30TH – Up till after 1 o'clock this morning,
talking politics in lamp-light with the Captain and his li-
entenants (sic). The conversation – in English, French and
Arabic, with Masraff translating as middle-man – returns
again and again to America, the U.S.A. And, as in the Arab
Middle East, the questions are all directed at me, as an

American. The old question, why did America carve a homeland for the Jews out of the Arab world, instead of Europe,
South America, or the U.S.A.? Why does America give more aid
to little Israel than all the Arab nations combined, more
per capita than any other nation in the world? Why didn't
America stop the Anglo-French-Israeli attack on Egypt before
it started? Why does America, a former colony, support what
they call British and French colonialism? I know the answers
to these questions, and try to answer them. But, still, the
questions continue. Finally, as always, I reach the usual
point and ask why it's always America; why virtually everyone in the world today - especially the Arab world - blames
America for anything and everything. The U.S., I point out
in simple terms, has been the first country in the world to
spend billions of dollars trying to HELP the rest of the
world. No one, I add, could ever accuse the Americans of
evil, really evil, intentions abroad . . . naievite (sic),
perhaps, but not evil. Why then, I ask, does everyone accuse America of responsibility for every trouble in the
world today? A Lieutenant answers at length, in painfully
obvious sincerity. All the little countries, he says, look
to America as one, the only, stronghold of real liberty,
of the closest thing we know to democracy today. Therefore,
he explains, we feel let down, we feel cut to the heart,
when America's foreign policy doesn't follow those principles for which we stand. We feel, he adds, like a son
whose mother suddenly does something wrong, horribly wrong,
something against everything she has taught him is right.
We are not critical, so much, the Lieutenant emphasizes,
as we hurt; we still believe in America, but we are hurt.
This comment explains, better than millions of words, the
average Algerian's attitude toward America today. They
understand that America did not furnish arms and equipment
to France for use against the Algerian people. They understand that these arms and equipment were intended to help
France fulfill her role in the cold war drama, in NATO. But
the Algerians claim that 4/5ths of the French forces are in
Algeria, using these forces, and NATO arms, mostly American
arms, against the Algerian people. The Algerians cannot
understand why America has never protested against this
mis-use (sic) of NATO arms. And they find it difficult to
understand how America insists she cannot interfere in the
Algerian undeclared war, when American guns, ammunition,

planes and bombs are being used against the Algerians every
day and night. Here in the mountains, watching American
B-26's and B-29's flying overhead almost constantly, and
watching American P-38's strafing, it's difficult for an
American reporter to argue this point. And I, for one, am
particularly surprised that these Algerian officers and
soldiers can still be quietly logical about this situation,
that they still bear no real ill-feelings toward America,
still hope for help and understanding from America. The
soldiers they are fighting, after all, usually wear American
uniforms, including helmets. They carry everything from
Colt .45's to our old M-1 rifle and Thompson sub-machine
guns; they ride in American jeeps and trucks and half-
tracks; they use American ammunition, drop American bombs,
fly American planes, strafe with American guns. And yet the
Algerians are not bitter against America . . . yet. They
still have hope. After our long talk last night, another
officer joins us in our long bed. And, on the ground, the
three boys adopted by the Captain and the camp, three small
figures shivering under one blanket, a sub-machine gun near
their heads. For some reason, the sight is even more effective than all the arguments; it's a sight which moves the
heart, as well as the head.

Today, we spend part of the morning working around camp.
Then, down the mountain to make a TV report on what kind of
arms the Algerians are using, where they get them. The answer, of course, is simple. The Algerians ARE buying some
arms abroad, but they are comparatively few, so far. Our
patrol, for example, has only one Beretta sub-machinegun
(sic) from Italy, two World War I rifles from Germany, a
machine-pistol from Czechoslovakia, several British Lee-
Enfields.[35] But the vast majority of the arms, 17 out of 25
to be exact, are French or American, mostly American. And
they've all been taken from the French, taken the hard way.
We also film some soldiers eating, and make arrangements for
a mountain trip tomorrow to visit some villages allegedly
razed to the ground by the French.

Just finished filming and interviewing four Algerian
refugees, chosen at random from those constantly moving
through these mountains. Four men, the eldest named Asfour
Ahmed, tall, gaunt 62-year-old grandfather. I say interview, but really, it is an interrogation, for we are
anxious to dig up facts, not propaganda. Question upon

question builds up an unshakeable story, a story of obvious and unrehearsed truth, the story of a typical Algerian
refugee. Ahmed comes from a village near Duvivier,[36] in
Eastern Algeria. He was a farmer, with a home, a family,
and 15 hectares[37] of land full of wheat, tobacco, and so
forth. All of his four sons did secret work of one kind or
another for the FLN. Early last year, he says, the French
captured and later killed his eldest son, Othman, 41,
father of six sons. Ahmed says he found the body himself,
in the forest. The second son, Mohamed, 29, father of two
boys, immediately took off for the mountains and service
with the FLN army. Hearing of this, the French, according to Ahmed, raided his farm, found only his third son,
Amor, working in the fields. Ahmed says the French burned
his farm to the ground, took Amor off to a nearby village,
where, according to people there, they tortured and killed
him. He was 26, left two sons. This past July, Ahmed says,
the French finally caught up with Mohamed in the mountains,
and killed him. A fourth son, Ali, who is 38, is back in
the mountains now after undergoing torture by the French,
who later released him, according to Ahmed, who adds that
his 65-year-old wife is now in the mountains with this
only remaining son. Ahmed claims that all of the men and
young boys of his village are either dead or in the mountains fighting with the FLN; out of a population of some
200, he says, only a few women and babies are left. And
all the women, he adds casually, and insists, indignantly,
despite persistent questioning have been raped at least
once by French soldiers. His farm burned to the ground,
his home gone, three sons dead, his wife and only remaining son hiding in the mountains, this 62-year-old grandfather has taken to the mountains himself, always on the
move. His grandsons, he says, were begging in the streets,
until the FLN arranged to give them food and clothes
every month. Ahmed himself, still as tall and dignified as
a Saudi sheikh, rides an Arab stallion through the mountains. For more than a year now he has been spinning out
his final years of old age in this manner, leading three
other refugees, finding their food every sundown from civilians or FLN army units. Where is he going now? He shrugs.
Tunisia, I ask, or Morocco? No, he replies, I want to stay
in Algeria . . . this is my country, my land. And he mounts
his horse, rides off through the oak and cork forest. No

comment is needed — Ahmed's story, the story of a typical
Algerian refugee chosen at random, speaks for himself.

THURSDAY, AUGUST 1ST — Now, we're REALLY convinced the
Algerians have an army, a real army. The soldiers and officers in the mountains are as tough, disciplined and experienced as any in the world . . . more, than most. They're
soldiers, real soldiers, and they're part of an army, a
real army. Now, we have proof that, like all armies, this
one is sometimes sabotaged from the rear, its front-line
soldiers sometimes trapped on fly-paper created in the rear,
by desk-soldiers and Higher Brass. By an incredible "Snafu"
we are back in Tunis. Tuesday, we worked 14 hours straight,
up in the Algerian mountains, without letup, finishing up
by flashlight at 8:30 p.m. One hour later, just as (we)
finished dinner and prepared to climb into bed, completely
exhausted, a breathless courier arrived. An urgent message
for the Lieutenant in charge . . . from the Captain, who
had crossed the frontier into Tunisia earlier in the day.
The two journalists, he read out in the lamplight, are to
return to the border headquarters in Tunisia . . . immediately . . . with all their equipment. An order, a direct order; without explanation. We can only assume that
an extremely grave situation has arisen . . . that headquarters, perhaps, has information the French are going
to attack our camp, that very night. At the same time, we
have personal misgivings, afraid this is another in a chain
of delays and changes of plans which have plagued us from
the start of this trip. Regardless, "c'est la guerre," we
pack up equipment in the dark, load it on the mules, and
start the long trip down the mountains, back twoard (sic)
Tunisia. This time, a truck meets us at a rendezvous and
in two hours we are across the border, a part of our trip
which required 5 days coming, afoot, through the mountains.
At the border village, our Captain can offer no explanation, reads out his own orders, which add only that we
have been working in the wrong zone. He says we are to go
on to the next town and spend the night. Okay. But at the
next town, the FLN man in charge is frankly astonished to
see us, knows nothing whatsoever of our order. Thoroughly
disgusted, completely exhausted, we insist upon returning to Tunis to get the whole thing straightened out. It's
almost daylight when we arrive. Even so, the little hotel

looks like a palace. We hand every stitch of our clothing
to the night porter, clothes we haven't had off for a week,
and sit around wrapped in towels, waiting anxiously for hot
water . . . and our dream, a shower. Yesterday, our contact
was to appear at 6:30 p.m. But no one showed up. We enjoyed our first real dinner, especially beer and sole. Then,
when no one arrives to explain WHY we have been pulled off
the mountain, we go to bed, thoroughly disgusted, ready to
give up the whole thing. This morning, the FLN men finally
appear, a public relations man and two colonels. We have
a frank showdown. And the FLN men apologize, insist these
things happen in war. But they DO want us to go to another
zone, as we suspected. And they swear they still don't know
where the mysterious order came from. We say we want only
one thing . . . to return to the mountains, to the spot
where we started our work. We're not concerned with zones,
we emphasize, we're not concerned with politics of the
higher-ups; we simply want to get back where we were, and
resume our work. Finally, "d'accord" - they agree. We can
pick up where we left off. Not tomorrow, because Masraff,
completely exhausted, is not feeling well. I'm not Bernarr
McFadden, myself.[38]

FRIDAY, AUGUST 2ND - Masraff spent a sleepless night, suffering from some sort of chest trouble. Happily, we've made
most of our purchases here in Tunis. Yesterday afternoon,
we went downtown to buy two air mattresses, flashlight batteries, and so forth. Both of us, incidentally, reluctant
to part with our beards, now have goatees. This afternoon,
while Masraff recuperates from his sleepless night, I spent
3 hours shopping . . . for canteen, two heavy shirts and
two sweaters for the cold mountain nights, for some heavy
blue-jeans. I also cable our wives, and CBS News in New
York that we're alright. Slight distortion of facts, perhaps; but reassuring to all concerned. Our last civilized
dinner, and now to bed. Tomorrow, the war, again . . . even
more reluctantly, this time.

SATURDAY, AUGUST 3RD - Up at 6 a.m., off for the border
about 8 a.m., in two small cars, accompanied by several
officers, including the two Colonels. Arrive early morning, but due to the usual snafu, it's late afternoon before we start out across the actual frontier. Even so, our

departure comes off only because Masraff raises the roof;
despite all promise, they had wanted us to spend still
another night in Tunisia. Finally, everyone in vile tem-
per, barely speaking we start off. En route, we meet two
Algerian soldiers who've been wounded and are returning
to Tunisia for treatment. Farther on, we meet a file of 150
ragged-looking soldiers dragging along the road toward
Tunisia. These men, it turns out, have just completed an
incredible 750-mile march into deepest Algeria, and back,
to deliver arms and ammunition carried on their own backs.
Each man carried three rifles, for example; his own, and two
for the men in the mountains. Now, many have no weapons.
Why? Because, we're told they felt the men in the mountains
needed them more than they did, so they left ALL their
arms there. Only a few had arms for the long, long march
back. Yet they fought five pitched battles with the French
en route, lost only five men and claim they killed around
110 French soldiers. 750 miles over some of the rough-
est country in the world, mostly by night, through an area
crawling with some 15-thousand French soldiers, covered
by jets and bombers sun-up till sun-down, country studded
with barbed wire and mines. Once again, you have to believe
pretty strongly in a cause to make a trip like this. It's
a poignant, moving sight, these 150 weary soldiers marching
along the road . . . a silent comment on Algeria's soldiers, and a picture of War, since wars began. We're crest-
fallen that our cameras are 'way up ahead, with a patrol;
we've missed some terrific film. It's dusk, however. And by
the time we reach the big mountain, our mountain, it's completely dark. This last stage of our trip back takes almost
two hours, up the last mountain, straight up, in the thin
moonlight. But we're happy to be back in Algeria, where
we can resume work once more. And our welcome at the camp
is warm and cordial, almost boisterous. The air matresses
(sic) and the sweaters feel good in the sharp, bitter mountain cold. And we're going to sleep to the murderous tune
of artillery shells . . . 105's, American 105's . . . tha-
rumping in the distance. They sound much closer than before, much closer.

SUNDAY, AUGUST 4TH – Awaken to the sound of a French observation plane buzzing the treetops over our heads. They tell

us the French now have a camp only 12 kilometers away, less than 8 miles from our camp.

MONDAY, AUGUST 5TH - Very little sleep again last night. First, long political talks. Then, the pounding of artillery, which sounded mighty close. Then, at 3 a.m., the officers talking Arabic in the darkness. Masraff says they are discussing the artillery fire, whether they should evacuate this camp, which seems to be a target. Later this morning, a scout comes in with a handfull (sic) of scrap metal. Everyone identifies it as the remains of an American 105 shell. Where did he find it? Less than one-third of a mile from here. He grins. You know the place, he says - where you spent the night when your patrol got lost . . . right there, exactly. The scraps are good souvenirs - but hardly reassuring. We wonder if the French artillery - American 105's - will come any closer tonight. Meantime, a long work-day, me on the typewriter about 9 or 10 hours straight, back breaking for want of a chair; Masraff busy filming recruits receiving uniforms and arms, and so forth. I checked and double-checked my information on the Algerian army and now feel qualified to discuss it. In brief, the ALN, or the Algerian army, IS an army, and its soldiers are real soldiers. The French picture these men abroad as bands of outlaws, as bandits. But here on the spot it's obvious they are soldiers, part of a well-organized, well-disciplined army. The majority are veterans of the French army itself, veterans of World War II and Indochina. They're young, mostly in their 20's - the official age brackets are between 18 and 35 - young because it takes young men to fight this tough, mountain, guerrilla war. Recruits get two full months of training. Then, apprenticeship, on-the-job training: covering patrols engaged in actual operations. A buck private gets 1,000 francs a month, just under $3. And the pay scale goes up slowly. The highest-ranking man in the army, a Colonel, gets less than $15 a month. Tops for an enlisted man are still under $6 a month . . . hardly enough to justify French claims these men are fighting for money. Men with families get a special allowance, under $6 monthly for wife and each child. The Army's organization is pretty intricate, and thorough. All Algeria is divided into seven (Wee-lay-ette), or Departments. Each department

is sub-divided into sectors, regions and zones. The smallest unit is what we would call a squad, what they call a
group . . . the usual patrol, 11 men, including a Sergeant.
Three groups make a Section. A company has about 150 men
headed by a 2nd Lt. who is also chief of his geographical
region. Next comes a battalion, which has 3 companies, plus
mortar and machine-gun sections, the usual headquarters
outfit, a Medical officer. A Captain commands this unit, has
up to 500 men, and is in complete charge of a zone. Topping
this whole pyramid is the regiment, 3 to 5 battalions headed by a Colonel who is chief of a complete department. Each
of these units has three special officers, one a military
chief, another the political chief, and the third in charge
of intelligence. The Algerians have no planes, like the
French . . . no American B-26's, P-38's, Piper-Cubs. They
have no battleships, no navy for the long Mediterranean
coastline. They have no artillery, no American 105's
and 155's. Their biggest weapon is a mortar. No jeeps,
no tracks, no half-tracks . . . only mules. And they're
'way-outnumbered. The French have at least half-a-million
soldiers in Algeria, more than they ever had in Indochina,
most of their NATO commitment, which belongs in Europe.
They have another 1 or 2 hundred-thousand in their tremendous police force, territorials, and the armed colons. The
Algerians count their soldier in groups, or patrols, not
in battalions or divisions. The exact number is secret.
We've heard everything from 30-thousand to 100-thousand.
Regardless, they're outnumbered, out-equipped, anywhere
from 5 to 10 to one. Yet we've never heard a single, soli-
tary Algerian soldier use the phrase, "IF we win." It's
always "AFTER the war." Anyhow, now the sun is going down;
time for dinner, bed, and another night of wondering how
much closer the French artillery will come. Tomorrow, we
shoot several sound-film stories for television. Then, tomorrow night, we move off deeper into Algeria. On inquiry,
I learn there are about 30-thousand French troops around
here, in this department, as permanent garrison; right now,
today, they say there are about 80-thousand. This is the
sort of area we're going to travel through. I also learn
our artillery shells are coming from a French camp less
than 8 miles away, and another about 9 miles away; about
2,000 French in both these camps. This particular area,
we're told, has been attacked 18 times already this year

by forces ranging up to 7 and 8 thousand French troops.
And 29 days ago there was a French camp less than 2 miles
from here. Unwilling to reflect on these thoughts, I can
only report that these soldiers are so tough we've seen one
remove a bottlecap, another open a sardine can, with their
teeth. One sad note today: Two boys, 12 and 14, one of whom
has no family since the French killed his father, have been
here for several days, as camp mascots. They made their way
up here alone. And the whole camp has grown fond of them.
This afternoon, they had to leave; the Captain is sending
them into Tunisia, to school. The eldest cried, when he
gave up his guns and said goodbye to the Captain. I had a
big rock in my throat myself, I must admit. And the Captain
followed them up the trail, alone, staring glumly into the
forest long after the patrol had disappeared. These are
the children he could have had, but for war. Obviously, he
is deeply moved, even shaken. In Algiers tonight, or Bone
or Oran or Constantine, a couple of little French boys may
lose their fathers. It happens on both sides, in all wars.
I wish the politicians who talk so big about war, in all
countries, could see these little dramas . . . which, in
some ways, are worse than battles.

TUESDAY, AUGUST 6TH — Saw our first forest fires last
night . . . huge red fires, 7 or 8 miles away, sending
pillars of smoke into the clear star-filled sky. This is
a typical French tactic, incendiary artillery shells, or
incendiaries from planes, or napalm bombs, to literally
smoke out suspected Algerian hideouts. Saw two more forest
fires today as we (were) working filming three sound reports
for television — working 6 hours, non-stop. Returned to
camp completely exhausted to find marching orders — we're
leaving in half-an-hour. Frantic packing and at 5:15 p.m.,
we're off. For the first time, I'm offered a mule — and take
it. It's worse than hiking, downhill; but pure luxury, up
the steep rocky mountains. See our first burned out farm,
destroyed by the French. En route, down the mountains and
into the valley, find some water; it's from a filthy water-
hole, and we drink it from a rusty tin-can . . . but it's
delicious. About 8:15 p.m., after a 3-hour hike, we stumble down a particularly steep mountain — and find an entire
company drawn up to meet us in the darkness. This is the
Deuxième Companie, 2nd Company, commanded by "Indochine."

A good, banquet-style dinner in the dusk - we all sit on
blankets and eat from a communal bowls (sic), 6, 8, and 18
to a dish - then, bed-time. I go on a midnight patrol with
Indochine, mountains beautiful in the silver light or a 3/4
moon, but ominous now, so near French troops and possible
ambushes and patrols. Indochine ches-out (sic) several
groups for not being more vigilant; shows one how he
would have crept up and cut down the lot with his sub-
machinegun; shows another, by tossing a rock in their
midst, how they could be wiped out by a sudden grenade.
Back at our camp-site, a rocky field in a valley, sleep is
as elusive as ever. The sky is studden (sic) with stars.
But the mountain silhouette above is threatening. And every
noise in the night is alarming. To the West, deeper inside Algeria, another tremendous forest fire gets the whole
night skyline aflame. This is another of the many tragedies
of this undeclared war . . . the firest (sic) fire, a standard French tactic. The oak-like cork tree is one of the
mainstays of Algeria's economy, provides most of the cork
- everything from bottle corks to soundproofing. Yet one
salvo of incendiary shells, one bombing run with incendiaries or napalm, can wipe out an entire mountain forest in a
matter of hours. And it takes at least 20 years to replace
just one cork tree. Tonight, brilliant red in the darkness,
another forest is dying.

WEDNESDAY, AUGUST 7TH - Unable to sleep till after 3
o'clock this morning . . . then awakened at 5:30 a.m., by
a B-26 on patrol, scouring the mountaintops and valleys for
Algerian soldiers. After only 2 1/2 hours sleep, run for
cover before I know what's happening. Everyone takes cover.
The B-26 returns for another look - then disappears. If he
didn't see us, nothing will happen. If he DID see us, we'll
know soon enough . . . artillery shells, bombing and strafing. It's a funny feeling to be an American, crouching in
a bush, while an American plane roars overhead . . . also
a funny feeling to have everyone shouting at you, jubi-
lantly, yet accusingly . . . "Américaine, Américaine—Bay-
Vingt-Sees" (American, American B-26 . . . see!" (sic)
Masraff films our Captain changing into Arab sheikh's robe
and turban for an air-raid alert. This is one of the French
headaches . . . any Algerian soldiers can change into the
simple Arab civvies in a matter of seconds. Also film family

of our host of last night and today, a farmer who literally makes his home ours, in true Arab hospitality. Also,
some shots of four civilian women, squatting beside a hut,
kneading in hand-carved wooden bowls the dough for the flat,
round, wheel-like Arabic bread. Their silver bracelets and
necklaces and earrings tinkle musically as they work this
bread for the soldiers. Later, film for TV an entire company . . . 3 groups, or squads . . . 33 men . . . zigzagging
down one mountain, single-file; up another, silhouetted on
the skyline, (and) then climbing down the cliff-like mountainside. Hard, tough soldiers, they know every inch of
these mountains and climb over them like human mountain-
goats. Also shoot company on parade, marching - then,
suddenly, their run for cover as a plane comes overhead.
Afterward, lose a little appetite as we see our farmer-host
slit the throats of two goats - fresh meat, our lunch. Soft
thoughts for a bloody, no-quarter war like this. At 9:15 in
the morning, we have finished 3 hours of hard, fast photography. Later: We've just finished lunch . . . fresh goat
stew, and bread . . . the goats we saw killed an hour or so
ago, the bread we saw them making earlier. Here, you realize how the Algerian soldier is down to the basic essentials . . . eating, sleeping, and fighting. None of us has
bathed nor shaved for days now; we've hiked and slept and
sweated in these clothes, these filthy clothes. Breakfast is
a cup of coffee in the morning . . . and it has to last a
long time. Bread is really the staff of life - I've never
eaten so much bread in my life. And, water: Water in this
baking daytime heat, in the August See-O-coe[39] (sic) - water
becomes beer, champagne and wine mixed into one wonderful,
life-saving drink. Life for the Algerian soldier is, as I
say, reduced to the barest necessities. Another point: We
realize now that this undeclared war is, for the Algerians,
a night-time affair. French planes, mostly American planes,
are overhead sunup (sic) till sundown. And many an American
World War II veteran remembers what it's like to fight
without air cover, the frustration of having no planes of
your own, not even any ack-ack.[40] So, the Algerians fight at
night, travel only from sundown till sunup (sic). For the
Algerians, this is strictly a war in the dark, a war of individuals, fighting exactly like Indians, against one of the
biggest and most modern armies in the world. . . . It's a
nighttime war of rifles against artillery, of mules against

trucks and half-tracks, of camouflage against air attack. In short, it's an Indian-like army, fighting a super modern, jet-age army. And most of the battles, big or small, take place in the night, after dark. The Captain tells us the Algerians are comparatively quiet right now because it's harvest time. Otherwise, he says, if they start up ambushes and other operations, the French start firing the fields, wreaking vengeance, and the Algerian farmers lose their precious harvest. . . . It's noon now, time for a few hours' nap, and hiding from French planes. Then, about 6 o'clock, just before sundown, we move off again, deeper into Algeria . . . our next stop is at least 15 miles from here, 15 miles through mountains, in the dark, through the French army.

THURSDAY, AUGUST 8TH — Last night was our worst march yet. Even the afternoon was miserable, before we started, as hot as the Western desert, partly because of the Sirocco, but mostly because of hot furnace winds blowing in from the West, from forest fires started by the French. About 7 p.m., we start out . . . in bright moonlight. The going's not so rough, in the beginning, because we're travelling up a valley, through rolling, cultivated fields and orchards. And we have a strong force with us, about 300 men. But, you feel almost naked traveling in the open, spotlighted by the moon, a perfect target for any French forces hidden on the dark mountainsides. And most of the early hours of this march is through this bright, semi-daylight, thru open country. This time, I'm on a mule, so I don't suffer so much, nor does Masraff. But the pace is fast through this dangerous section of our journey. And the panting of the soldiers is even louder than the mules' hooves clattering on rocks. At one point, we pass right between two French camps, about 1500 French troops on each side, only half-a-mile away in each direction. It's a delicate point, and the sudden barking of village and farm dogs sounds like an alarm. For the first time, I, for one, feel frankly scared . . . a gigantic target at least 12 feet tall. But, as the Algerians have always claimed, the French apparently have no taste for sudden night-fighting. They certainly can hear us, perhaps even see us. But there's no trouble. The night, and the mountains, apparently belong to the Algerians. There's a brief, thunderous artillery

barrage at one point, but the shells are nowhere near us.
We plod on into foothills at the end of the valley, between forest fires burning brightly on the mountaintops to
the north, south and west. After a while, the march becomes
a nightmare, as the Captain drives us on and on twoard
(sic) the safety of the mountains and the forest, before
daybreak. Hour after hour, without letup. Both Masraff
and I are tired, dead-tired, but we are riding; the soldiers are walking, over rough, rocky terrain, hour after
hour. In fact, we march all night, with only two real rest
stops . . . 8 hours of straight marching. First, up-hill,
then up steep mountains, even after the moon has gone down.
Finally, at 3 o'clock in the morning, on a thorny mountaintop, our section seems lost, and we bog down. Masraff collapses on the ground like a wounded elephant, and refuses
to move any farther. The soldiers and I agree, and we all
pass out till first early-light. Then, heavily, we're off
again, up another mountain, dragging toward the forest
and camouflage from air attack after dawn. An hour later, we
reach the edge of the forest here, 4500 feet above sea-
level . . . and fall asleep immediately. Later, they tell
us 3 different French planes buzzed this area, but we
didn't move an eyelid. For the first time, we know the full
meaning of complete exhaustion, complete, utter exhaustion.
I mention this NOT as a purely personal comment, but to TRY
to explain what kind of soldiers these are, young men who
can march 8 hours straight, thru mountains, in the dark,
without a single word of complaint. These are soldiers,
fighting men. Our 17-year-old, on his first march, cries this
morning, his body sobbing with fatigue. Later, our first
food in over 12 hours is a bitter cup of Arab coffee from a
farmer . . . and some baked corncobs, green corn, but it's
food. Then, one soldier asks us, shyly if we have any alco-
hol or iodine. Eight wounded men are tucked away in a woods
less than a mile from here, he says. One has his jaw shot
away, he adds, and some iodine would be helpful. Masraff
and I empty our two first-aid kits packed by our wives,
and take off. In one ravine, we find four of the wounded.
One has a hole in his swollen right jaw, where a bullet
entered, and a raw, gaping open wound in his upper jaw,
where the bullet came out. I dissolve some penecillin (sic)
tablets in a spoonful of water, and spoon-feed him, hoping it will help his face wounds, plus another in his leg

and still another in his side. When I start to sprinkle
penicillin powder on the raw open wound in his side, the
others say to save it for another man, who has little face
left. We leave a bottle of strong penicillin tablets for
the 4 wounded here, including a boy with part of his heel
shot away. Then, on down the ravine to a little thicket.
The smell greets us first, the oldest odor of war, rot-
ting flesh. Peering in, we see him, a man with half a face,
uttering pitiful animal cries of agony. I try to explain
the penicillin tablets, but feel ashamed and inadequate
when I understand he can't drink or eat. Yazid carefully unpeels the stinking bandage and pours all our penicillin powder on that raw half-face, teeth, mouth and jaw
gone, only half a lip hanging down from the shreds of his
face. Only the eyes are alive and human, yet animal-like,
sunken in pain, questioning, searching. Masraff leaves
first, after a few film shots which seem as blasphemous,
before those eyes, as a curse in Church. I'm next, as the
near generous smell finally rips into my stomach. Yazid,
as gentle as a professional nurse finishes the job. Later,
I find appetite vanished at lunch, at the sight of fresh
meat. Both Masraff and I have seen a lot of war, a lot of
crushed and broken bodies both in war and peace. But we're
each moved, and shaken, beyond description, by the plight
of this pitiful piece of human being, choking on his own
stench, unable to eat or drink or take medicine — and,
above all, without drugs. Politics and war aside, it seems
such a horrible crime . . . a man alone like this, suffering tortures of the damned, uttering helpless, animal-like
cries. Every soldier should have drugs and medicines. But
the Algerians, fighting what the legalists call a rebellion, or an illegal, undeclared war, have little medicine
for their fight against the jet-age army of the French. And
this man, who's dying, was strafed while walking across an
open field, strafed by an American plane. I don't feel very
proud to be an American today . . . not very proud, in
fact, to be a human being.

FRIDAY, AUGUST 9TH — For the first time since leaving
Tunis, we're in something resembling a house. Left our
last camp at 3:30 in the afternoon, the Algerians rarely
travel in strength thru open country in daytime, because
of French planes. But, as a special, slightly unnerving

favor for us, we travel in daylight this time to photograph our caravan, our march. First, up and down steep,
forest-covered mountains, thru August heat, then down into
a long, open valley. Masraff gets some beautiful shots of
our company deploying down the last mountain. But when HE
starts down, alone, a hulking target in the wheat field, a
B-26 suddenly appears. A soldier yells at the mule, which
becomes confused. Masraff is thrown, head over heels, onto
the rocky ground. A hard fall, but happily, no broken
bones. At the start of the valley we photographed farms
and "Meshtas," groups of farms, destroyed by the French.
Nothing but low stone walls left standing in the gutted
houses, the rich valley fields overgrown with weeds. The
whole place has an eerie, lonely atmosphere . . . broad
daylight, and rich farming country, but the atmosphere of
a graveyard at night. Once, this was a thriving, farming
valley . . . 5,000 people. Four months ago, our officers
say, the French came here in force. First, strafing and
incendiaries on every thatched-roof farmhouse . . . then,
artillery barrages . . . then, all-out assault by masses
of soldiers. Now, the farms are dead, the valley is dead.
We feel especially conspicuous filing through the fields in
broad daylight, taking cover from occasional curious
B-26's . . . and a particularly suspicious helicopter. But
the chief of the region, a Lieut., meets us and escorts us
for the last, final, fatiguing stage up the end of the
valley, in growing darkness. Even the Captain and
Indochine take mules. And the soldiers are sagging,
stoop-shouldered, feet dragging. But, once again, I'm
amazed at the stamina of these soldiers. The wounded man
we saw yesterday had marched 72 DAYS before he was
hurt . . . then, even with his face shot away, he had
hiked 18 miles. On this particular march we have made
exactly 102 kilometres . . . almost 65 miles . . . 65
miles of mountain country, really rough going, almost all
of it at night. One night alone we made almost half of
that, about 30 miles. And the Captain has told us, just
now, that night we slipped by a French ambush. The French
apparently had advance information a company was coming
thru that night, but Algerian intelligence had advance
information on where the ambush would be set up. So, our
route was changed, and we slipped by the ambush - an
ambush of armored cars. Even more disquieting, the

Algerians have information the French are mounting a huge
"Ratissage," a big encircling, or weeding-out operation,
of this area we're in right now . . . 10, 20 or perhaps
as many as 30,000 troops, plus planes and artillery . . . a typical Ratissage. And it's planned for
today or tomorrow, within 3 days at the latest. So,
we're moving on late this afternoon . . . fast . . .
back to the Captain's regular camp. He says we're going
straight thru this time . . . one night, for a murderous
trip that has taken 3 nights of hard marching enroute . . . almost 65 miles in one night. Our welcome here
last night was fantastic, the warmest I've ever experienced anywhere, in any country. Among other things, officers sat us down on rocks outside, put a rock under each
of our feet, and then poured cold water for us while we
washed our feet for the first time in days. Then, into
this building, the closest to a house we've seen since
Tunis . . . and chairs, real chairs, and a table. And a
meal which can only be described as a feast. As we go to
sleep, stretched out on the floor, the 5th Company's political officer is delivering a lecture outside our open
window. It's 11 p.m. And gathered around him in a circle,
on the ground, are white-turbaned civilian leaders of this
district . . . an unforgettable picture in the moonlight . . . but, unfortunately, one too dim for our cameras. This morning, a wash in cool mountain water, and we
feel like new men. French planes overhead from time to
time, but ignored. We spend hours talking with the officers
here. It's fascinating, because this mountain region, a
"Douar,"[41] is well-inside Algeria, and somewhat typical.
Three months ago there was a French camp near here. It was
under constant attack by the Algerians, and finally, when
French intelligence learned the ALN here had received
mortars, they decided it was time to move on. Before The
Trouble (sic), this area had about 4,000 people, mostly
farmers. The Algerians say their official records show that
374 persons have been killed by the French, almost all
civilians, mostly women and children. Others have been
interned, or have gone away, wandering through the mountains. Only about 1,000 are left. There are some 6,500
French troops in this region. Yet the ALN company here
attacks without letup. Two sections, 36 men, are special-
ists in sabotage. The Lt. in charge of this work, a tall,

deceptively mild-mannered and soft-spoken man, says casually that his men sabotage the trains once a week . . .
and that it takes the French 2 or 3 days to repair the
damage each time. Also, saboteurs regularly topple electric high-tension poles, or pylons. They saw through 3
legs of one pylon, then some legs of others, and, usually,
with one dynamite charge bring down at least 3 or 4 poles
and the wires. This company also attacks a French camp at
least once every 10 or 12 days. In its spare time, it sets
up ambushes and carries out other, secret, operations.
They say they have spies right inside the French units,
know in advance every move the French plan. The civilians
not only cooperate; most are part of the ALN itself, in a
way, according to the officers here. One civilian came in
this morning carrying a basket of precious drugs and
medicines stolen from the French. What happens if a civilian doesn't cooperate? The question arises so seldom,
they say, that it's not a problem. These people have seen
first-hand the way French troops operate, they say – almost
all have lost members of their families – and they're more
enthusiastically anti-French then (sic) the ALN, if possible. But, I insist, it's normal for many people to
remain neutral in a situation like this – for a few to
collaborate. What happens to these? An officer shrugs. The
neutrals, he declares, we leave alone. As long as they
don't actually HELP the French, he says, we leave them
alone. And if they do help the French? In wartime, the
officer says, in any country, a civilian who actively
collaborates and helps the enemy against his own people,
is condemned to death. This answers the question. Here, as
everywhere behind the Algerian lines, I am convinced that,
rightly or wrongly, the Algerians have an almost pathetically sincere conviction that sooner or later, the United
States, the Americans, will help them achieve independence. Individually and collectively, politically and
personally, they look to America as the only real source
of aid for for (sic) their cause. "We want America to be
the means of our achieving independence, thru the U.N.,"
one officer adds this morning. I find the Algerians the most
logical and realistic of all Arabs. They admit it's tough
to believe in America when you're being bombed or strafed
by American planes, shelled by American artillery, shot at
by American rifles and sub-machineguns. But, even so, most

say they realize this material was sent by the U.S. to
France, for use in NATO, not against the Algerian people.
They also say, as they did just this morning, that even the
lowliest peasant knows the difference between communism and
democracy. They say they know, for example that America
made it clear in the beginning that for many reasons she
could not interfere in North Africa, could only try to
mediate between both sides. But they say they also know
Russia was not so honest, that she offered political help
– and even arms, which have been turned down so far – only
when it suited Russia's policy. "We are always teaching
our people," the political officer here just said, "that
Americans are our only home, the only people, the non-
colonial people, with whom we can cooperate." I can't
report in detail all these long, long conversations. But I
can report, in absolute honesty, that, despite the experienced correspondent's natural cynicism, that despite continual mental probing and interviewing tricks, I find these
people tragically hungry for independence, ready and willing to fight to the death for that independence . . . and
nothing less. "These people say they will not accept any
compromise package for independence from FRENCH hands," the
political officer says. "After the price we've paid already," he continues, "we want nothing less than independence through the UN . . . guaranteed by the UN. And we
hope," he adds, "we pray, that America is the MEANS of our
achieving independence thru the U.N. America," he con-
cludes, "is our one hope, our only hope."

SATURDAY, AUGUST 10TH – To escape French encirclement, a
Ratissage, we've just marched all night, a fast, hard,
forced march of 60 kilometres . . . almost 40 miles . . . in
one night. And, Thank God, we've made it. Yesterday, in the
early afternoon, we went up a mountainside to watch and film
ALN officers distributing food to civilians of the region.
French planes overhead, so they gathered under the trees.
About 75 men, squatting under the trees, and some 50 women
and children huddled at the bottom of a stone cliff.
Practically all barefoot, in rags, children without under-
pants . . . an incredible contrast to the rich farmland in
the valley below; farmland now out-of-bounds because of
French operations. Each family gets a bucket of corn, and a
little cash according to the size of the family . . .

usually, about 1000 francs, less than $3. The men squat
stolidly, listening to a lecture by the political officer,
who talks at length about America, and how we have come to
report the facts of this situation to the people of America.
The women, carrying and leading somber-faced babies, pick
up the corn and money as the family name is called. This is
also the time for the 6-month ration of clothes, a new
cotton dress for each family, for the wife or to be cut up
for clothes for the children. As we start to leave, the
distribution breaks up and there are loud protests from the
men, who are standing now, aroused. Perhaps I'm suspicious,
but I suppose this distribution was staged just for us, for
our cameras, that it's not regular distribution time, that
the ration is not as plentiful as that we've seen. Such
thoughts are washed out, however, by thunder and darkening
skies . . . a storm coming up. Regardless, we pack up and
start out, at 4:30 p.m. But, at that moment, the storm
breaks . . . heavy, slashing rain, and strong, driving
winds. It's a gloomy, uncomfortable, ominous start. But the
rain doesn't last long, returns only occasionally in small
gusts. We're wet, but not soaked. And the equipment is
well-covered. Darkness comes early, with the storm. And the
moon, almost full, appears only occasionally from behind
dark clouds. The usual forest fires are burning on several
mountaintops and the smell, the sad smell, of burning wood
is strong in the night air. The march goes on and on, hour
after hour, at a fast pace, over shortcuts to avoid French
ambushes. No one speaks. Even the usual hushed banter of
the soldiers is missing. Everyone is too preoccupied with
keeping going, with putting one foot in front of the other.
Occasional civilians appear in the darkness, speak quietly
to the Captain, point out a new shortcut away from French
troops. Our only stop is on a mountaintop, early in the
march for a bit of food and rest. The food is a dish full
of butter, covered with honey; we dip hunks of bread into
the butter, then the honey . . . and this is dinner. The
rest of the night is marching, forced marching. Several
times I dismount, aching from the unaccustomed mule's back,
and march a while for a change; each time, I wonder how
these soldiers can keep it up, hour after hour. Sometime
after midnight, both Masraff and I take on board a weary,
half-sick young soldier, the only two unable to keep up the
rigorous pace. Gradually, the march slows down, past the

danger point, and past human endurance. Finally, even the
Captain realizes no one can go much farther. We file into an
apple orchard and stretch out. It's 2:30 in the morning;
we've been marching steadily since 4:30 in the afternoon:
10 hours. In seconds, every single man - except the poor
sentries - is asleep, sound asleep. Then, in what again
seems like seconds, we're awakened. Night is thinning out
and, the Captain tells us, we have to find better cover
before daylight, before French planes are overhead. Stiff
and awkwardly, we start out again and, within an hour or
so, arrive at a stream bed with shrubbery as cover. Here,
the Captain tells us, we'll spend the day. Everyone stretch-
es out, asleep in seconds. Everyone except Masraff and I,
who find it difficult, even in our fatigue, to fall asleep on
a teeming anthill. As we wander around looking for a place,
any place, to sleep, the Captain takes us to the hut of a
farmer, where blankets have been stretched on the mud-floor.
All of us TOO tired (to) sleep, we talk. Is it true, I ask
the Captain, that the days, the open country and the skies
belong to the Algerians? Partly true, he explains. But the
French, he adds, have only part of the day, from about 7
a.m. till noon or 2 p.m., when it's too late for them to
mount a big operation against any sudden, specific target.
The rest of the time, he says, 17 out of 24 hours, belongs
to the Algerians. And even in the mornings, the Captain
declares, the Algerians often launch their commando assaults against camps and other priority targets. The commandoes, he says, proudly, are our guided missiles. What, I
ask, is the Algerians' most formidable weapon? "Unity," he
replies at once. "Unity of the people and the army . . . our
Will, and our Faith." Later, noticing that we're watching
him read a note just handed him by a courier, he hands the
paper off. "Read it," he smiles. "This might give you some
idea of our intelligence." Written in French, in small
precise letters on four large sheets of paper, the so-
called note is an "Intelligence report" on a village in the
area, a regular, military-style intelligence report. And
its detail is fantastic. This Algerian agent, a civilian,
lists every French military post in the entire area, the
number and caliber of each gun, where attacks would be
possible and where retreat after attack would be difficult.
He pinpoints each French blockhouse, each searchlight, each
mortar, each strand of barbed wire. Typically, the French

have virtually surrounded this village with barbed wire and
checkpoints; residents have special passes to leave by one
of the six gates each morning, return each evening. The
Arabs, it seems are specially incensed over these passes,
which are written out for, and I quote, "French Moslems."
In other words, Arabs. This is one of the many reasons
Algerians snort at the French claim Algeria is an integral
part of France, that Algerians are French citizens with
equal rights. Algeria, they say, is not part of the French
Third Republic, Algeria is the Deuxième, the Second
Republic . . . and its people are only second-class citizens. The writer of this intelligence report also lists
carefully some persons he regards as "Mouchard," or Stool-
Pidgeons (sic). He names a number of farmers, shopkeepers,
café owners, etc., as particularly bad people from the FLN
standpoint. And I note with special interest that he includes in this list a man accused of being a Communist;
this fits with the Algerians' constant claim, here on the
spot that they have nothing to do with the communists, want
nothing to do with the communists, want nothing to do with
them. This agent warns his superiors he is being closely
watched by the French, that it's more and more difficult for
him to collect money for the FLN for this reason. As for
his accusations against alleged stool-pidgeons (sic), he
adds a solemn footnote for any Moslem: "By Allah," he
swears, "I will never accuse anyone unless I have checked
and double-checked, as God is my witness." He signs off
"Long live the F.L.N., and the glorious Army of Liberation."
It's an impressive document, this intelligence report, and
it typifies the fantastic intelligence, because they had the
same thing in France during World War II, when they were
fighting an enemy within their own country.[42] All of us
eventually drift off into fitful sleep, fitful because of the
extreme heat, compounded of Seer-of-coe[43] and hot winds from
the forest fires, almost unbearable. At 5 p.m., after a bit
to eat, we start out again. I give up my mule to a weary
soldier and march over half of the way, and arrive back at
our main camp with the first contingent, tired, dead-tired,
but somehow happy at being back at what we now regard as a
sort of Home. The rest arrive half an hour later. Our
equipment, we learn, has been moved to a well-guarded
building about a mile away; the officer in charge here
was worried about a possible French attack in our absence,

and thought it safer to move our stuff. It's returned,
and after dark, however, and we all go to bed early.
But sleep, blocked by fatigue and nerves and aching
muscles, comes slowly. I'm trying again now, but not
very hopefully.

SUNDAY, AUGUST 11TH — Sunday, here in Algeria is a long,
long way from the American Sunday of the thick Sunday
paper, the comics, the late breakfast, big lunch or dinner, radio or TV, perhaps a Sunday drive. Heavy artillery
fire from early morning, on the other side of this mountain. And rocket-fire at some sort of target on the ground
over there. The sun turns a queer yellow, because of some
smoke clouds from forest fires, and the sunlight filtering
through the forest here is deep yellow, almost amber, as
viewed through a camera lens cloud-filter. The very morning
we ache to sleep, late, the Captain rouses us early, anxious, I suspect(,) to get us out of here, to be rid of the
terrific responsibility for our safekeeping. So, from early morning onward, we both work non-stop all day, almost
dropping from fatigue, spurred only by an equal anxiety
to finish up here, to get back home, to normal civilized
life, and our families, and peace. I spent the day at the
typewriter; Masraff, on the camera. Among other things,
I want to record assorted miscellaneous notes unrecorded
till now. The fact, for example that the ALN has its own
guardhouses, and prisons. The former are for soldiers —
such as one here the other day who shot off his rifle just
for fun, although misuse of ammunition is a comparatively
severe offense; he got 8 days in the guardhouse for wast-
ing that one cartridge. The guardhouse, incidentally, is
literally underground, for prisoners' safety; probably
a cave. Both these and prisons, for captured soldiers,
etc., are top-secret, for obvious reasons. The Algerians,
by the way, claim they treat French army deserters even
better than their own men, see that Italians and Germans
and so forth with the French army get passage back to
their own countries. Here again, they decline to discuss
details. As for casualties, I have pursued this subject
for one month now, both at Cairo and Tunis headquarters
of the FLN, and at lower levels, among both officers and
soldiers. The figure varies somewhat, but it levels off at
around 400-thousand, consistently, from all sources — some

400-thousand Algerians killed in this war already. Most of
them, according to the ALN, are civilians, killed in bombing and strafing attacks, in all-out assaults against villages and farms, and so on. Around 400,000. There's no way
to check this figure. And even the Algerians have no real
idea as to French army losses, which, they say, the French
treat as top-secret. Once macawbre (sic) footnote: Every
Algerian soldier has a nice wristwatch, French or Swiss,
taken from dead French soldiers. Officers' watches, usually more expensive, are especially prized. A grim reminder
that this is war, real war. I forgot to mention yesterday that in the hut, our last stop on the long march, a
young boy wandered in. And we awakened to find him singing
a song, a song in which our Captain, deeply moved, joined
in on the chorus each time. On inquiry, we discovered the
boy had composed the song himself, as a wandering minstrel
would. Translated, the song told of how his father and
mother had been killed by the French, in a village about
3 miles away, and how he hoped to join the army and, as he
put it, free his country, under our Captain. It was a sad
song, a true folk song in the making. I recorded part of
it for CBS News. When we asked the boy's age, he replied,
"16." We looked incredulous, for the boy looked no older
than 12. The Captain laughed. "It's always this way," he
explained. "They all know they have to be 18 to join the
Algerian army, so they start moving up their ages gradually, hoping to bluff their way in." His smile disappeared.
"Most of these boys have had part, or all, their families
killed by the French. They can't wait to grow up and fight
the French." Today, I might add, in this camp, a youth of
12 appeared; this is a dangerous criminal, one officer here
explained; he's wanted by the French. Why? For what crime?
For giving food to Algerian soldiers. 12 years old. Sent
off into the mountains by his own parents, afraid for his
very life. A wanted criminal, at 12, by French standards.
Everywhere you turn in Algeria these days, it seems,
you're confronted by the sad and tragic. The horrible red
locust is here this summer, for example; the entire countryside and the forests are suffering from the plague.
You suddenly find the sun blacked out as hordes – millions – of the huge red insects fly through the sky, looking for new lands to conquer. Sitting under a tree, you
think it's starting to rain, till you look up and realize

the noise – like that of the first drops of rain – is the
sound of locusts devouring every leaf on a tree. The ALN,
on the other hand, keeps fighting, not just militarily,
but in the field of economics. Last night, an ANL soldier
who is a forester explained how he oversees a group of
civilians cutting cork bark from the trees. By law, the
forests belong to the Government, to what the Algerians
regard as "The French." But, every day, the forester here
has his workers on duty. During artillery barrages, or air
attacks, the workers go underground; or, if the attacks
continue, work elsewhere. Regardless, the FLN harvests
cork bark right under the noses of the French; harvests
the cork, smuggles it out through French army units in
the countryside, through the mountains, and into Tunisia.
Then, it's sold abroad, mostly to America, where it's pul-
verized and turned into cork as we know it. And the profits
go into FLN funds. Once again, it's difficult to describe
this sort of organized activity, as the French do, as the
work of criminals and bandits.

MONDAY, AUGUST 12TH – The power-pack for our sound camera
(sic) is gone, finished. And Masraff takes off on a long,
tiring journey to the nearest village with electricity, to
charge the batteries. The village is hours away, through
the mountains and back across the border . . . always a
ticklish and somewhat dangerous trip, especially the bor-
der-crossing. The last newspapers we saw quoted Algiers
and Paris officials as saying the French are sealing off
the entire Tunisian border . . . they plan to erect barbed-
wire barriers all along the frontier, and, at crucial
areas, plant minefields. So Masraff's trip, just to charge
the camera batteries, is hardly a pleasure trip. Just hope
and pray he makes it OK. I spend the day typing at a makeshift desk, our camera case, sitting on a box, itching,
scratching, wiping away perspiration, trying to ignore an
increasingly painful back-ache. Nine hours straight typing,
with only a half an hour off for lunch consisting of to-
matoes and onions. Stop at sunset, barely able to stand up
straight. And now, to bed.

TUESDAY, AUGUST 13TH – More typing, almost ten hours
straight today. Nervous all morning and afternoon, because
Masraff hasn't appeared . . . over-due. Everyone says it's

all right, he'll show up soon; but I'm worried. Finally,
about 5 o'clock in the afternoon, I look up from typewriter to see a sagging Masraff coming down the path astride a
weary mule. Thank God. Terrible trip, he says. Seven hours
going, yesterday; eight hours coming back today. But, he
adds, he drank his fill of good, clean, fresh water, at the
village. The water here, incidentally, is so bad that we're
only drinking enough to keep alive, filtering it through
a swab of cotton; it's murky, dark with dirt, cloudy and
smelly. Masraff also says he slept in a bed last night, a
real bed . . . and, biggest thrill of all, had a bath. The
whole trip was almost worth that bath, he declares. Anyhow,
he's back safe, and the batteries are ready. Both of us to
bed early, dead-tired.

WEDNESDAY, AUGUST 14TH — Another day of hard work, me typing, Masraff shooting silent film all over the mountain.
Entire camp depressed, as news arrives that the French have
launched a huge, all-out attack against the 5th Company,
some 60 miles from here. This is where we were the other
night, where we had such a wonderful meal, and sat on
chairs, real chairs — the place we had to leave next day
because of reports the French were planning an encircling
operation. The reports were right, it's clear now. And,
if we had stayed . . . well, we would've remained forever, under the ground. They say something like three to five
thousand French troops are taking part in this Ratissage.
First, air attacks, the bombs and incendiaries and napalm;
then, heavy artillery barrages; then, a tightening circle
around the entire area, moving in for the kill. So far, the
boys here say they've heard only that 45 ALN men escaped.
About the rest, no one knows. Moving on the other day
really, and literally, saved our lives, Thank God. Things
brightened up a bit here in camp tonight, as four nurses
arrived, four young women in soldier's uniform, knapsacks
full of drugs and medicines. All four are friendly, cordial
and competent. And dinner, bad as it is in the dimly-lit
hut, is warm and pleasant, enlived (sic) by our female
guests, and conversation is a little lighter. Once again,
however, we are struck by the fact that these girls are
accepted as comrades, more as sisters than as girls, as fe-
males. These Algerian soldiers, have, in a sense, renounced
all normal life, much as monks would; it's incredible. Most

of them have been living this tough, mountain life of bare
essentials for one or two years now, far, far from civilization. I don't know a lot of Arabic, but I know a great
many of the curses, the Bad Words. And yet I've never once
heard one of these soldiers curse, really curse. Masraff,
whose Arabic is perfect, agrees, somewhat in awe. We've
both seen several wars and we've seen a lot of soldiers
of many nationalities. Yet these are the first we've ever
encountered whose conversation is not peppered with curses,
with rough, tough talk. After dinner, over a cigarette in
the darkness outside, we ask the Lieutenant about the nurses. It doesn't seem normal, we point out. There's no boy-
girl play, no boy-girl talk. The Lieutenant, who has been
around, everywhere from Algiers to Saigon, agrees. It's
difficult for outsiders to understand, he says. But, until
after the war, we've given up everything, EVERYTHING. These
women, he says, are soldiers, just as we are soldiers. We
call ourselves brothers, and they are sisters; we're a
family. I know, he declares, that it's almost impossible
for you to understand . . . coming from the city, from civilization, where there's such freedom. But we're absolutely devoted to our cause. Besides, he chuckles, the penalty
for any trouble between a man and a woman, in our army, is
pretty severe - the death penalty.

THURSDAY, AUGUST 15TH - We get up early, for a hard day's
work, shooting some sound film reports for TV. Masraff
nudges me. "Look!" It is a sight. Everyone else is still
asleep. And our bed is crowded, a bed which is sort of log
table about 12 or 15 feet long, the branches laid over the
top as a mattress. It's only 6 a.m., and everyone is still
sleeping soundly - several officers, and the four nurses,
each wrapped up in his or her blanket. Masraff grins. "Our
wives will never believe this - four women, and four or
five men, in one bed - and nothing happens!" He's right. The
work-day starts off bad. We both feel sick, really sick.
By the time we set up our sound equipment on a mountaintop,
Masraff is bent-double, with cramps. And I have to break
off the start of our first report to turn and vomit. We do
the first report in fits and starts, as Masraff keeps sitting
down, doubled-up with pain, and I interrupt my report to
do the same. Then, French planes start scouring the skies
overhead. And we have to stop every few minutes or so to

take cover. The soldiers camouflage our equipment for us,
with pine branches. But, every time, we have to break-off,
cover up the equipment, hide in the bushes, then, when
the plane's gone, come out and take off the camouflage and
start over again. Five minutes later, another plane, the
same story all over again. Hardly ideal working conditions.
Then, in the middle of a report on the Algerian army's
technique, Masraff collapses. It's a kidney attack and
he writhes in pain, unable to speak, unable to stand. We
get him back to the hut, in bed. "Morphine," he whispers.
"Morphine – it's the only thing . . . I know . . . had
this same thing 3 years ago!" He breaks out in a sweat,
then shivers with chills, groaning with sharp acute pains.
At the first-aid infirmary, I learn, to my horror, there is
no morphine . . . no pain-killer stronger than aspirin.
And it'll take at least 24 hours for a patrol to get back
across the border into Tunisia, to get a shot of morphine.
And it's absolutely impossible to put Masraff on a mule,
in this pain where every step of the mule would mean excrutiating (sic) pain. Deep in despair, I go back to the
hut, to find Masraff worse. Water, he cries, keep giving
me liquid . . . it's a kidney stone . . . and I can feel
it moving down . . . I've got to get rid of it. So, for an
hour or two, we fill him with water, and watch helplessly,
as he rides it out, alone, really alone. After a while, the
pain becomes unbearable and nature provides her own anti-
dote: sleep. He sleeps fitfully, shivering and groaning; but
asleep. Later, he awakens . . . and the crisis is over.
"Let's get back to work," he declares. But we make him rest
a couple of hours, tell him to forget about work today.
Within two hours, however, he feels better and insists upon
returning to work. So we go back on the mountaintop and,
between air-raid alerts, between pauses for Masraff's kidney pains, my stomach pains, continue our TV reports. Then,
suddenly, a new crisis – our power-pack is gone, no power
to run our camera. And the extra power-pack sent from New
York for this trip, the spare battery, turns out to be the
wrong size! It's the final blow. Neither of us is in good-
enough shape to make the 15- or 20-hour trip back across
the border to re-charge the battery . . . and we're already
'way past our one-month deadline on this story. In short,
it's time to call it quits . . . to leave. . . . to go
home. Both of us have "had it."

SUNDAY, AUGUST 18TH — We're in Tunis, Thank God. And lucky
to be here. Our trip out of Algeria, and across the border, was all arranged before-hand, and should've been very
simple. The ALN had arranged for a truck to sneak across
the border and meet us inside Algeria, so we could ride
out in comfort and speed. But everything went wrong. Our
actual departure from camp was moving, and somewhat emotional. The Lieutenant arranged a parade in our honor,
presented the entire company to us in a simple, poignant
ceremony. Then, finally, we start on the way back, down the
last mountain. About an hour out of camp, a French plane
buzzes the forest-tops. There, in the woods, it's no problem. But later, starting down the last mountain, what we
call THE mountain, the forest thins out and there are only
occasional trees. And another French plane appears. Even
so, it's simple, at first, to take cover. Then, suddenly, the plane starts shooting. About 200 yards away from
our party — not far, but out of sight. "Probably shooting
cows," one of the soldiers snorts. Close as the shooting
is, it doesn't bother us much. The pilot, it's apparent,
is not very serious about the whole thing; he's firing
single-shots, not rapid-fire. Then, just as we reach a
cluster of trees, a soldier comes running down the mountainside and says a civilian, a farmer, has been shot in
the back. The pilot apparently has been pot-shotting at
him, just for fun. We all feel a little sick. It's so
senseless, a man working in the fields, and a pilot chasing
him around the fields, firing single-bursts, apparently out
of sheer boredom. Meanwhile the Lieutenant announces that
our truck hasn't appeared. He points to the dirt road down
below — nothing. The rendezvous was set for several hours
ago. But there's no truck. "Just hope these planes haven't
strafed him," one soldier mutters. Another says this is
probably the reason for the plane overhead this morning;
one, he says, must have seen and attacked the truck — now
they're looking for the rendezvous group . . . us. So,
for almost three hours, we wait there on the mountainside, sweating and taking cover under the nearest tree
or rock every time a plane swoops low. Masraff gets some
good shots of the planes, but we all keep worrying for
fear a ray of sunshine will reflect from the lens, bring
the planes in big numbers. About 1 o'clock someone shouts;
"C'est La! It's there!" We all stare down, and see it — a

small van, with a canvas top . . . our truck. At the same
time, a sad procession appears above us . . . four men
carrying a stretcher made of logs and branches. Atop it
lies the wounded civilian, flat on his stomach, mute with
pain and shock, his clothes soaked in dark-red blood;
the bullet is still in his back. The plane is still overhead, curious, suspecting. Buzzing overhead, flying away,
then circling back for another look; over and over again.
Cautiously, we move down the mountainside . . . running
from tree to tree, through open fields, each time the
plane flies away, then huddling under the tree each time
he returns. Finally, we make the stream-bed which has cut
the valley at the bottom of our mountain. Then, start
up the other side, toward the road, a hillside without
trees. Here, where there is no cover, where the truck is
an open target on the road above, we all feel This is It,
that we haven't a chance. But suddenly, for some unknown
reason – maybe simply because it's 1:30 p.m., lunchtime
– the pilot veers away in a big circle . . . and disappears. Either it's the biggest break of our lives, or he
has gone back to bring more planes. Nervously, we help put
the stretcher and the wounded man in the truck, say quick
goodbyes to our Lieutenant and our patrol, and take off.
The road is rough, rough as only a real mountain road can
be . . . full of ruts and stones and boulders. Because
of the wounded man, our driver creeps along in low-gear,
about 6 or 7 miles an hour. We scan the sky anxiously,
looking and listening, straining every nerve for first-
sight or first sound of a French plane, or a squadron of
planes. If anyone ever asks me about the worst ride in
my life, this is it. Every bump a pain, thinking of the
man there with the bullet in his back. And every minute an hour, straining, listening, looking for the first
plane overhead. In this truck, on this dusty road, we're
a perfect target for any strafing plane – one strafing run
and we've had it. Slowly, however, the road gets better,
and we go faster. And, finally, the frontier, unmarked, but
nevertheless, the frontier. We're in Tunisia again, out
of Algeria . . . safe. Further on, the Tunisian guard at
the customs post waves us on gaily, obviously familiar
with these secret travelers, raises his gate and salutes
smartly, grinning. Our grins stretch ear-to-ear. At the
first village, we have a lemonade, bottled lemonade, from

an ice-box, fresh and clear and cold. Then, on to the next
town, where the wounded farmer is lifted out gently, still
on his makeshift log stretcher, then taken into a hospital
for an emergency operation. We are taken to a secret office
of the FLN, where we wait for hours while they try to find
a car to take us to Tunis. At dusk, they find a taxi, a
small French station-wagon barely big enough for us and
our equipment. And, by 9 p.m., we're back in Tunis, at our
old hotel, which now looks luxurious beyond imagination.
We toss all our filthy clothes onto the balcony, stand in
the shower for more than half-an-hour, gulp down a buffet-
dinner and gallons of cold, fresh, clear, clean water —
then, to bed, in a real bed.

MONDAY, AUGUST, 19TH — Both of us seem to be in a daze,
almost a state of shock. Too nervous to sleep, yet too
exhausted to do much. For one thing, we're just beginning to realize how lucky we are to be here, how lucky we
are to come out of this thing alive. A story in the Paris
newspaper is a good reminder. It says briefly that during
a French military operation near Laverdure,[44] in Algeria,
a "chief rebel" named Djebrane Mabrouk has been killed.
Mabrouk was the soft-spoken sabotage leader who urged
us to move out of his area fast, because of an impending
French operation. Thanks to him, we did move out — that
was the time we marched all night, 10 straight hours, to
escape French encirclement. But Mabrouk apparently didn't
move fast enough. And now, he's dead. This sort of thing,
and our flight down the mountain the last day, hiding from
French planes which shot a civilian only 200 yards away,
has left us still taut and nervous. Also, we're beginning
to realize how little food we ate in the mountains, food
which we couldn't stomach. Our civilian clothes here at the
hotel are all too big for us; we've each lost at least 3 or
4 inches around the waist, and our trousers droop ridicu-
lously. Lack of food, and lack of sleep, in the mountains,
has left us somewhat gaunt . . . and utterly exhausted.
Every muscle hurts, it's impossible to get comfortable in
bed. And instead of being excited, exhilarated, at getting
back safe, at being back in civilization, both of us are
sunk in deep, black clouds of depression. To top everything
else, our TV interview with President (Habib) Bourguiba,[45]

head of the Tunisian republic, is called off. Bourguiba is
leaving, suddenly, for Switzerland, for a rest.

TUESDAY, AUGUST 20TH — We've got reservations on the next
plane out of here — Thursday — and feel better. At the same
time, an FLN official tells us to be careful around Tunis,
that the old French counter-terrorist group here, the "Red
Hand,"[46] is still active. They probably know you've been inside Algeria, reporting our side of the story, the official
explains. And, he warns, these old die-hards in the Red Hand
are capable of anything . . . anything. Taking special measures to guard our precious film, we shoot some scenes at an
Algerian army hospital near Tunis. The hospital is barren,
pitifully equipped. Some of the patients lie on the floor.
But the operating room is well-equipped. And the surgeon is
probably the best in all North Africa, a young, dedicated
Algerian who studied in a number of countries abroad, including Philadelphia. Among other things, he's a prominent
and talented plastic surgeon. The proof of his talent is a
man lying in bed there — the same faceless man we thought
we left dying in the mountains. The doctor has given him
an entirely new jaw, a plastic jaw, and now he has a face,
can eat and drink and even speak despite a partially artificial tongue. The Algerians, we learn, have well over one
thousand hospital patients here in Tunisia, most of them
surgical patients, for the removal of bullets . . . some,
however, are the inevitable amputees. And others said to be
victim of gas attacks. An FLN official promises us what he
describes as a document full of facts and evidence on alleged French use of poison gas in the Algerian fighting.

THURSDAY, AUGUST 22ND — Our plane leaves in a few hours.
It's time to sum up, to sort out our impressions. We're
certainly no experts. But we have spent some six weeks with
the Algerians . . . in Tunis, along the frontier, and inside Algeria itself. And, inevitably we find ourselves coming
to certain conclusions. First of all, we know now that this
is a war. No matter what you call it . . . rebellion, civil
war, or undeclared war . . . this is war, real war, bloody,
no-quarter war. Secondly, no matter what the French call the
Algerians, they have an army, a real army . . . a well-
organized, uniformed, armed and disciplined army fighting

under definite tactical and strategic direction. And its soldiers are as tough as any we've ever seen. Most are ex-French
army men, veterans of Indochina and, some, of World War II.
And in this terrain, in this particular war, they're practically unbeatable. They know the mountains, are experts in
mountain fighting. And, it must be reported that our one big
impression is that most of these people are sincere, absolutely convinced they are fighting for a just cause, for what
they regard as the liberation of their country. Not fanatic,
as I suspected before coming here, but devoted, determined,
dedicated . . . in a quiet, logical, almost unemotional way
unknown among Arabs of the Middle East. We've fenced and
boxed all around this question, even slugged. Not only in
formal interviews, but also on the march, at meal-time, and,
above all, in long nightly bull-sessions. Yet we've found
no evidence of communist leadership among the Algerians, no
evidence of communist arms . . . Yet. There is, however, evidence that the communists have offered arms. Definitely. So
far, the Algerians insist they have turned down this offer.
They say they want no part of communism that they're well-
aware of what it means. But, if this war drags on and on,
without any sign of help or sympathy from any part of the
West - the United States in particular - the Algerians warn
frankly that they may HAVE to accept arms, and other help,
from the east, the communist east. Meantime, it's plain that
the Algerians are getting help, a lot of help, from the Arab
nations. From what we've seen here, the Tunisians cooperate
in practically everything except the shooting. There's no
question about this. And the Algerians say it's the same in
Morocco. Other help comes from Egypt, from Libya and Syria
and Saudi Arabia . . . even Southeast Asia. Most of it,
though, from the Arabs. Regardless of French law and over 100
years of French history, it's difficult, inside Algeria, to
go along with the idea that the country itself is an integral
part of France, that its people are Frenchmen. Except for the
European minority, the Algerians are Arabs. Many think and
speak in French, but they're Arabs. Also they are Moslems and
this is a Moslem army, through and through. So far, there's
little talk of a holy War. But, here and there, you hear
occasional fanatic talk of a Jee-Had (sic), a Holy war. And
it's significant that most, if not all, of the political officers are more Arab, more Moslem than the others. As for the
reasons for this fighting, this war - they're deep-rooted,

and ill-defined. Basically, the Algerian is rebelling against
what he calls a Second-Class citizen, in what he describes as
the Deuxième, Second Republic to the Third Republic, France.
Soldier after soldier speak of school days, of teachers who
treated them as second-class students, teachers who respected and encouraged European pupils but looked down upon the
Arab students. And you hear the same complaints about daily
life. Basically, the Algerian declares, he simply wants to
be treated as an equal, to BE an equal, to enjoy real fra-
ternité and liberté. Now, after almost 3 years of fighting,
the Algerian has a new bitterness toward the French, a bitterness over French conduct in this rebellion, or war. The
Algerian is especially bitter over French destruction of
the country's valuable oak forests, of whole villages, and
groups of farms. He accuses the French of atrocities inde-
scribably, of making war on civilians. And now, the Algerian
says that after the price his people have paid . . . between
2 and 4 hundred-thousand civilian deaths alone - the people
of Algeria are not prepared to accept any compromise. They
say they won't take a package-deal, like Tunisia and Morocco.
Bitterness and distrust is so deep now, they declared, that
the Algerians will not even accept full independence, if it
comes from France. They insist on full independence recognized and guaranteed by the United Nations. Meanwhile, any
conscientious American correspondent in Algeria must report
that Washington statements claiming the United States cannot interfere in this fighting sound somewhat ridiculous.
Especially when you're listening to an artillery barrage from
American 105's, or hiding from an American B-26. A large part
of the French army is American-equipped. Some Algerians know
these arms were sent to France for use in NATO. But they say
they've heard no violent protests from Washington against
the French diverting these arms to Algeria. And the average Algerian knows only that most of these arms being used
against him are American. Either way, he laughs at non-
interference statements out of Washington. And many an
Algerian asks, pointedly, what is the difference between
Algeria and Hungary?[47] Which leads to another point. Despite
all this, the Algerians are almost pathetically hopeful that,
somehow, the United States will still come to their aid.
Here they are, attacked daily by American arms, yet, they are
still pro-American, still clinging to ideals about America.
It's a fantastic, unbelievable faith, faith against facts and

bullets and bombs, heart against mind. And it's the biggest single impression of this trip, this almost desperate
faith, against all odds, in ideals for which our forefathers
fought. . . . But, this faith is being murdered slowly, day
by day. Time is running out for America. One last point. The
French claim all this is strictly internal affairs. But the
bulk of her war machine in Algeria is furnished by America,
diverted from the international effort known as NATO. The
refugees pouring into Tunisia and Morocco are fast forming an
international problem which soon may become as big and difficult and tragic as the Palestine refugee problem. All the
countries giving aid to Algeria lend further international
color to the Algerian problem. And the communist offer of new
arms, more and more tempting to Algerians hungry for arms,
Algerians fighting Indian-style against a jet-age army, looms
more and more ominous in the background. Communist participation in this fighting could lead to another Korea . . .
or worse. In brief, the Algerian war . . . and it is a
war . . . has been going on almost three years now. Neither
side is giving an inch, or gaining an inch. Neither side
will accept any kind of compromise, neither side will give
the other a way out. Yet, every day, the situation becomes
more international. To a determinedly neutral observer who
has just come from inside Algeria, it seems obvious that this
is a war . . . that it's becoming more international every
day . . . and, that it's high-time to recognize the Algerian
problem AS an international problem . . . before it becomes
an international war. END END END END

CHAPTER SIX

"Evidence of Considerable Interest"

The next day—August 23—Frank Kearns and Joe Masraff were safely tucked into rooms at the exclusive Hotel Excelsior, known locally as "the magnificent white palace," which is situated in the famed Via Veneto district of Rome, Italy, not far from the Spanish Steps, the Villa Borghese Gardens, and the US Embassy. Kearns said that he looked "like a fugitive from the Dachau concentration camp, damned near dead."[1] Plagued by illness (kidney stones), Masraff had lost twenty-five pounds during their seven weeks of news-gathering and lugging heavy television and radio gear around the rugged mountains in Tunisia and Algeria. Both men arrived in Rome with waist sizes that had dropped by four inches each. But for their sacrifices, they left North Africa with a television first, the vivid images and voices of the nationalist rebels showing and telling their side of the three-year struggle. They had positive proof that the FLN and its army were real. It was not a puppet of the Soviets, nor was it caught up in the East-West tug-of-war. But it could wind up there if something wasn't done.

Now able to eat properly and get some rest, Kearns started to type out a six-page letter to his foreign editor, who was back in New York anxiously awaiting delivery of their "unrealistic . . . impossible" story.

Meanwhile, Masraff carefully boxed up a large package bound for the next available flight to New York. It contained 9,600 feet, or sixteen hours, of film—half of it sound-on-film (SOF),[2] dozens of audiotapes, and a variety of scripts prepared in the field by the network's Cairo-based, part-time news team. All that was missing was Kearns's detailed account of the past seven arduous weeks in Tunisia and Algeria. Masraff had yet to process dozens of rolls of still photographs taken for their private use during their trip, something he planned to do when they returned to Cairo.

As he tried to collect his thoughts about what they'd heard, seen, and been through, Kearns struggled to summarize it in only a couple of pages. After all, this was not your typical news report. His inspiration came from the excitement he wanted to share with his boss back in New York, and after reflecting on what Masraff and he had accomplished, he started to type:

```
Dear Ralph,
First of all, let me say that this is the first-ever real
report on The Other Side (sic) of the Algerian story. It's
the first sound TV report, for sure. And I'm equally sure
it's the first real report in depth. We've spent some six
weeks with the Algerians, in Tunis, along the Tunisian bor-
der, in No-Man's Land along the actual frontier, and inside
Algeria itself. And I think we've really got the story,
that we're the first to get this story.

It's not sensational in the bloody, gruesome sense. . . .
The Algerians offered to set up a real ambush for us, with
real French victims. But we refused, on moral grounds, and
assume y'all, on sober reflection, agree. Instead, we have
continually probed for "The Other Side," the human story, a
story and a documentary.³
```

Like the patient instructor that he would become after retiring from CBS News, Kearns carefully described where the editors back in New York could find key parts of their story among the sixty-six rolls of film and audiotapes that were prepared "under these adverse and sometimes impossible conditions." He knew that sorting it all out would be a formidable job, so he provided his editors with "dope sheets, in duplicate," written details of each and every shot captured over the previous weeks.

He also gave them rough scripts in typed, carbon-paper duplicates to go with the sound-on-film commentaries he and Masraff recorded. Included in his notations were an "opener" to establish the importance of the story and a "closer" to summarize what they discovered throughout their investigation behind the lines. Individual story "cut-ins" about arms shipments was provided for the documentary, for radio commentaries, and/or for whatever news holes might be available to them on the fifteen-minute nightly newscast, *Douglas Edwards with the News*.[4] Their detailed coverage revealed everything from the rugged conditions that the rebels endured in their mountain camps and hideaways to suspicions of communist infiltration, and most importantly, to documenting the existence of a trained Algerian army already conducting combat missions and believing so much in the idea of a free Algeria that they would fight to the death of the very last man.

His report continued:

(The diary) proved to be one of my biggest chores. And I realize full well it's much too long, often much too personal. But I believe it will be invaluable for scripting the documentary, for scripting any silent Tv (sic) reports, for everything connected with this whole story. . . .

The diary has been written down, at great expense of physical effort alone, primarily to guide (the) script. . . .

The Algerian war (and it IS a war, no mistake about that!) is unique. And covering it is a unique experience. There are no war correspondents and we were traveling illegally, of course, inside Algeria, traveling without passports. If we had been captured, Masraff was a dead man, as an Egyptian; that's sure. And I'm equally convinced I would've been knocked off, too, publicly explained as a victim of "rebel" action. That's not overly dramatic; just simple statement of fact. It'd be worth a million bucks to the French to stop this story . . . and this has been one of our main hazards.

The sheer physical demand and intellectual depth required for this type of work seemed to take Kearns by surprise. After all, he was an experienced writer and newsman, and he knew that such an assignment would be challenging but not nearly so hard to translate from story idea to actual storyline:

Back in Cairo, it seemed clear enough. But, as we got into Algeria, into the story, I realized it wasn't clear. Also,

```
I realized that I could never, alone in the mountains,
physically and mentally exhausted(,) write and shoot a com-
plete sound documentary woven around our film; your letters
left the "special show" somewhat open, as a possibility,
didn't even mention length. So, finally I realized it was
completely impossible for me to write (let alone record,
with our precious-little power) an entire documentary. And,
thereafter, we shot separate commentaries or reports, for
double-system, to be used as special reports on news shows
and, at the same time, tailored for inclusion in a long
documentary, every possible phase of life in the mountains,
of the Algerian story. I've put all this rather clumsily,
but believe you'll understand and, I hope, agree this was
the only way.
```

As the letter continued, Kearns started to expose the raw emotional impact of his experience. He understood that this wasn't an ordinary story. His grasping for words really didn't work. It was an adventure that has to be seen and heard and felt to be understood. It's not told like a story typically filed from foreign locations, where they are usually reporting after the fact from towns and villages, because in Algeria these were in the hands of the French. Instead, CBS relied on veteran Paris Correspondent David Schoenbrun to tell that side of the story. Kearns's subjects lived in makeshift camps hidden under trees. They moved nightly in small, mobile units through dangerous mountain passes, and they were constantly on the run, traveling as much as forty miles in a single day. The masses of people they encountered heading to refugee camps in Tunisia were pitifully malnourished, seriously in need of medical attention, yet supportive of the young men and women who chose to stay and fight along the sometimes violent and rocky slopes of the Atlas Mountain Range, pressing harder and harder against their French adversaries.

```
We have, I think, some really fantastic film, and a some-
what fantastically complete story. Among other things: a
really moving SOF report on Algerian refugees, some poi-
gnant scenes which have to be seen to be believed. . . . Our
trip from Tunis to the border . . . Our first Algerian army
camp . . . Marching into No Man's Land . . . An overnight
camp . . . Across the border . . . some wonderful shots of
life, soldier life, everything from eating and cleaning
```

```
rifles to praying, in a group, toward Mecca . . . On the
march . . . Our first camp inside Algeria, a permanent camp
. . . Patrols . . . Camouflage . . . an Algerian army
"parade" inside Algeria . . . Taking cover from French
planes . . . New recruits being taken into the army . . .
Soldiers in action . . . Our long marches, up and down moun-
tains, taking cover from planes, burned out farms, distri-
bution of rations to civilians, soldiers' pay-day, shots
of attacking planes, horribly wounded men without drugs or
medicine, etc., etc.
```

Page after page, Kearns reminded Paskman that this isn't a typical news report. Their equipment "is in shambles . . . battered and torn." The not-so-subtle message: Expect to replace everything. Bills were mounting.

More than that, he and Masraff were just stringers, part-time employees. They were paid a set amount per story, and this one was unusually difficult to obtain, both physically and financially. The danger that came with their mission they accepted. It was "part of the game":

```
I must say, in all understatement, we've stuck on this
story, through all the incredible frustration and physical
torture and war strain, only because we're reporters. No
amount of money could pay for this kind of work, no amount
of money could, ever, persuade either of us to go through
anything like this again. We were both all thru (sic) World
War II, and we've been around since then. But: Nothing like
this. . . .

Suffice it to say that we are both completely, utterly,
physically, mentally and emotionally exhausted . . . thank-
ful to be alive . . . but, in another sense, dead. We're
holing up here to get everything straight and to await word
that the film is there, in NY, then word on how it shapes
up, if it's OK.⁵
```

Once they caught up on their rest, Masraff departed for Geneva, Switzerland, to pick up new camera gear. He ruined two of his own Bolex 16-millimeter cameras while shooting this story. Kearns, meanwhile, stayed put. He was looking forward to the arrival of his wife, Gwen, and their seven-year-old son, Michael, who were joining him from their home in Cairo.

As he closed his letter to Paskman, Kearns asked about publicity for their trip because "in a reporter-infested place like Rome, it's impossible to remain underground any longer." He also expressed concern about what he called "an awful stink from the French" when they find out about the story that CBS is holding:

```
At the very least it outlaws us from France for a long,
long time. And North Africa, I expect the French to call
us every name in the book, everything from spies or mer-
cenaries to paid agents of the Algerians, or what have
you. . . . We don't give a damn. This is a story, the OTHER
side of an important story, and we're reporters. Period.
```

The timing of their report was very important. Kearns reminded his boss that the United Nations would be meeting in less than a month and sure to take up the Algerian question, forcing the United States into—at last—taking a position. He had provided viewers and his government with good documentation about the Algerians fighting for their independence.

```
. . . I can say in all honesty, understating, that both of
us have done our best on this story, we've done more than
can be expected of any two mere humans, we've done the best
we could under the worst of circumstances. Can't do more
than that. . . .

Meanwhile, we're grateful for just being alive, believe me.
And awaiting anxiously your reports on The Job.⁶
```

Now alone in Rome, Kearns sought medical care. He was diagnosed as suffering from an enlarged liver, anemia, low blood pressure, atrophied muscles, and a shrunken stomach. Over the preceding weeks he'd lost nearly 15 percent of his body weight. In a letter back to his parents in Ashburn, Virginia, he described himself as being "skinny as a skeleton."⁷ The doctors gave him a choice: either go into the hospital or get complete rest. So when his family arrived, they headed south to Positano, a small Italian village near Capri. For three weeks, he ate large meals, took various prescription medicines, and did nothing else: "didn't even lift a finger or touch a pen or typewriter."⁸ When it came time to return to Cairo, Kearns and his family were delayed another week while he remained under additional doctor's care. Finally, they caught a Trans World

Airlines flight to Athens, experiencing yet another delay, but finally boarding an Ethiopian Airlines plane that was headed back to Egypt and everyday life at the Cairo outpost of CBS News.

In New York, Paskman coordinated his incoming reports with CBS executive producer David Zellmer, producer Edwin Hoyt, and assistant director of CBS News Malcolm Johnson. They were working on "a big special show" that was planned for airing on Sunday, October 13, 1957. Half of it would be given over to the story that the tall, Hollywood-handsome Kearns and his dashing and eloquent cameraman Masraff had developed; the other half devoted to what was happening on the French side, as reported by the short, mustachioed, and dapper Paris correspondent David Schoenbrun. His crew consisted of Paris-based cameraman George Markham and soundman Paul Habans. From the studio, chief Washington correspondent Eric Severeid would anchor the program, and his commentary would tie the two-sided story together for viewers. Arguably, Severeid was among the best writers and thinkers at CBS. His presence would provide the story with the necessary gravitas it needed to indicate how much importance the news department placed on it.

In early October, "the publicity mill has started grinding and there's already evidence of considerable interest,"[9] Paskman wrote to Kearns. He could hardly contain his enthusiasm upon seeing the rough cut of the upcoming program. He told his reporter, "This one is going to be really good."

The documentary was scheduled for a 5 p.m. airtime across the television network. The CBS News Press Information office described *Algeria Aflame* as the "first detailed camera coverage of [the] grim war in Algeria."[10] The subhead read: "Newsmen endure disease, vermin, shells, bullets to get exclusive film of life with 25,000 troops of Algerian army for hour-long CBS News Report."

A radio version of the story was edited and scheduled for broadcast on CBS Radio a week later at 9:30 p.m. on Monday, October 14. In New York, it aired an hour later, wedged between an interview with Israeli Foreign Minister Golda Meir and actor Anthony Perkins on *This Is New York* and the local station's overnight classical music program, *Music 'Til Dawn*.[11] For the radio broadcast, correspondent Blair Clark served as anchorman with Blaine Littell producing and directing.

These programs "represent the achievement of a journalistic goal set by CBS News Director [John] Day ever since the outbreak of fighting in Algeria three years ago—to tell the full story of the grim struggle to the television and radio audiences of this country," the press release exclaimed. CBS was clearly proud of the work delivered by its news team in North Africa. Years later, foreign Editor Paskman would say of Kearns, "He was my favorite reporter—a real pro . . . and a gentleman."[12]

Taking a chapter from his diary, the producers decided to open *Algeria Aflame* by having Kearns describe his initial encounter with representatives of the FLN in Tunisia who would take Masraff and him across the frontier and into the mountains. It sets up the program for the next hour:

```
Saturday, July 13th - We will have to wear uniforms, it
seems; otherwise, the Algerian rebel units, or the Algerian
villagers, might shoot us. This seems logical, and we
agree. Then we're asked, what kind of arms do you want?
Rifle, revolver, sub-machine gun, or what? Here, we dis-
agree. We're journalists, not soldiers; we're foreigners,
not Algerians; we're reporters, not partisans. One of the
men points out that the French don't acknowledge this as
war; therefore, there's no such thing as a war correspon-
dent. Besides, he adds, if they start shooting close, you
can hardly defend yourself with a press card. He has a
point. But we insist, no arms; uniforms, okay; but no arms.
```

The producers and editors had every reason to be happy with this achievement. It was a grand, highly risky, and groundbreaking effort that paid off. They handily beat their competitors who persisted in covering the story from the French side. The reviews were positive and the story was exciting. It was television news at its very best. *Time* magazine said that the program "brought a tragic stalemate into sharp focus."[13] *Variety* pointed out that it "came up with a kind of searching reporting rarely found."[14]

A week after the program aired, Eric Severeid penned a note to Kearns on his personal stationery from his office at Broadcast House in Washington, DC. He told his colleague "how much I admired your work for the Algerian show. I think you told this country something it did not know and needed to know. This was a reporting best in the classic manner . . . everyone concerned [at CBS] is aware of your accomplishment."[15]

That same year, CBS News received an institutional award for providing "news in depth by going behind current happenings to identify related problems, underlying causes, and influential individuals—as exemplified by the exclusive Moscow interview with Khrushchev on *Face the Nation*; the documentary filmed behind the rebel lines, *Algeria Aflame*; and such series as *See it Now*, *20th Century*, and on its New York radio station, *This Is New York*. In recognition of this depth and range, with a special nod to each of the programs just mentioned, a Peabody Award for News—Radio and Television—is hereby presented to CBS."[16]

On April 3, 1958, Long Island University announced that Frank Kearns and Yousef Masraff won the coveted George Polk Memorial Award for "distinguished achievement in journalism" for their courageous coverage of the rebel fighting in Algeria. Polk was a CBS News correspondent killed in Greece in 1948 while trying to reach rebel Gen. Markos Vafiados for an interview. Kearns and Masraff received their bronze plaques commemorating the occasion at an awards luncheon held on April 15 at the Hotel Roosevelt in New York City.

A second major award was given to them two weeks later on April 29 at the Waldorf-Astoria Hotel in New York City when the Overseas Press Club of America (OPC) cited them for "Best Foreign Reporting on Radio and Television" for their crucial contributions to *Algeria Aflame*. Correspondent David Schoenbrun also won an OPC award that year for his best-selling work of nonfiction, *As France Goes*. A year earlier, OPC cited the excellence of Kearns's work with cameraman Paul Bruck when they provided the first on-the-spot sound television coverage of foreign riots in war-torn Cyprus and violence at the Suez.

When he arrived in New York to accept his awards for *Algeria Aflame*, Kearns was greeted by a letter from Abd-el-Kader Chanderli, who was a representative of the Algerian National Liberation Front and a friend of Sen. John Kennedy. The diplomat, who was proving to be an expert in media spin in favor of the FLN, congratulated Kearns "for your recent award . . . [which] you richly deserved for your excellent and extremely fair presentation of the Algerian problem."[17] In a handwritten postscript, Chanderli invited Kearns to lunch, saying, "I'll be very pleased to know you."

Beyond outside peer recognition, Kearns and Masraff earned the attention of an even more important audience for them: CBS management. In June, Kearns met in Rome with Sig Mickelson, who was vice president of News and Public Affairs. Mickelson talked with his reporter about his stellar performance and what the future might hold for him. Before returning to Cairo, Kearns went on back-to-back assignments inside of the next seven days, first to an armed camp preparing for war with the Turks in Nicosia, Cyprus, once again and six days later to Beirut, Lebanon, where he was caught up in a dramatic shooting war.

Afterward, Mickelson told him, "Your film piece from Beirut . . . was one of the great conversation pieces of the summer. I don't know how many times it has been run but I am sure that millions of people have seen it by now."

His work there even earned a special letter from CBS, Inc. president Frank Stanton, who told him, "We broadcast your superb coverage of the Beirut street battle. Congratulations for an excellent job. This was television news reporting at its very best, as well as a fine display of personal courage under exceedingly dangerous circumstances. Accomplishments such as yours over the years have won for CBS news the highest honors in broadcasting and its reputation for the best broadcasting news organization in the world."[18]

On September 25, 1958, Kearns received the details of his new contract with the network. He was named to the prestigious position of staff correspondent. It included a regular weekly salary, separate compensation for commercial programs on which he appeared, and a benefits package, including a pension and health insurance. David Klinger, director of business affairs at CBS News, told him in a letter, "I have seldom seen such unanimous approval and enthusiasm about a promotion."[19]

Joe Masraff was invited to join the network on a full-time basis, too. He went on to become one of the most reliable and resourceful cameramen and then a producer at CBS News. Stories of his later exploits are legendary.

"He used to get really excited about doing something daring, like smuggling out narration on the magnetic striped film leader that the censors never checked," remembered Scotti Williston, the Cairo bureau chief for CBS News in the late 1970s and early 1980s. "Joe was issued a passport from Lebanon and it was number two—the second one they issued as a country! I've never known anyone to have a single-digit passport. But that was Joe."[20]

"Once he got into a royal cavalcade in Saudi Arabia by hiring a limousine and slipping into line," Patricia Bernie, the retired bureau chief in Rome, laughed as she retold the story. "Everybody thought he was part of the royal court!"[21]

Another time he and a news crew from the Paris bureau conducted an interview with American chef Julia Child. Each time she added wine to a recipe, everyone on the crew would have a drink. By the time the interview was over, the entire crew was drunk.

Kearns stayed in Cairo until February 1961, when the network decided to close down its full-time operation there. Egyptian government censorship of news reports from the Middle East capital made it harder and harder to rely on accurate and timely dispatches. Masraff was transferred to Paris, which would remain his base of operations until he retired from CBS News in 1981.

While he debated with managers in New York about where to move his base, Frank Kearns was given a temporary assignment at headquarters back in New York to re-familiarize himself with American culture. Before returning there, however, he spent five weeks in Moscow, filling in for Marvin Kalb, who was the bureau chief and staff correspondent in the Soviet capital. Kearns moved from there to Paris to cover domestic uprisings. It would take two more years—March 1963—before CBS management agreed that he should become the Africa bureau chief, based in London, where access to airports to connect to the massive continent would be within easier reach.

The impact of the first-ever broadcast news report from behind the lines in Algeria by Frank Kearns and Yousef Masraff provided an entirely new and different view of what was really happening in Algeria and Tunisia. After their report ran on television and radio, American interests began to tip in favor of the rebels, and their battles took center stage in diplomatic circles in Europe and at the United Nations. By 1962, the Algerians had succeeded. The world turned in favor of the FLN and its war-weary representatives. The last vestiges of French rule over them were gone. France had no more political will to hold on. Algeria had earned its fragile independence.

Over the ensuing years, Kearns and Masraff returned to that part of North Africa over and over again. In 1962, they covered "the final days of OAS [Organisation de l'Armée Secrète] in Algeria, a period of all-out, bloody massacre."[22] According to Pulitzer Prize–winning journalist Ted Morgan, the OAS was "a terrorist mix of renegade officers and ultras that hammered, through their lunatic violence, the final nails in the *colons'* coffins."[23] The next year, they went back into the war-ravaged mountains near Kabylie to cover a clandestine resistance movement, called the Front des Forces Socialistes (FFS), which was organized by Hocine Ait Ahmed, a Kabylie opposition leader who quit the Algerian National Assembly in protest over the direction that independent Algeria's new president Mohamed Ahmed Ben Bella was taking the country.

From there they moved west to cover the frontier war between Algeria and its neighbor, Morocco. In the midst of the fighting, they got lost for three days in a scorpion-infested no-man's-land between the warring factions, and once again, they faced certain death if captured.

In the midst of a firefight one night, Kearns later remembered, "I hit the rusty metal bed of the truck so instantly and without thought or feeling that [the terror] was instinctive. (Only later, much later, did I discover all the bruises on knees, shins, elbows, wrists and jaw where body smashed into steel as though that truck bed were foam rubber.) I heard and felt a bullet hit my tape recorder. And somewhere deep inside, assumed *I* had been hit. . . . '*This is it!*' There was no time for a flashback of my life, for quick regrets of all the things I still wanted to do, for thoughts of loved ones. There was no prayer; no hint of God or religion. Not even a thought of escape—for there seemed no hope of escape, not with all that shattering noise, all those flashes of fire, all those explosions. The sole reaction was one of terror . . . mindless, instinctive, animalistic terror."[24] It was one of the 114 times he was nearly killed while reporting for CBS News.[25] Masraff "emerged bleeding from the navel, from grenade concussion."[26]

They tried to escape, but the truck in which they rode with other journalists from Radio Havana, London's *Daily Express*, Reuters, *Le Figaro* of Paris, Algerian newspapers, ABC News, and *Life* magazine crashed into a ditch a short distance from where the ambush took place.

"We all scattered and ran and stumbled and fell and ran and stumbled and fell again . . . until, quite literally, we couldn't move any farther," Kearns recalled. "I was so far gone I could stretch out and watch calmly, with a Moslem's sense of detachment and *maktoub*,[27] as a pair of scorpions slithered across my legs, my stomach, even my chest. And I watched with almost resigned disinterest as, every few minutes, artillery barrages from the Algerian and Moroccan sides expressed through the beautiful star-crammed desert sky right over our heads."

Writing years later in an unpublished, first-person short story he planned for *Reader's Digest* about that night in the firefight, Kearns remembered that while looking toward heaven Masraff saw the Southern Cross, also known as Crux. The small but distinctive, kite-shaped constellation of stars can be easily seen in the southern region of the night sky, and Kearns's cameraman, a Roman Catholic, began "to speak directly to God, first in French and then in English:

"Look God," he said in a soft voice. "You know what our situation is here. And we need your help. We desperately need a sign, any kind of sign, to tell us which way to go. One way might mean we're safe. The other way probably means we're dead. Can you give us a sign?"

He stared up at the heavens. I snorted, but looked up, too.

Suddenly, a brilliant shooting star arched across the sky, falling and fading in a direction to our left.

We were both silent. "Look, God," Yousef said finally. "I want to believe that was a sign. But maybe it was just a coincidence . . . just a shooting star."

He—we—waited.

Another shooting star blazed across the brillant (sic) night sky, in the same direction.

I was awed. But Yousef still wasn't content. "Forgive me, God, but even two could be a coincidence, at this time of year. As a real sign—your sign—would a third be too much to ask?"

I shivered in soul-thrilling wonder as we watched a third shooting star seared in the sky . . . in the same direction.

"Thank you, God. Thank you." He stood up. Nodding at me, he said to the others, "I've just prayed. And we're going that way." He pointed to what we both now believed to be the East.

They headed off, the story continued, until they encountered a small band of Algerian soldiers. There was lots of shouting in Arabic and French.

These anxious sentries had been looking for them all night, but were afraid that the Moroccans had gotten to them first and shot them. When they arrived safely back at their hotel, Masraff said, "I promised God, silently, that if we came out of this, I would wear a gold Southern Cross crucifix on a chain around my neck . . . the rest of my life."[28]

And so he did. Frank Kearns did, too. Their experiences in Algeria and many other dangerous parts of the world bound their deep, abiding friendship and professional respect for one another. When they returned to their homes in Cairo, each man gave a gold-chain necklace to his loved ones. "From it," he said, "hangs the Southern Cross, the Saharan and West African version of the true cross."[29]

For the rest of their natural lives, they wore this "recognition of Someone or Something far beyond me or other human," Kearns said. "Without it, I would be lost, as lost as [we] were in that desert."

In the typical way that Kearns approached his job, just hours after he was rescued and wearing the protective evidence of safe passage around his neck, he participated in a live interview with Algerian president Mohamed Ahmed Ben Bella on *Face the Nation.*

In his twilight years, looking back on the night of their crossing the Tunisian-Algerian frontier for the first time, as fear occupied him, Kearns remembered that "at that moment, I was as *alive* as at any other time in all my life. Life was almost unendurably sweet and precious. The very thought of willing myself to stand up and to go forward was equally unendurable, as was the very thought of a storm of rifle and machinegun fire, or artillery, even, and mortars and grenades and buried mines. Yet, in a sense, the joy of being alive overpowered the horrible feeling of fear. And to this day I can recall – even reconstruct, behind my eyes, in memory, so intensely it becomes both a picture and a feeling, an emotion, in front of my eyes – the exquisite beauty of an evening drop of dew on a blade of grass just beyond my nose. I can see the crystal clarity of that dew-drop, its prisms of light and color, the texture of the blades of grass. I can smell the perfume of the earth, and evening, and see the excruciatingly lovely sunset, the shadows, the darkening sky. And, again, I can remember perfectly the wonder of each breath, the . . . *thankfulness* . . . for everything. . . . And since then I've tried consciously to recapture that sense of wonder each day."

At the start of their journey from Tunis to the Algerian border, an FLN soldier escorting Frank Kearns and Yousef Masraff greets one of an estimated 4,600 barefooted and undernourished refugees, mostly women, who carried with them only the rags on their backs as they crossed Algeria into the sunbaked village of Tagerouine, Tunisia, 125 miles south of Tunis.

The FLN assigned a special army unit working in close cooperation with the Tunisian government to sneak Frank Kearns and Yousef Masraff across the frontier into Algeria.

A small convoy of soldiers cross into Algeria, carrying some of the nearly four hundred pounds of pared-down gear belonging to the CBS News crew.

An Algerian National Army (ALN) unit marches on a mountaintop in eastern Algeria. They count their soldiers in groups, or patrols, not in battalions or divisions, and the exact number is kept secret. (Photo by Yousef Masraff. Courtesy of Sara Kearns.)

FLN rebel soldiers are trained in organized guerrilla-style mountain fighting. They know they are outnumbered and out-equipped, but they believe they are better prepared for conflict in the inhospitable Algerian countryside. Kearns reported that FLN officers and soldiers possess "a solid, unshakeable belief that theirs is a just cause, a right cause . . . plus an indescribable brotherhood . . . and absolute optimism."

When accepted for service, new recruits receive whatever uniform and gun is available at that moment and begin physical training right away.

Considered one of the Big Four global powers in 1957, France had one of the most modern armies in the world. Many of its weapons were supplied by the United States for NATO defense. Yet, for nearly a decade the Algerian army managed to fight on and tie up the French. Every day, American-built reconnaissance planes flew overhead and tracked ALN movements, often interfering with reports that Frank Kearns and Yousef Masraff were trying to record.

Many of the Algerian soldiers that Kearns met were veterans of the French army and served in World War II, Indochina, or both. He said they were well-trained, well-disciplined, and they have their own commando units. Not bandits, as the French referred to them, but they fight under definite strategic and tactical plans. In addition, Kearns saw that "the Algerians have an intelligence network which can only be described as fantastic."

A squad leader traveling with Kearns and Masraff gives instructions to his unit. He knows that his army is outnumbered by as much as fourteen to one by the French, who have at least a half million soldiers in Algeria in 1957, "more than they ever had in Indochina," according to Kearns. One of their most effective weapons was the ambuscade (ambush).

Life in an Algerian rebel camp is pretty much like life in any army camp anywhere in the world. Each soldier regards himself as "a nationalist, a patriot." Part of the day is spent performing military duties, and "like soldiers everywhere, the Algerians spend most of their time in camp talking and arguing, in resting and sleeping, and eating." Chow time is the most important hour of the day, and one meal is the most a soldier can expect. Food comes from neighboring villages that "contribute to The Cause."

On payday, a private receives 1,000 francs per month—just under $3. The pay scale goes up slowly. A master sergeant gets just under $6 a month. A colonel, the highest rank since there are no generals, receives $15 a month. Those soldiers with wives or children have a family allowance of under $6 monthly for each person.

Kearns observed that "one of the things that holds these volunteer soldiers together is their religious faith, their faith in Islam, in Allah, or God and his prophet Mohammed. Usually, they pray alone, on mountaintops and facing the East, and Mecca."

In camp, soldiers smoke cigarettes and try to catch up on the latest news whenever a newspaper reaches one of their transient camps. Kearns noted in one of his reports that "soldier and officer alike, they call each other Brother, and mean it. It's the warmest relationship I've ever seen in any army, anywhere." (Photo by Yousef Masraff. Courtesy of Michael Kearns.)

New recruits come from all over Algeria. "Like any volunteer," Kearns reported, "they represent a higher standard than draftees. Every man here came to the mountains of his own free will, for his own good reasons." Most are in their twenties. The age limit is eighteen to thirty-five. For this type of mountain fighting, anyone over thirty-five is considered to be too old, as Kearns experienced while traveling with this army. At the time of this assignment, Frank Kearns was forty years old.

Officially known as the National Liberation Army of Algeria (ALN), Kearns was embedded in one of the two largest of seven military departments, called *Wilayats* (pronounced Wee-lay-ette). Each department is responsible for geographic regions. Kearns was in the Eastern Zone, along the Tunisian border. The Western Zone of Oran covered the Moroccan frontier. There also were zones in the North (including the major battle site of Philippeville and the ALN headquarters in the Collo Mountains), the Grand Kabylia, the Aures Mountains, the Sahara Desert, and one for Algiers, the capital.

Each military department is divided into subsectors, sectors, regions, and zones. The smallest unit of an army is a squad, or what the Algerians call a group, comprising eleven men, including a sergeant, who is in charge. (Photo by Yousef Masraff. Courtesy of Michael Kearns.)

Soldiers undergo hard practical training learning to use a variety of weapons for this special type of war.

Orphan children made their way alone to a rebel camp and became the camp mascots for a few days before being sent to Tunisia. Kearns said that he "had a big rock in my throat" as he watched them leave.

Epilogue

....

he assessment of many colleagues and competitors is that Frank Kearns was a remarkable reporter. Dan Rather called him "a legend" at CBS News. His foreign editor said he was "among the best foreign correspondents at CBS."

He stoically went about his job of news gathering without getting the recognition that others received, but he experienced deep frustration when his hard work didn't make it to air. This is attributable to where he worked—Africa and the Middle East—and how long it took his stories to get from remote locations to New York and on the air, which was sometimes weeks or months, and the general indifference with which his editors and the American audience viewed that part of the world during his tenure with the network. Today, of course, the view is very different. Kearns's contribution to the body of work at CBS News during its developing years in television has been underappreciated. He conducted himself with humility, earnestness, and a tremendous amount of professionalism in some of the most difficult spots on earth. He went to places others declined to go. He risked his life in order to do his job. Along the way, he provided a framework, or perspective, in which others could follow behind.

With that said, however, it's hard to know the precise impact of the news reports from inside Algeria that Frank Kearns and Yousef Masraff produced during their weeks of living in the mountains with the rebels. We do know that the timing of their radio and television stories coincided with what appears to be the tipping point for international pressure being exerted on the French, especially as it came from sources inside the United States government.

Initially the world looked the other way. The Algerian issue was a French problem. But their catastrophic failures in Southeast Asia and with the British at the Suez in Egypt began to wear on the governmental leaders in Paris. France seemed to lack the political will and the calculated capability of managing its way out of this crisis. The nightmare that was staged in the weather-beaten mountains and moved into the explosive urban areas of Algeria played into the hands of the ambitious Egyptian President Nasser, who was seeking to coalesce Arab countries into a single, unified, Pan-Arab world, and thus the leaders of the FLN had a natural ally with access to money and weapons. Nasser's success at the Suez helped to cement his power with the nonaligned, developing countries and put Washington on notice that influence over the Middle East rested in Cairo.

But all of this was being staged during an intense period of the Cold War between the United States and its NATO allies and the Soviet Union and its satellite states in Eastern Europe. Hungary tried to turn toward the West and was crushed. A barbed-wire fence already had been erected in Berlin to separate East from West. Each side watched the other in a never-ending bid to influence developing countries.

All over the world a strong, anticolonial sentiment was prevailing. Morocco and Tunisia were free at last. Indochina had been lost by the French. Budding countries across Africa and elsewhere were building resentment against their European protectorates from Belgium, England, France, Holland, Portugal, and Spain. Revolutionary winds were blowing in the Western hemisphere, too, with Cuba as a litmus test. Fidel Castro and his rebel army were set to overpower Gen. Ruben Fulgencio Batista y Zaldivar, Cuba's reigning dictator.

For all of the good that France brought culturally, economically, and educationally, Algeria was nevertheless a divided country. The breadbasket industries that fed Paris with goods and services through southern Mediterranean ports created opportunities in Algeria that were not wanted or welcomed without bringing with them self-determination. But millions of French citizens had moved to Algeria. France was determined to make it part of the mother country, albeit without as many rights.

American interest was aroused as France began to lose its grip. The fear was that if the United States didn't support Algeria's independence, if France lost this war, and if Algeria's neighbors—Morocco and Tunisia—expressed interest in the tumult going on between them, then the door would be opened for the Soviets. President Eisenhower and his chief adviser on foreign affairs, Secretary of State John Foster Dulles, surely didn't want that to happen on their watch. It was for this reason that they conceived the so-called Eisenhower Doctrine in early 1957, in which the president told the world that the United States was prepared to use arms to support any Middle Eastern country—including those in North Africa—that asked for help against meddling by the communists. Kearns and Masraff provided solid evidence on which the Americans could make strategic decisions in that region of the world.

The job of more closely watching over the various actors on this stage was given to the younger brother of Secretary Dulles, Allen Welsh Dulles. Allen Dulles was the director of Central Intelligence, i.e., the CIA. His primary operative in Egypt in the 1950s was Miles Copeland, who had been a member of Kearns's counterintelligence corps in London during World War II and with whom he lived as a bachelor, along with another CIC officer, James Eichelberger.[1] All three arrived in Cairo at approximately the same time, according to Copeland. He worked undercover as a consultant with Booz Allen Hamilton, an American management consulting firm. Eichelberger was an economic attaché at the US Embassy but really functioning as one of several CIA chiefs of station, and Kearns was fresh off the airplane as a Prentice-Hall contracted author and as a stringer for CBS News. Historian Scott Lucas described the three as being "right out of a Graham Greene novel."

Unlike the other two who worked directly for the US government, Kearns "refused to accept any official status with the CIA, but he readily agreed to co-operate with both Eich and me," Copeland wrote in his memoir, *The Game Player.* The three men and their families spent time together socially in Kearns's "luxurious Zamalek apartment . . . as a headquarters," Copeland recalled.

Michael Kearns, the journalist's son from his first marriage, confirmed growing up with the Copeland children. The youngest son, Stewart Copeland, is closest in age to Michael Kearns. He was the drummer for the globally popular band, The Police. Older brothers, Miles III and Ian, also played major roles in the entertainment industry, while sister Lennie is a writer and film producer.

It's not a stretch to see how the activities of Kearns and Masraff in Tunisia and Algeria could be monitored quite casually from the ground in Egypt, and whatever bits and pieces of information gleaned by Copeland, Eichelberger, and others proved beneficial back in Washington. But aside from Copeland's musings, there's no evidence that either Kearns or Masraff were complicit in such an arrangement. What happened to their reports when they arrived back at CBS in New York was a different matter.

Writing in his own memoir in 1979, entitled *As It Happened*, CBS chairman William S. Paley acknowledged that during the Cold War there was "a tradition of cooperation between journalists and government agencies concerned with threats to our national security from abroad."[2] CBS was a party to such an arrangement, but it "was terminated completely in 1961," he said.

"The Agency asked that CIA representatives be permitted to screen, and in some instances to purchase, certain CBS news films. On occasion, the CIA was permitted to view material which was of interest to the Agency but was not broadcast.... Agency representatives also were permitted to listen to radio transmissions from some of our overseas correspondents prior to their being edited and actually broadcast," he wrote. "At the Agency's request, CBS News foreign correspondents, upon their return to the U.S., sometimes met with CIA officials and briefed them on the countries they covered." A favorite meeting place was the Alibi Club in the West End of Washington, DC, near George Washington University, the World Bank, and the Bureau of National Affairs. Its membership was a veritable "Who's Who" of the nation's capital and a favorite of the Dulles brothers.[3]

In addressing this issue, Paley mentioned that "Frank Kearns was alleged to have been in the employ of the CIA while working as a stringer for CBS News," a fact claimed to have been discovered by CBS News president Sig Mickelson when he was considering Kearns for a full-time staff position in 1958. This may have been at approximately the same time that Kearns was back in the United States to accept the awards for *Algeria Aflame*. However, the date of a Kearns-Mickelson meeting in New York can't be established.

Investigative reporter Carl Bernstein, writing for *Rolling Stone* in 1977, said that "The Columbia Broadcasting System—CBS was unquestionably the CIA's most valuable broadcasting asset. CBS president William Paley and Allen Dulles enjoyed an easy working and social relationship.... Once a year during the 1950s and early 1960s, CBS correspondents joined the CIA hierarchy for private dinners and briefings."[4] He said that Dulles "sought to establish a recruiting-and-cover capability within America's most prestigious journalistic institutions. By operating under the guise of accredited news correspondents, Dulles believed, CIA operatives abroad would be accorded a degree of access and freedom of movement unobtainable under almost any other type of cover." Media organizations mentioned by Bernstein included, but are not limited to, ABC and CBS, the *New York Times*, the *Washington Post*, the *Los Angeles Times*, *Time* and *Newsweek* magazines, the *Louisville Courier-Journal*, the *Copley Press*, and others. Another organization that is sometimes mentioned as serving as a front for the CIA was the American publisher Prentice-Hall, the sponsor for Frank Kearns's never-written book about Egypt, the idea of which he carried with him in the form of a contract to Cairo in 1953.

According to Bernstein, "Paley's contact for the Agency was Sig Mickelson" and "according to Mickelson, he did so."

The nature of the network's close relationship with the CIA was "found in Mickelson's files by two investigators" working for Richard Salant, Bernstein wrote. Salant, a Harvard-trained corporate lawyer, had been an unlikely choice to replace Mickelson as CBS News president in February 1961. He wasn't a journalist like those before him had been. But his investigative work was thorough, and because of it, the name of Frank Kearns surfaced during the CBS-CIA inquiry years after Kearns's retirement from the network. Salant told Bernstein that Kearns "was a CIA guy who got on the payroll somehow through a CIA contact with somebody at CBS." Kearns, he said, was an "undercover CIA employee, hired under arrangements approved by Paley."

Initially, the story went, Mickelson "was told by one of our correspondents that one of our stringers was really an agent of the Office of Naval Intelligence, the ONI."[5] The correspondent, Bill Downs, who was based in Rome, told his boss "that our stringer in Cairo, Egypt, who'd had quite a bit of work recently, was actually a full-time staff member of the Office of Naval Intelligence." In a conversation that took place around New Year's in 1956 in a suite at the Berkshire Hotel, across the street from Mickelson's office at 485 Madison Avenue, Downs said to his boss that he had been told by others, whom he did not name, that Kearns had been sent to Egypt by ONI.[6] So Mickelson asked CIA chief Allen Dulles about it, and the spy chief agreed to check out the story.

"He called back a couple of weeks later and said, 'Your man doesn't work for ONI. He works for us,'" Mickelson wrote in the notes for a planned but undeveloped second memoir. "I replied that I thought that, even though Kearns was a stringer and not a staff member, he should not work for both. Dulles urged me to take no action for the moment but to give him some time to work it out.

A couple of months later, two men showed up at my office (they always seem to travel in pairs), presented their credentials and handed me a hand-written letter from Kearns.

"Kearns wrote that he preferred working for CBS to the CIA and was hence resigning immediately," Mickelson continued. "The CIA men told me that the resignation was accepted and that he was free to qwork [*sic*] for CBS. We destroyed the letter. I sent Kearns a contract and he was now a staff member. I have frequently wondered whether the resignation was genuine, but I took it at face value.

"In April, I visited Keanrs [*sic*] in Cairo," his notes concluded. "He would not talk in his apartment nor in his car wherehis [*sic*] driver could overhear him, so we went for a long walk. He explained that his assignment was overt rather than covert and that Nasser knew for whom he worked and the nature of his assigmnent [*sic*] there but that he preferred to work for CBS with no other commitments." A black-and-white, silent 16-mm film of Kearns and Mickelson meeting in Cairo and walking together was found in the Mickelson archives at the University of Texas Library, and it is used in the documentary *Frank Kearns: American Correspondent*, a coproduction of Greenbriar Group Films in Columbia, South Carolina, and West Virginia Public Television.

Former CBS News president Van Gordon Sauter, who worked with Yousef Masraff in the Paris in the mid-1970s, said that the cameraman told him, "Kearns was CIA. Nasser was told about it by his security team, and he told [Joe] about it at the first interview that he gave to Kearns in 1954. Consequently, Nasser was very guarded about what he revealed."[7]

On February 10, 1976, *The CBS Evening News with Walter Cronkite* reported a story about the CIA's use of the media. During the network's coverage of the Church Committee Hearings (the US Senate Select Committee to Study Governmental Operations with Respect to Intelligence Activities), Daniel Schorr reported that Frank Kearns was one of two former CBS News stringers in the 1950s who worked for the network and the CIA. The other reporter was Austin Goodrich, who couldn't be found. He said that Kearns denied the allegation, which was attributed to Mickelson, but he refused to elaborate on it beyond a prepared statement. It was outlined and delivered to inquiring reporters from notes on a series of three-by-five-inch, yellow index cards. On them, he typed in his reporter's shorthand:

During all the years I was a CBS News staff correspondent I had no connection whatsoever—NO—NONE—with the
CIA or any other intelligence agency. And I will sue—
sue hard—sue the arse off anyone who makes such a false
charge, a lie, in print or on the air or on the screen.
(You are damaging) my reputation, my career, my life.

Thank you for the chance to deny it—which I do, completely. But (I) won't have (a) chance to go into detail. (There was a) death in my family last night.
Besides . . .

Every foreign correspondent (is) accused, sometime. All
foreigners believe it. But: (We) live with it. (For)
example: (A) colleague who told everyone I was ONI had
to ask what it was. (The) only connections with (the)
U.S. Navy (was) trying to enlist, covering (a) Marine
landing in Lebanon, and several stories w(ith the)
Sixth Fleet. Where do you start? Where do you stop?

(I am) at (a) loss to understand these attacks. Not
just (on) me, I gather. Others, even W(alter) Cronkite
and J(ohn) Chancellor (have been accused). (It's an)
attack on all the media, really. I don't believe in
plots, but . . . why? Newsmen (are) being used to dis-
credit newsmen, and the media.

Personally, (I) don't believe any legitimate news man
employed by a legitimate news organization should have
any connection whatsoever (to do) with any intelligence
agency. Absolutely not.

(What's) even more bewildering . . . all these
false charges, accusing everyone of working for the
Americans. (I) could understand, MAYBE, if (it was a)
charge of working for C(ommunist)s. (It's) more like
(the) McCarthy era . . . (or) . . . John Henry Falk.

The joke—the irony: (I) must've been naïve, but (a)
number of times (that I) expected I would be approached, or debriefed, after being in a hot spot or

```
having an exclusive story. But, to my knowledge: Never,
not even once. Not in Algeria, Congo, Cyprus, even
Moscow. Not only (have I) had no connection, but not
ever, not once, (have I been) knowingly approached, in
all my years as a staff correspondent for CBS News.⁸
```

For the most part, the West Virginia media where Kearns then lived left him alone. Following a stiff rebuke, Mike Wallace at CBS News never pursued the story for *60 Minutes*.

More than a year later, though, Kearns's name was still in the press. On May 27, 1977, Robert Scheer, writing for the *Los Angeles Times*, interviewed Richard Salant, who said that his internal investigation "led to Kearns . . . [who] seemed to have been placed or had some sort of relationship to the CIA and was a reporter for us. I don't think it would be strong enough to say he was a spy. He was just one of those people that, when he found out things, he would pass it along to the CIA." What is striking is that this description of Kearns and the CIA is much softer, less accusing than Mickelson's earlier position in his testimony to Congress.

In responding to Scheer's inquiry, Kearns read from another series of notes that he had prepared:

```
I have been deeply, deeply hurt, and mystified, and an-
gered, by this recurring smear on my former career as
a foreign correspondent, a career of which I am very
proud. I am not alone, apparently, in becoming a vic-
tim of this strange campaign. But, once again I most
emphatically deny that I had any connection with the
CIA whatsoever, or any intelligence agency, official or
unofficial, in any place, at any time, in all the years
I was a staff correspondent for CBS News. And now, I
have taken active legal advice about suing, massively,
anyone who has made or makes such a false accusation in
print or on the air.⁹
```

After that, the story disappeared from the headlines.

When asked whether they think Frank Kearns had worked in dual roles with CBS and the CIA, his family members, friends, and former colleagues issue a split decision. Even though he died almost three decades ago, the CIA still won't confirm or deny this allegation. Another copy of Kearns's signed 1958 letter resigning from the CIA, which was supposedly shown to Sig Mickelson, has never been discovered.

Whether Frank Kearns was or was not working in any official capacity for a US intelligence agency while at the same time reporting for CBS News is an issue that cannot be answered until the government provides a firm *yes* or *no* to the question or until CBS produces evidence one way or the other. However, in the matter of the journalist's role with respect to fairness, objectivity, and prejudice in favor of one's government—not to mention collusion—will continue to generate debates within the profession. But there is a very fine line between working *with* and working *for* the government.

The argument made by those who have admitted working in this dual capacity points to the mindset at the time. The United States had just endured a brutal war on two fronts, in Europe and in the Pacific. The Cold War–era with the Soviets had begun. Many of the journalists working overseas in the 1950s came from roles in the US military and pure reportorial objectivity was infected with patriotism. CBS chairman Bill Paley had worked for the Office of War Information where he helped to set up the Allied propaganda mechanisms used as the troops advanced across the European Theater. After the war, he gave his approval for CBS reporters to cooperate with the government in matters of national security. Besides, having such close relationships produced good news sources, and reporters trade information with their sources all the time.

Whatever Frank Kearns did, one thing is known: The quality of his reporting speaks for itself. It was of the highest caliber, according to his superiors. He worked in a dangerous area of the world, so having a good working relationship with various aspects of the US government—and other governments—no doubt helped him to do his job effectively and, in some cases, may have saved his life and that of his news crew. Analysis of his television stories reveal a changing focus over the years, starting with what can now be called "the CIA's view of the world" and what emerged after the Algerian success as a more thoughtful attention to the growing independence and security needs of each emerging country rather than the ongoing struggle of the West versus the communists.

Over his seventeen-year career at CBS News, Frank Kearns conducted chief-of-state interviews with Gamal Abdel Nasser and Anwar el-Sadat of Egypt, David Ben-Gurion and Golda Meir of Israel, Jomo Kenyatta of Kenya,

Haile Selassie of Ethiopia, Ian Douglas Smith of Rhodesia, Edward Wilson of Great Britain, Mobutu Sese Seko of Zaire (the Congo), Gen. Chukwuemeka Odumegwu Ojukwu of secessionist Biafra, Saddam Hussein of Iraq, King Juan Carlos I of Spain, US President Richard Nixon, and Mihail Makarios of Cyprus.

Among his noteworthy reports were coverage of the Suez crisis and the Six-Day War in the Middle East; an extended interview with Dr. Albert Schweitzer in Gabon; the Kennedy-Onassis wedding in Greece; the funeral of Sir Winston Churchill; a report from the Montes Lunae ("Mountains of the Moon") in Uganda prepared for the day that Neil Armstrong landed on the moon; US presidential trips with Eisenhower, Kennedy, and Nixon; Sicilian, Iranian, and Yugoslavian earthquakes; papal installations in Rome; the first TV report from a Soviet naval cruiser; the Algerian-Moroccan frontier war; life in Moscow; the Cold War in Afghanistan; safaris in Kenya; life on a US Sixth Fleet submarine in the Mediterranean, independence of African countries; mothers of babies in Europe and Africa with birth defects from thalidomide; the Aberfan mining disaster in South Wales; and many, many more.

When he'd finally had enough adventure for one lifetime, Frank Kearns told his bosses at CBS News that he was ready to do something else. He wanted to do softer, human interest stories around the world similar to the roving domestic correspondent in the United States, Charles Kuralt. In response, they offered him the opportunity to go to Vietnam or to return to the United States to work as a national news correspondent. Neither option appealed to him.

After all of those years with the network, soon to be divorced and living in one of his favorite cities—Rome—Frank Kearns was ready for a different challenge. He was tired of bloody civil wars, volatile international conflicts, and seeing all of the many ways people could brutalize each other. He was fed up with being the network's go-to guy for dangerous stories in Africa and the Middle East. It was time that they found someone else. What was to come next he wasn't sure. But he was starting to get pressure from his old chums to come home. Kearns saw them whenever he went back to visit his aging parents, and their draw was powerful.

Over the years, he had accepted invitations by officials at West Virginia University to be a guest speaker at the campus during Journalism Week. Each time he did that, he left feeling a little more homesick and, in turn, he also left a good impression on those with whom he met there, especially university

President James Harlow, who suggested to Dean Guy Stewart that the School of Journalism recruit him to the faculty. By the time that Dean Stewart was able to reach Kearns, the correspondent already had left the campus and returned to covering events in Africa. But eventually they talked about it.

"'I don't have to think about [your offer] for very long,'" Stewart remembers Kearns telling him. "He just came back from covering Nigeria. He had spent some time in a Nigerian prison, and he had some real health concerns after they let him out. So he said, 'I sat there in prison, and I started counting up all of the times that I had someone shoot at me and about the number of close scrapes I had and, literally, I'm just lucky to still be here.' . . . 'I'd love to come to teach.' So we struck a bargain on salary."[10]

On August 16, 1971, the fifty-three-year-old Kearns became one of ten Claude Worthington Benedum professors at West Virginia University. He moved into a small, L-shaped basement office in Martin Hall at the School of Journalism, his alma mater. Framed photographs from Algeria, including ones used in this book, and from other assignments, along with salutations and best wishes from former colleagues and competitors, lined the walls of his office. There he regularly met with students and rapidly grew into a success in his new profession, teaching the next generation of broadcast journalists. It was an opportunity to move back home to look after his aging parents and aunts, to enjoy time with old friends, and to start a new chapter in his life.

"If you do one job all your life, it's a pretty narrow street," he said. "Maybe I should stress that what I am doing is certainly not retirement. It's not a bitter thing. It's partly re-learning, reaching the end of a period. I think it would be wrong to continue at something just because it's the job you happen to know best at that particular point."[11]

While on a vacation five years earlier in Bermuda with his teenage son, Michael, Kearns was introduced by friends to a sparkling and spirited Englishwoman, Sara DeMaine Ginders, who eventually left her flatmates in London—one of whom, Tim Rice, would later be knighted by the Queen of England and become known throughout the world for his creative partnership with Andrew Lloyd Webber—to join Kearns in Rome. Although not yet divorced and involved in a second relationship with a former Israeli lieutenant, Varda Ackerman, whom he met during the Six-Day War and who was attending college classes in New York, Kearns agreed to share his impressive apartment overlooking the beautiful Baroque Fontana di Trevi (Trevi Fountain) with Sara Ginders. She gave up her job with British Overseas Airways Corporation and traveled with him doing crew work on some of his less risky assignments. When Kearns asked her to go with him back to Morgantown, she agreed. With that move, his divorce was settled and she became his new wife.

A popular professor, Kearns "tried to shy away from the I-was-there lecture circuit, the self-appointed role of cocktail and after-dinner raconteur,"[12] although he knew that was a part of his job at the university. For the most part, he kept those stories to himself and promised everyone who asked that one day he'd write them down in a memoir.

For thirteen years, he taught undergraduate and graduate courses, mostly classes in broadcast news. He even created a summer course for graduate students to introduce them to international news broadcasting at the source, first in Rome in 1975 and later in London. To make the seminars and workshops more meaningful, he called on former colleagues and competitors at American and foreign news organizations to work with his students and to share their experiences. In Rome, Leslie Stahl, Bert Quint, and Tom Fenton were guest lecturers from CBS News, along with cameraman Mario Biasetti and bureau chief Patricia Bernie.

In 1983, he retired for a second time. He cashed in his CBS and university pensions and moved with his wife to a seaside villa in Sardinia that was owned by his former CBS News colleague and then *60 Minutes* senior producer in London, Bill McClure. There he liked to take lunch on the home's breezy veranda, sip a cold drink, watch the ships of the US Sixth Fleet, which he once covered, pass on the water in front of his house, and compose pages of short stories and work on the outline for his promised memoir, which he never completed.

Frank Kearns died on August 1, 1986, at Memorial Sloan-Kettering Cancer Center in New York. He was only sixty-eight years old. For two years, he was in and out of hospitals with the painful, exhausting illness of oral cancer, but wanted to be near home in the end. His cameraman and best friend at the network, Joe Masraff, died five years later in France.

That night on *The CBS Evening News with Dan Rather*, the anchorman called him "a [legend] around here."

Acknowledgments

....

I began this book as an offshoot of the research I was doing for my documentary, *Frank Kearns: American Correspondent*. It came as quite a surprise to discover a typewritten version of the hand-scrawled notes from Algeria that Frank Kearns tossed into a shoebox years ago. The process of researching, organizing, and preparing various drafts of this book took a decade of on-again, off-again effort, but the work really began three decades earlier. From my very first graduate proposal in the fall of 1975 to do a film on the life of Frank Kearns (and which he roundly rejected), I held onto some of the notes about him, his circle of friends and associates, and his employer without ever knowing whether any of it might lead to a published book or a produced documentary.

In April 2002, Sara Kearns told me that she had grieved her husband's death long enough. "I think it's time you do your story," she said. "I'll do what I can to help you."

Beginning in 2003, I conducted a number of interviews with people who knew Frank Kearns. Some of them were in the United States, but many were in Europe and Africa. Over the years, that number continued to grow. In the course of preparing this book and its companion documentary film, which was released to PBS stations around the United States, I have been most surprised by the many people who knew him but declined my request for interviews, either on or off the record. Those who did speak on the record, however, gave graciously of their time and did so openly and without hesitation at in-person interviews and in writing.

Therefore, I want to acknowledge the incredible encouragement provided by specific people without whom the various elements of the Frank Kearns Project—book, film, and soon (hopefully) a motion picture—would never be possible:

- Sara DeMaine Kearns, who enthusiastically suggested that I tell his story. Not only did she reinitiate the project that lay dormant in my mind for nearly three decades, but she shared her late husband's archives of notes, manuscripts, letters, photographs, and other memorabilia for investigation, called on his friends to lend their support, and maintained regular contact with me to answer questions and provide encouragement. Without her instigation, this book would not have been possible.

- Michael Kearns, Frank's son with his first wife, Gwendoline Shoring Kearns, provided an insider's look at his family life in Cairo in the 1950s, which few others could recount. He very graciously opened his personal archives, as well, in order to help tell his two children about their grandfather.

- Ivan Pinnell, PhD, the chairman of my (second) graduate committee at the P. I. Reed School of Journalism, showed tremendous patience, support, and resourcefulness throughout the project, organizing for me an outstanding editorial board from across West Virginia University, including Diana Knott Martinelli, PhD, the late George Esper, PhD, and Joe Super, PhD, who endured and shared their experiences, expertise, and intellectual curiosity. Regrettably Professor Esper passed away in February 2012, just two months after we last spoke by telephone.

- Chip Hitchcock, a Kearns student and my co-producer of the documentary at West Virginia Public Broadcasting, as well as a longtime friend with whom I have worked on other film projects, provided guidance, counsel, and support for some of the components of this book.

- There are people who gave freely of their time to share their knowledge of Kearns's life and work and insight into the network, especially Patricia Bernie, Tom Fenton, the late John Tiffin, Johnny Peters, Kurt Hoefle, the late Sandy Socolow, Van Gordon Sauter, the late Ralph Paskman, Scotti Williston, and Kevin Tedesco from CBS News.

- Sandy Gall, CBE, a former ITN anchorman (i.e., news presenter in the parlance of the United Kingdom) and foreign correspondent for Reuters, competed directly against Kearns in global hot spots. Consequently, he knew Kearns well.

- A last-minute but endearing contact came from Lorraine Copeland, widow of Miles Copeland Jr. Frank Kearns had been the best man at their wedding. I was connected to her through her sons Miles III and Stewart and daughter Lennie, and she graciously shared her memories of Kearns in Egypt during two days at her wonderful château in southern France. Sadly, Mrs. Copeland passed away in April 2013.
- Two longtime Morgantown friends of Frank Kearns—Betty Shuman and Leighton Watson, both of whom are now deceased—filled in some missing details about growing up with him.
- Clay Farrington, a former US Navy intelligence officer now writing a book on the government's use of journalists as spies, kindly shared some of his research findings as they related to Austin Goodrich, Sig Michelson, Frank Kearns, and others connected to CBS News.
- Anne Eichelberger Tazewell, whose father James Eichelberger was an important figure in Cairo in the 1950s, kindly helped me to understand her father's relationship with Frank Kearns.
- Scott Lucas, PhD, at the University of Birmingham, England, was extraordinarily helpful in providing narrative guidance regarding the working relationships of Kearns, Copeland, and Eichelberger, the "three amigos" from World War II and Egypt. He also helped to frame the way American broadcast news organizations covered the Middle East and the United States–Soviet Union standoff relative to what was going on in the Maghreb.
- Jeff Davis, my brother, offered comfortable accommodations and nourishment during my intermittent trips to Morgantown to work on this project. Happily, he now lives near Judy and me in South Carolina.
- My informal sounding boards—Tom Jamrose and my recently deceased childhood friend Mac Pritt who knew Frank Kearns at WVU, my inquisitive historian and longtime friend Mark Rozeen, PhD, in New York, and my creative consultant Andy Witt in St. Augustine,

Florida—suggested ideas about the overall project that had largely escaped my attention.

- I would be remiss if I didn't single out my editor, Carrie Mullen, who helped me to significantly improve the manuscript. She has been very patient and considerate in calling out where the story could be improved, and I trust she was right. Also, I'm grateful for the expertise of my copy editor Valerie Ahwee in Vancouver, BC, for showing the errors in my writing before we went on press.

It goes without saying that, but for my being in close proximity as a Kearns student, for serving as his undergraduate work-study assistant in the broadcast news labs, and for later his becoming both a mentor and a friend, none of this book would have happened, and Frank Kearns would remain largely unknown.

Finally, my wife Judy made it possible for me to take the time off to pursue this project, and I'm forever grateful.

Errors and omissions are mine alone to suffer.

Sound-on-Film Scripts from Algeria

[From Original Transmission Documents for *Algeria Aflame* written by Frank Kearns]

On the following pages, I have reproduced the actual scripts that Frank Kearns filed with the raw film and audiotapes that were sent from Rome to New York when he and Yousef Masraff left Algeria. Because of the condition of *Algeria Aflame,* which is stored in the archival vaults at CBS News, it's unclear how many of these reports actually made it to the final program. The condition of the program itself—without overdubbed narration, without music, and often without complete scenes, which have been permanently damaged or lost—it's impossible to know how much actually made it to the air. The following eleven reports make up what Kearns believed to be the most important information that CBS could share with its audience about what was happening inside Algeria at that time. These reports form the core of the diary itself. For that matter, they are worth reading and studying, as they tell the truth in Algeria as Frank Kearns experienced it.

1 — SOF (sound-on-film) "Opener" for Report on Algeria.

2 — SOF Report on Algerian refugees.

3 — SOF Report on Algerian army.

4 — SOF Report on life in a Rebel Camp.

5 — SOF Report on type of person fighting in Algerian army (profiles).

6 — SOF Report on techniques of Algerian army.

7 — SOF Report on question of Communism among Algerians.

8 — SOF Report on devastated farms, distribution of rations.

9 — News SOF Report on mysterious Algerian leader.

10 — News SOF Report on Communist offer of arms to Algerians.

11 — SOF "Conclusion," or Summary, to end Report on Algeria.

(PAGE 1 – Algeria Report: SOF OPENER)

This is Frank Kearns, reporting from Algeria, with the Algerian army.

The French side of the fighting in Algeria has been well-publicized, well-reported. But, there are always TWO sides to any argument, two sides to any fight, two sides to any war. And, till now, the OTHER side, the Algerian side, has not been reported in depth, on the scene.

Reporting both sides of any story is in the best tradition of American journalism in general, and of CBS News in particular. And this is a sincere attempt to report objectively the OTHER side of the fighting in Algeria, the Algerian side.

Unfortunately, both sides disagree about the nature of this fighting. The French say it's a rebellion. The Algerians say it's a war. Legally, perhaps, the French view is correct. And there are no war correspondents.

But, to report a fire, you go to the fire. And to report a war, you go to war. In this case, reporting the Algerian side means going to UNDERGROUND, sneaking over the frontier into Algeria, with the Algerian army.

It all starts with weeks of cloak-and-dagger negotiations with officials of the Algerians' National Liberation Front, the FLN, in Cairo.

(Film: Shots, which Kallsen was to take and send, via Emile, showing FLN offices in Cairo, under sign of stamp-dealer, brick air-raid wall in front of entrance)

Day after day you sneak through a doorway under the sign of an Egyptian stamp-dealer — a scene straight out of a Hitchcock mystery — and work out details. The weeks drag by. It all takes time, FLN officials say, because this trip is so important that all communications between Cairo and FLN headquarters in Algeria must be carried by hand.

(REPORTER)

Then, one sweltering afternoon, the only English-speaking man in the office tells you, "Mabrouk! Congratulations! It's all set. You and your cameraman, Mr. Masraff, will leave Cairo this Thursday, Thursday at midnight. Your first stop is Tunis."

(FILM: Scenes of Tunis, the bay, downtown landmarks, our feet walking around Tunis, then the FLN office in Tunis)

(PAGE 2 — Algeria Report: OPENER)

Several days later, you arrive in Tunis, a beautiful city gleaming in the moonlight beside a bay strikingly similar to that of Naples.

Here, you put up at an inconspicuous little Arab hotel. And spend the days exploring the capital, which has an informal, seaside atmosphere, a city of white walls and blue shutters, a city half French, half Arabic, with a colorful Casbah. Most of the time you hike for hours in the heat . . . hiking as training for the marches ahead . . . and, to work off increasing nervousness. At the third-floor office of the FLN, there are continual delays, changes of plans. An officer explains these delays and changes are due to sudden movements of French troops along the frontier.

(REPORTER)

Meanwhile, you keep hearing about Algerian refugees in Tunisia, and suggest a visit to one of the border camps. FLN officials agree, and you drive southward, for a firsthand look at this aspect of the Algerian problem. This is what you find:

(INSERT S-O-F REPORT on Algerian refugee problem, Rolls 1-5, Incl.)

(REPORTER)(OR, shots of Tunis to change scene, then reporter)

Somewhat subdued, you return to Tunis more impatient than ever to move into the country from which these refugees have come. Instead, you find more delays, more changes of plans.

Then, finally, an FLN official shows up at the hotel with a document. It's of somewhat dubious value from the French, or legal, viewpoint — but, among Algerians, very official. You read it.

(FILM: CUs, 3 stages, on Roll No. 49 of laissez-passer)

Written in both Arabic and French, it's an official
laissez-passer authorizing travel to Wilaya (Wee-lay-a)
No. 2, North Constantine, Algeria. It holds the army chief
of each zone responsible for offering all facilities. It's
good for leaving and reentering Tunisia, signed by the commander of the Algerian base in Tunisia — specific evidence
the Tunisians cooperate hand-in-glove with the Algerians.

(PAGE 3 - Algeria Report: OPENER)

(REPORTER)

That night, there's a meeting with an Algerian Colonel
and friends in a crowded Tunis café. In answer to questions, he says you are free to go anywhere, see anything,
ask anything. No censorship, no security, no nothing.
You'll be completely free, he declares; we ask only that
you tell the truth. We have nothing to hide, he adds; the
truth is our story. It's a fantastic press freedom for any
army, for a war zone, and speaks volumes for the Algerian
side. At the same time, you're proud to tell him your instructions from CBS News, say your editor is counting on
you for what he calls your usual thorough, hones (sic) and
objective reportin (sic). We have no axe to grind, the
editor has written; we want nothing more or less than the
truth of what is happening in Algeria — so really lay it
on the line.
And the next day, after lunch, you take off . . .
looking for the truth . . . headed for the frontier . . .
Algeria . . . and war.

(PAGE 1 — Algeria Report: ALGERIAN REFUGEES)

This is Frank Kearns, reporting from Tunisia. The
tragic Algerian problem is creating a tragic new refugee
problem.

Nationalist circles claim that at least 300-thousand
refugees have poured out of Algeria already. Some 100-
thousand, they say, have headed west, into Morocco. Twice
that many . . . 200-thousand . . . east-ward, in this
direction, into Tunisia.

This is how they come across the border. On foot . . .
most of them BARE-foot . . . with only the rags on their
backs. This is a typical point of entry, a sunbaked little
village called TAGEROUINE, 125 miles south of Tunis.

So far, 46-hundred Algerian refugees have crossed into
Tunisia here. Other thousands are spread all along the border, wherever there are villages, or any kind of mud huts.

The whole story is in these refugees' faces . . .
their feet . . . their torn clothes . . . their stumbling
walk . . . their children . . . their babies . . . their
aged.

This ancient old man, for example, struggling across
the last ditch. His name is Tahar Derbal. His age:
87 . . . 87.

As you can see, there are few young men or wom-
en in this sad procession. Most of the young and able
are dead . . . or up in the mountains, fighting with the
Algerian's guerrilla army. These are the unwanted, the
widowed, the poverty-stricken, those who have lost homes,
lands, husband, fathers and brothers.

By far the majority of Algeria's refugees are wom-
en . . . women with babies. Some have walked as much as
100 miles over mountains and valleys, travelling mostly at
night, to avoid French patrols and control points.

Practically their sole benefactors are the Algerian
Red Cross people — the Red Crescent. And they have pitifully little money, pitifully little food, pitifully little
medicine.

This tiny courtyard, with its mud wall, is the so-
called hospital. Two doctors, Algerian refugees themselves,
make-do with what they have.

Doctor:

A young boy is treated for foot trouble. . . . Eye-drops for trachoma in a tiny baby's eyes . . . and an old woman. . . . Another baby has bronchitis — and gets a priceless injection. An old woman gets a shot for heart disease. This is a refugee hospital . . . this dirty, fly-infested piece of desert.

Doctors and Tunisian authorities alike fear the coming winter, the first for this camp. Already, they say, it's strictly a case of survival of the fittest. And winter, they warn, may wipe out even the strongest of these undernourished refugees.

(PAGE 2 — Algeria Report: ALGERIAN REFUGEES)

Undernourished is the right word. The daily diet here defies all laws of minimum nutrition. Right now, the refugees get two so-called meals a day . . . one at noon . . . another at 7 o'clock at night. The menu is simple. One hunk of bread. And one small hunk of tuna-fish. That's it.

Even so, spirits are surprisingly high. Some of the youngsters have formed their own little Liberation Army, with toy arms and imitation drills. And they sing out lustily with the nationalists' liberation song. . . .
    SONG
One line of this song translates, "O God, O God, why don't we have the same liberty as people in other countries?!"

The answer to that question is political. But the answer to this refugee problem is non-political. Already, it's festering on the world's conscience . . . and becoming a problem, not for just Tunisia, and Morocco . . . but for the world.

This is Frank Kearns, reporting from the Algerian frontier, in Tunisia. Now back to CBS News, in New York.

Approximate script for SOF script on Algerian army:

(Alternate opening: If live-sound on beginning of Roll No. 20 is OK, suggest opening with this live-sound shot of Algerian company marching on mountain-top "parade ground," behind their flag, singing forbidden national anthem. If neither this, nor a repeat to be taken before we leave here, is OK, then have to open direct on reporter as usual)

(REPORTER)

The men fighting the French in these Algerian mountains are soldiers. And they have an army, a real army, in every sense of the word. These are the two most important facts immediately apparent to an American reporter traveling through these mountains searching for facts.

(FILM: Some shots to stress uniforms, arms, military appearance and actions of Algerian soldiers. E.g., LS, then MS's and CU's of soldiers in quadrangle of flag-raising ceremony on mountaintop; and/or at similar ceremony in rebel camp; or individual soldier saluting officer; shot soldiers marching by, showing different hats, etc., but all armed and uniformed and trained.)

The French picture these men abroad as bands of outlaws, as undisciplined bandits. But here on the spot it's obvious that these men are soldiers, part of a well-organized, well-disciplined army. The majority, incidentally, are veterans, veterans of the French army itself, veterans of World War II and Indochina. They're trained soldiers, veteran soldiers, and, now, past masters at planned, organized guerrilla, or mountain, fighting. Soldiers.

(FILM: Shots of individual civilians, and groups of civilians arriving in mountaintop forest camp. Then, at pertinent points, shots of civilian registering, getting uniforms, getting arms.)

New recruits come from all over Algeria. To keep up the youthful standard of the army, most are in their 20's. A recruit cannot join until he is 18. The age-limit is 35; for this type of fighting, anyone over 35 is too old . . . as we ourselves can testify. If accepted, the recruit receives whatever uniform is available at the moment — and his gun.

(FILM: Shots of recruits in training, with weapons, etc.)
Then, like recruits everywhere, he starts training. Two full months of hard, rough, practical training to prepare him for this special type of war. After two months, what you might call on-the-job training — covering a patrol engaged in actual operations.

(Page 2, SOF report, profiles of Algerian army)

(REPORTER)

Recruit or veteran, the Algerian soldier joins up, not because of a draft, but, usually, because he's on the run for anti-French underground activities . . . or, more often, because he simply aches to fight the French, to fight for what HE regards as the liberation of his country. At the same time, he gets a soldier's pay:

(FILM: Shots of soldiers lined up, receiving pay)

A buck private receives one thousand francs monthly . . . just under $3 . . . hardly enough to justify French charges most of these men are mercenaries and bandits, fighting just for money. The pay scale goes up slowly. Tops for an enlisted man, the equivalent of our Master Sergeant, is still under $6 a month. And the man with the highest rank in the Algerian army, a Colonel — there are no generals — a Colonel gets less than $15 a month. Those who have wives or children have a family allowance, under $6 monthly for each person.

(REPORTER)

Officially, this is known as the A.L.N.A., initials of the French phrase for the National Liberation Army of Algeria, or the A.L.N. But in popular language it's known as the F.L.N., initials which stand for the National Liberation front, the political group of which this army, the A.L.N., is the military branch.

(STUDIO ART WORK, A MAP to illustrate the following, map based on information and sample to be furnished by us; suggest finger or baton pointing to various sections as mentioned, and/or block groups or soldiers figures appearing as appropriate groups are mentioned)

All Algeria is divided into seven Wilaya (Wee-lay-ette), or Departments. The two biggest ones, the most important, are: This one, to the East, along the Tunisian border, and the Western Zone of Oran, along the Moroccan frontier. There's another big one north of Constantine, which includes Philippeville and the ALN hqs in the Collo mountains. Another is the Grand Kabylia (CAB-A-LEE); another, the Aures (OR-ESS). Also a department for the vast Sahara, to the south, and a separate one for Algiers, the capital.

Each department is carved up into sub-sectors, sectors, regions, zones.

(FILM: Patrol marching through mountains)

The smallest unit of this army is a squad, or what the Algerians call a "group" . . . 11 men, including a Sergeant who is in charge of a sub-sector.

(Page 3, SOF report, profiles of Algerian army)

(REPORTER)

Next comes a "Section," composed of three squads, or Groups . . . 33 soldiers, plus three Master Sergeants and an Adjutant, roughly a Warrant Officer, in charge of the sector. One Sergeant is military; the second, political; the third, intelligence . . . each responsible for his field throughout the sector.

(FILM: Company marching on mountaintop parade ground, or grouped in quadrangle at flagpole)

A company has about 150 men headed by a 2nd Lt. who is chief of his region. He has the three sub-chiefs, Warrant Officers, for military, political and intelligence affairs. He has a supply group, a group of engineers, a headquarters group, and three sections of infantry.

(REPORTER AND/OR FILM showing mortars, Captain)

An Algerian battalion consists of 3 companies, plus
mortar and machine-gun sections, the usual headquarters
outfits, a Medical Officer and the three political, military and intelligence officers, 1st Lt's. A Captain commands
a battalion, in charge of up to 500 men and in complete
charge of his geographical zone.

(REPORTER)

Topping this organizational pyramid is the regiment,
3 to 5 battalions headed by a Colonel who is chief of a
department, militarily and politically the head-man for his
department.

Obviously, this is an army, a complete, well-organized
military and political organization which covers every yard
of Algerian territory.

Like all organizations and all armies, of course, the
A.L.N. has its share of confusion, or administrative chaos
and mistakes. We ourselves have been involved in some incredible, Grade-A, Class-1 "snafus." But all these have
occured (sic) in rear areas, behind lines, in carbon-copy
and desk country.

(FILM: Quick shots, somewhere in montage, showing combat
soldiers on patrol, rushing toward camera, in camouflage,
etc . . . in action; CU's)

(Page 4, SOF report, profiles of Algerian army)

There's no confusion here in the mountains, in the combat
zone. These are soldiers, veteran soldiers. They're well-
trained, well-disciplined, and they fight in army units.
They have their own separate commando units, yet all these
soldiers can and do fight as commandoes. At the same time,
they fight under definite strategic and tactical plans, and
commands. French troops here in Algeria — not the politicians and propagandists in Paris — can testify these are
soldiers, this is an army, and — declared, or not — this
is war, all-out war.

(FILM: Soldiers dispersing, taking cover, during air-raid
alert. Then, appropriately, shot of patrol on march; shot
of mortar crew; CU of tough individual soldiers, various
poses, including one camouflaged in tree, etc.)

The Algerians have no planes, like the French . . . no
American B-26's, no American P-38's, no American Piper-
cubs. They have no battleships, no cruisers, no destroy-
ers, no navy for the coastline. They have no artillery,
no American 105's, 155's. Their biggest arm is a mortar.
Instead of jeeps, trucks and half-tracks, they have only a
few mules.

(FILM: If available and practical, here and perhaps just
above, some appropriate shots of French army and arms would
be most appropriate; here, especially showing French en
masse, in large groups)

Also, the Algerian soldier is outnumbered 5, 6 0 7
(sic) — perhaps 10, 12 or 14 — to one, by the French. The
French have at least half-a-million soldiers in Algeria,
more than they ever had in Indochina, most of their NATO
commitment, which belongs in Europe. They have another 1 or
2 hundred-thousand in their tremendous police force, territorials, and the armed colons.

(FILM: Patrol in action, or on march)

The Algerians count their soldiers in groups, or
patrols, not in battalions or divisions. The exact number is secret. We've heard everything from 30-thousand
to 100-thousand. Regardless, they're out-numbered, out-
equipped, anywhere from 5 to 10, to one.

(REPORTER)

Yet even the most neutral and cautious reporter
must report that every Algerian soldier has a weapon
which few French soldiers possess here in the mountains.
Namely, a solid, unshakeable belief that theirs is a just
cause, a right cause . . . plus an indescribable brotherhood . . . and absolute optimism. We've NEVER heard even
one Algerian soldier say, "IF we win." Instead, every time,
it's: "AFTER the war."

In short, the Algerians have a well-organized, well-armed, well-trained, veteran army.

This is Frank Kearns, reporting from the mountains of Algeria. Now back to CBS News, in New York.

Approximate script for SOF report on "Life in the Algerian army camp," filmed SOF somewhere in Eastern Algeria, Monday, August 5th, 1957:

(REPORTER, opening)

In some ways, life in an Algerian rebel camp is pretty much like life in any army camp anywhere in the world. The French call the Algerian fighter a rebel, or a fellagah, or even an outlaw or a bandit. But he regards himself as a nationalist, a patriot. And, whatever you call him, he's a soldier, a real soldier.
(FILM: Company lined up for flag-raising ceremony at camp, NOT open clearing; present-arms; saluting; Captain, etc.)
Life in one of the semi-permanent camps, like this one somewhere in Algeria stresses discipline. And, like soldiers everywhere, the Algerian spends part of his day in military duties. This is a typical flag-raising ceremony, with the entire camp drawn up in military formation. As you can see, these men are well-uniformed, well-armed, well-disciplined . . . soldiers.

(FILM: Some shots of soldiers cleaning rifles or sub-machineguns (sic), etc.)

And, like good soldiers, they spend a large part of their time in camp taking care of their best friends, their weapons. The Algerians, who are short of arms, and get most of them the hard way, from the French, respect and care for their arms even more than most frontline soldiers.

(FILM: Shots of soldiers peeling potatoes, fanning fire under kettle)

They also take turns attacking the universal enemy of every soldier, the potatoe (sic) . . . Kitchen Police . . . K.P., peeling spuds. . . . And they do time on other K.P. duties, everything from washing dishes to fanning the camp fire.

(FILM: Shots, first, of soldiers eating; then, talking, resting; then, sleeping, napping)

Above all, however, the Algerian – again, like soldiers
everywhere — spends most of his time in camp in talking
and arguing . . . in resting and sleeping . . . and . . .
eating.

Chow-time is the biggest, most important hour of the
day. On duty — which usually means patrolling, in the
mountains – the pickings are usually slim. One meal a day
is the most a man can hope for, at best of times. So when
he gets to a camp like this, food is important, chow-time
is important.

(FILM, if wanted: Shots of boy bringing bread into camp,
mule-back)

(Page 2, SOF report, life in an Algerian army camp)

Usually, in a camp like this, the food comes from a neighboring village. Bread, for example, comes in on mule-back,
daily. Officers here say they pay for all food and clothes
they get. But some of the soldiers say frankly they don't
have to pay for anything, that Algerians contribute everything to The Cause. The truth is elusive.

(FILM: Various shots of soldiers talking, smoking, reading
newspapers, etc.)

Regardless, after chow-time, soldiers in camp smoke
the usual cigarettes . . . read the usual newspapers . . .
and talk . . . and argue. Re-fighting old and recent
battles . . . talking politics . . . and, as usual, what
they'll do "after the war."
Then, the chief occupation of any soldier of any
uniform in any country: Sack-time. This is the best time
of day in a rebel camp, especially for men who sometimes
spend up to 3 months on the march, a march of up to 375
miles through rugged mountains and the entire French army.
Always, with arms close by, and sentries on guard.

(REPORTER)

But there's no garrison life in Algeria, except for the French. The Algerians have permanent, and

semi-permanent camps. But, basically, they're all, like
this one, transient camps.

(FILM: Shots of patrols coming in to, or leaving, camp;
refugees arriving and departing, etc.)

Every day, patrols arrive here . . . or leave. Some
come for rest, before going on another mission. Some are
just leaving on special jobs. Some are carrying arms and
ammunition into the deep interior, others returning from
jobs. Algerian refugees, condemned to a life of continual
wandering, pass through here mostly daily. And sometimes,
there are the wounded. The lucky ones get first-aid treatment, then return to their units. The unlucky ones are tak-
en on across the frontier, into hospitals in Tunisia.

(FILM: Shots of soldier writing letter, another reading
newspaper, then CU's of several typical soldiers)

There's no Red Cross in these camps, no entertainment. No dances, no drinking whatsoever, no pin-up girls,
no home-leave in a town or village where the soldier is
already condemned to imprisonment or death for joining the
FLN army.

(FILM: Shots of group of soldiers praying, led by Sergeant)

One thing holds these volunteer soldiers together is their
religious faith, their faith in Islam, in Allah, or God,
and his

(Page 3, SOF report, life in an Algerian army camp)

prophet Mohamed (sic). Usually, they pray alone, on mountaintops and facing the East, and Mecca.

(REPORTER, OR FILM showing soldiers greeting each other,
shaking hands, embracing each other)

Above all else, however, they are sustained by a
close, warm, personal relationship. Almost everyone knows
each other, either from before the Trouble, or from fighting
together in the mountains. Soldier and officer alike, they

call each other Brother, and mean it. It's the warmest relationship I've ever seen in any army, anywhere.

(REPORTER)

Furthermore, they're sustained by a singleness of purpose. Even the most neutral, objective reporter must report
that the vast majority of these men are here for one reason only . . . to fight the French, to force the French to
leave what they regard as their country. So, camps such as
this are only transient camps . . . mere stops along the
way to what these soldiers hope will be the independence of
Algeria.

This is Frank Kearns, reporting from Algeria. Now back
to CBS News in New York.

Approximate script for separate SOF report on type of person
fighting in Algerian army: Profiles.

(REPORTER)

What kind of person is fighting the French in the mountains of Algeria? It takes a while to find the answer to
THIS question.

(FILM: Shots of several particularly rugged-looking, tough,
fierce types. Then, shots of Kearns, and Masraff, traveling,
in camp, eating, etc.)

At first glance, they look like a pretty rough, tough
lot, these Algerian soldiers. But living with them, eating and sleeping and talking with them, marching over the
mountains with them, you begin to know and understand the
Algerian fighter. And, like any soldier in any army, he begins to fit a pattern.

(FILM: Our Captain; various shots appropriate to script,
such as scene directing parade, another shouting orders,
receiving communications, embracing children, greeting civilians, etc.)

This Captain served France 14 years, 14 years with
the French army. He fought for, and with France, everywhere from Bizerte to Dienbienphu. For 14 years he proved
his courage and his loyalty to France. Recommended for the
Legion of Honor, he has a private collection of 12 Croix de
Guerres.
Back in Algeria, however, unable to stomach operations
against his own people, the Captain rebelled. After a battle in which 16 Frenchmen in his unit were killed, he took
his entire company to the mountains, 92 men and all their
equipment; everything from 200 rifles to Thompsons, mortars
and walkie-talkies, loaded on 36 mules.
Politics aside, he is one of the best professional officers I've ever met. He's a touch disciplinarian, yet, in
the best tradition, tireless in looking after the welfare
of his men. And, childless, he is pathetically loving with
the orphaned Algerian boys who constantly make their way
to this camp. He's a tough, ruthless man, when necessary,
I'm sure. But he's also sad, with the complete fatigue of

the professional soldier who has seen too much war, who
has simply seen too much, period. His pay is less than $12
a month, so you can hardly call him a mercenary. And he
says that after the war, all he wants to do is work with
his hands, as a laborer. So you can hardly call him ambitious. In all objectivity, you can only describe him as a
professional soldier, and, by his standards, a patriot.

(FILM: One of the Capt's officers, tall gaunt, hollow-
cheeked man with Aussie-type hat, identified in dopesheets
(sic) and on film can.)

Or take one of the Captain's officers, a gaunt, hollow-
cheeked, born fighter, nicknamed "Indochine." This man spent
5 years in Indochina with the French.

(Page 2, SOF report, profiles Algerian types in army)

But, like the Captain, he found French actions against
his own people, the Algerians, too much to stomach . . .
and walked out.
Hardly a clean-living Tom Swift, or Rover Boy. But a
born fighter and leader of men.
"Indochine" claims the French have wiped out his entire family — mother and father, 4 sisters, one brother,
4 uncles — 20 in all. Yet when I asked him, immediately,
what he thought should be done with The French in Algeria,
if and when the war is over, he replies soberly: "All we
want from them is our liberty, to let our young ones grow
up free and equal. We shall forget the past," he declares,
"and work for the future."

(REPORTER:)

The men here in the mountains come from every walk of
life, And (sic), like anyvolunteer (sic) group anywhere,
they represent a higher standard than draftees. Every man
here came to the mountains of his own free will, for his
own good reasons.

(FILM: Shots of Yazid, former bookshop owner now PR man)

Yazid, here, for example, owned a café and bookshop
before the trouble. He says he joined up simply to help

free his country. His uncle was arrested in a French round-up, he adds, and killed on the spot as soon as the French learned he was related to Yazid.

(Start of new 400 ft roll here)
(FILM: Shots of straw-hatted soldier, looking like Mexican gaucho, "Rafal.")

This man, who says he knew many American soldiers in Algiers during World War II, is nicknamed "Rafal" (Raaf-all) for the murderous burst of his Czech sub-machinegun. He says frankly he has killed 15 or 20 Frenchmen with his gun. But he's an individual, more than a soldier. And the FLN has given him a lone-wolf job . . . supervising work-ers who cut cork bark from the trees here, under the noses of the French, and smuggle it into Tunisia for sale abroad. The profits go into the FLN treasury. Raaf-all was a busi-nessman before the war, has been in the mountains two years now, has a wife and four children.

(FILM: Shots of Abdel Kader, young man in civvies)

This 22-year-old, whom we met in Tunisia before en-tering Algeria, was studying mechanical engineering until early last year. Then, he says, some French soldiers opened fire on some students during an argument; 18 Algerian youths were injured, one killed. The latter was the cousin of this young man, who, a month later, took to the mountains and joined the ALN. Among other things, he is most bitter over how the French, according to him, treated the Algerians as

(Page 3, SOF report, profiles Algerian types in army)

second-class people in school, gave all advantages and en-couragement and politeness to French pupils.

(FILM: Shots of Youssef, crew-cut, young man)

Youssef, this 27-year-old with the American crew-cut, was a student when the French raided his village..and, he claims, shot his sister in cold-blood when she couldn't tell them where to find the village FLN leader. Youssef has been in the mountains ever since, over a year now. He re-members most a battle in July, 1956, near Bone.

He says the ALN had won the battle, when the French called up air cover to prevent further attacks. Then, he claims, the French sprayed his section of about 90 men with gas. He can't name the type of gas, but alleges that the first symptom is itching, then nausea. Some soldiers went mad, he claims. Others, he charges, died — 30, altogether. Some are still in a Tunisian hospital, he adds.

(FILM: Shots of Akila, young girl, who does hospital work)

This 21-year-old girl is typical of the few, dedicated girls and women, perhaps 100 at most — who serve with the ALN. A nurse, she worked secretly for the underground in a coastal town until one of her best friends was arrested for trying to throw a bomb into a cinema. This girl immediately headed for the mountains, has served as a nurse ever since. She's known as "The Little One," or "Sister," among the men, and insists most of her work is among wounded civilians, that ALN casualties are rare. When and if the war is over, her dream is to run a mobile clinic among the villages, to bring modern medicine to the people.

(REPORTER)

Always, the same pattern. The backgrounds vary. But the veterans are ex-French army men who refused to carry out operations against their people. The younger ones are often students, with personal grudges against the French, against French treatment of Algerian Moslem. And almost all have lost friends or members of their families in this undeclared war. Few angels, but, at the same time, few devils . . . normal human beings.

This is Frank Kearns, reporting from an Algerian army camp. Now back to CBS News, in New York.

Approximate script for SOF interview with Rushdi, sole
English-speaking Algerian encountered in almost six weeks with
Algerians:

Ad-lib, after all . . . story of why he left Algeria, what
events led him to leave, etc. Introduction in main documentary script, not here.

Rushdi, from Bone. Father, lawyer and writer. Arrested
(Father). Wanted to leave, but Mother said you're all we
have left. French controls. Curfews. Stay inside. Papers.
Police station. Applied for school in Tunisia (student);
refused, told comes from Bad family. Final straw: Aug.
20th, last year, when each French family took in a French
soldier for Sunday dinner. Much drinking. That evening,
drunken soldiers started shooting up town. Killed __,
wounded __. Went in Turkish bath, pulled out all men, naked, jeered, then shot each in head. Impossible to walk
on sidewalk. Decided to leave, got permission go to France
(French didn't know he had passport), boarded Tunis-bound
ship at Marseilles. Now studying in Tunis, working for
FLN (not ALN), civilian not military. 17 now, 18 come
August 29th.

Approximate script for separate SOF report on "Technique of the
Algerian army," how it fights, ties up great French army:

(REPORTER: Opening)

Abroad, there are many questions about the fighting
here in Algeria. But for the average man, probably, one of
the biggest questions is this: How do the Algerians tie-
up the big, modern French army now in Algeria? It's a good
question.

(FILM: Stock film of French army, including, if possible,
shots of French AF, paratroopers, naval units, etc., to
stress mass and modern)

France is usually referred to as one of the Big Four
powers of the world. Her army is one of the biggest, most
modern in the world. She has over half-a-million soldiers
here in Algeria, more than she ever had in Indochina.
She has every type of modern weapon from radar and
flame-thrower to rockets and napalm bombs. She has commandoes and paratroopers here, infantry and armored divisions, helicopters, a powerful air force including jets,
even deadly naval units along the coastline. Furthermore,
the French have been in Algeria over 100 years now, pre-
sumably know the country and its people and have a first-
rate intelligence.

(FILM: Appropriate shots of individual Algerian soldiers,
in action, and civilians)

The Algerians, on the other hand, have no modern, in-
dustrialized state with which to wage war. Their government
is illegal. They have no air force; not a single plane.
They have no artillery whatsoever; their biggest weapon
is a mortar. No planes, no artillery, two of the biggest
factors in any war. They have no trucks, jeeps or armored
cars, certainly no naval units. They are out-equipped,
out-numbered, by fantastic proportions. By all military
logic they should have been WIPED OUT long ago.

(REPORTER)

Yet the fighting drags on . . . three years, this
November. The Algerians are still typing-up this great
French army, which costs France, in money alone, some 3
million dollars each and every day. How do they do it?

(FILM: Studio map of Algeria, perhaps with map of Texas
superimposed for comparison; any stock film of the country,
and/or dissolving to some scenic views of mountains and
valleys from our film)

For one thing, Algeria is big, really big. Texan GI's
who hit Algeria during World War II were always chastened
to learn that Algeria is bigger than Texas . . . three
times as big. And, like the U.S., it has every type of
geography, from part of the vast Sahara in the

(Page 2, SOF report on techniques of Algerian army)

south to beautiful Mediterranean coastline in the north.
Above all, however, it has mountains, real mountains, huge,
savage mountains tailor-made for guerrilla fighting.

(REPORTER)

Secondly, the Algerians have an army. Not a jet-age
army, by a long shot. But an army created especially for
this country, this kind of warfare, this particular war.

(FILM: Shots to stress that Algerians are soldiers, part
of an army — saluting, drilling, parading, lined up, flag,
etc. Plus, if required, studio chart described and pre-
scribed for SOF report on Algerian Army)

The French have successfully propagated the idea
abroad that the Algerian fighters are Fellagah, or wild
outlaws. Here on the spot, it's obvious nothing could be
further from the truth. These soldiers, trained soldiers,
well-disciplined, most of them veterans of the French army
itself, of World War II and/or Indochina. And they are
well-organized, from patrols, or "Groups," on up through
Sections, Companies, Battalions and Regiments.

(REPORTER)

More important, they fight as soldiers, as an army, according to definite tactical and strategic plans. They fight a guerrilla-type warfare, a hit-and-run warfare. And this is the secret of their success.

(FILM: Shots of rebel camp . . . plus shots of patrol in forest . . . and views of mountains)

The Algerian army bases in the mountains. Despite artillery bombardments, despite forest fires, despite air attacks, despite occasional mass operation involving thousands of French troops, the mountains belong to the Algerians. Their headquarters and their camps are in the mountains.

(FILM: Appropriate shots of patrols, or training, and/or camouflage, etc.)

And every soldier is trained as a mountain soldier, trained especially for mountain warfare. He knows every rock and tree . . . and civilian . . . and path in his area. He's an expert at forest camouflage, forest living, forest fighting. And, to put it mildly, Algeria has plenty of mountains.

(Page 3, SOF report on techniques of Algerian army)

(FILM: Stock film of French army, to stress jeeps, trucks, half-tracks, tanks, and other mechanized equipment)

In this sort of terrain, French mechanized equipment . . . such as trucks and armored cars and tanks . . . are useless. The mechanized part of the French army is in the same position here as Britain's General Braddock when he marched his parade-ground troops toward Pittsburgh, ambushed and massacred by Pennsylvania mountaineers.

(FILM: Shots of Algerian soldiers, mountaineer-style . . . climbing or hiding in tree . . . camouflage . . . patrolling through mountain, etc.)

As a matter-of-fact, that's what this is, a mountaineer, or Indian-style warfare. Based, firstly, on soldiers
who can fight as individuals, like Indians . . . and, secondly, on tactical, strategic direction of army units.
As a result, the French only come into the mountains in
force, by thousands. And the mountains still belong to the
Algerians.

(FILM: from stock, of scenes in Algerian towns and cities, especially Algiers, showing French security measures,
street scenes, and/or results of acts of terrorism)

In the town and cities, the Algerians use the civilians' oldest weapon against any army . . . terrorism . . .
fires, grenades, murders, the whole bloody arsenal. The
Algerians say terrorism is directed only against the
French, and other Europeans; never against Moslem civilians, as the French claim. They say this is part psycho-
logical warfare against the French, civilian and military;
partly retaliation for French attacks against Algerian
civilians; partly designed to tie up huge masses of French
troops.
    Terrorism is, as always, horrible. But the Algerians
claim it is an historic weapon against the military . . .
as witness Cyprus, Greece, Yugoslavia, and France herself
under German occupation. The Algerians also say the murder
of an Algerian baby or mother by a French airplane over a
village is neither more horrible, nor less horrible, than
the murder of a French baby or mother by a hand-grenade
in town.

(REPORTER)

One of the Algerians' most effective weapons against
the French is the ambuscade, the ambush. They offered to
set one up for us, a real ambush with real French victims,
to show their military prowess in this type of operation.
We refused, of course, on moral grounds. We are here as
reporters, to report facts, the OTHER side of the Algerian
story. We are NOT here searching for sensational film. We
want no one, neither French nor Algerian, killed or even
hurt by our presence. We are spectators, observers, reporters; not soldiers, not participants on the other side.

(Page 4, SOF report on techniques of Algerian army)

(FILM: Shots of soldiers crouching in forest, hiding in trees, in camouflage.)

Anyhow, anyone who can read or watch a movie or TV knows what an ambush is. The point here: These Algerians are past masters at the ambush, a combination of the Indian-style ambush and the strictly army, or military ambush. No French convoy, no French patrol, not even a French camp gate is ever safe from ambush, sudden, unexpected, murderous cross-fire. This is one of the Algerians' most powerful weapons.

(REPORTER)

The Algerians also have large numbers of commandoes, special units trained in typical commando tactics, even attacks inside French army camps. No one here will talk much about these commandoes, who usually wear blue-denim uniforms. But one officer describes them proudly as "our guided missiles."
In addition, the Algerians have a large number of special sections - 11 men to a section - devoted exclusively to sabotage.

(FILM: Patrol of 11 men going thru forest, shots of commandoes down mountainside, etc.)

For obvious reasons, we cannot show them at work. But, at one base we visited, two sections of just one company spend all their time on sabotage. They claim they wreck or sabotage the Algeria-Tunisia train, usually mostly military, at least once a week that it takes the French 3 or 4 days to repair the damage each time. They also bring down electric power lines at least once every 10 days, and hit directly at French military camps a minimum of once every two weeks.

(REPORTER)

In addition, the Algerians have an intelligence network which can only be described as fantastic. I read one

typical report just a few days ago. Neat and military, it
described the number of French troops in the agent's village, the position of guards and blockhouses and search-
lights, the caliber of machineguns and mortars, which
persons were regarded as untrustworthy . . . on and on and
on, fact after fact. With millions of official and unofficial agents among the people, even in French camps, the
Algerians claim they know in advance every move the French
make. This, they say, explains why they have so few losses
in huge operations mounted by the French — they know where,
and when the French are coming.

(FILM: Algerian civilians. Especially those coming through
an army camp, those being greeted by an ALN officer or soldier, those feeding soldiers, etc.)

(Page 5, SOF report on techniques of Algerian army)

The Algerians have their normal share of neutrals,
whom they say they leave alone . . . and a few they regard
as active collaborators, whom they admit they kill. But, by
and large, I'm convinced, the civilian population cooper-
ates with the Algerian army . . . everything from carrying
messages, to providing food and shelter and intelligence.

(REPORTER)

This, of course, is the most formidable weapon of all,
civilian resistance. And it definitely exists.
Put it all together . . . civilian resistance . . .
organized terrorism . . . ambushes . . . sabotage . . . a
tough army created especially for this war, this mountain
country . . . and you begin to understand how the Algerians
tie-up a great, modern army like that of the French here in
Algeria.

This is Frank Kearns, reporting from the mountains of
Algeria. Now back to CBS News, in New York.

Approximate script of SOF report on Communism in Algerian Army, FLN:

(REPORTER)

One of the most serious charges leveled against the Algerian army and the F.L.N. is that they're a bunch of Communists. Some quarters charge the Algerians are led or dominated by Communists. Other circles claim the Algerians are armed and equipped by the communists. Some sources even claim that ALL F.L.N. members, ALL Algerian soldiers, are Communists.

(FILM: Various shots of Kearns, and Masraff, at work; going with patrols, talking to and interviewing soldiers, etc.)

For more than a month now, both here in Algeria and back in Tunisia, we have investigated these charges. The CBS cameraman, Youseff (sic) Masraff, and I, have, between us, more than 40 years of combined journalistic background. We know how to investigate, how to separate facts from propaganda. And, everywhere, we've dug after the truth about these charges of communism. In secret headquarters, in camps, on patrols . . . above all, in nightly bull-sessions, where arguments get hot and true thoughts emerge. This is what we've found.

(FILM: Studio chart, based on our data, showing organization of F.L.N. and A.L.N.)

The entire F.L.N. is headed by the C.N.R.A., the national committee of the Algerian Revolution. This top-level group has 34 members; 17 regular, 17 supplementary. Of this 34, five mysterious, unknown men form a C.C.E., a Coordination and Execution Committee.

(FILM: Stock, about two months ago, of five Algerian leaders at press conference in Cairo; or, still older stock, about 2 years ago, showing another group, including now-jailed Ben Bella and others)

No one knows who these men are. They could be these five who appeared publicly in Cairo some time ago, at a press conference. Or, SOME of these five. Anyhow, the five

members of the C.C.E., or executive council, are the top
boys, five shadowy figures who really run the Algerian nationalist movement.

(FILM: Back to studio chart, or, if we get it, shots of
Algerian village)

From this highest level down to the lowest level, it's
the same . . . committee of five. Each village still standing — not burned nor bombed, destroyed by the French —
has its committee of five. These are civilians, these five,
their identities highly secret. They are the underground
leaders most sought by the French.

(REPORTER)

(Page 2, SOF report on communism, Algeria)

Some quarters see in this praesidum (sic) of 34 members,
this higher council of five, and the village councils of
five, a distinct resemblance to communist organization, and
communist cells. The Algerians to whom we've talked reject,
and resent, this charge most vehemently. This organization,
they swear, is their own invention and copies none other,
especially not the communists.

(FILM: Back to studio chart of army, described in, and intended for, separate SOF report on Algerian army)

The military controls every section of Algeria. The
commander of a section is also chief of his sector. The
company commander is in charge of his region, the battalion commander is chief of all the regions which make up a
zone. And the colonel commanding a regiment is chief of an
entire department. Each of these officers has three aides, a
political chief, a military chief, an intelligence chief.
Civilians work directly under these men.

(REPORTER)

Some circles say this is a Red Army type of organization.
And they charge that these political officers with each unit
are all-too-similar to communist political commissars.
Here again, the Algerians say this is war, the military

control is necessary; but, that it's not the Russian system . . . it's their own. The political officers, they declare indignantly, are not commissars; they are just what
they're called, political officers . . . necessary in this
type of war.

(FILM: MS's and, especially CU's, of Algerian arms, soldiers carrying and/or cleaning and/or training on them)

The world press is often full of stories the Algerians
are receiving arms from the communists. We can't speak for
the entire Algerian army. Also, we have no knowledge of
what kind of arms they have stored, nor what kind they
have enroute. We can say, however, that all the arms we've
seen — and we've seen literally hundred — less than a
dozen were made in the Communist Bloc. These were Czech
submachine-guns, possibly from Egypt. The vast majority
of the arms we've seen are French or American, taken from
the French.

(REPORTER)

About the organization, we cannot say whether it is
based on communist framework, or with communist assis-
tance. For obvious reasons, we cannot prove whether the
F.L.N. is communist-led, communist-dominated, or even
communist-infiltrated.
We can say, however, in absolute honesty, that we
have come across no evidence of big communist arms shipments. . . . In all our dozens upon dozens of intimate conversations, we have not come across a

(Page 3, SOF report on communism, Algeria)

single Algerian soldier whose conversation or way of thinking reflects communist indoctrination. We have seen no red
literature, not even pink literature. We've found no one
listening to Radio Moscow.

(FILM: Various CU's and MS's of individual soldiers)
In private conversation, these soldiers admit frankly they're oriented toward the West, want no part of the
communist East. Their education, their lives, their way of
thinking is all French, Western. They're Arabs, and Moslem.

And, unlike their Middle Eastern brothers, they still, somehow, have a positive, constructive attitude toward The West. They say they're not going through all this to replace what they describe as French colonialism and imperialism, for Russian colonialism and imperialism.

(REPORTER)

What if this undeclared war drags on another year, maybe two years? Will the Algerians turn to the communists for arms, at least?

A 29-year-old former student, now an A.L.N. Lieutenant, answered this question bluntly. We HAVE received offers of arms from Russia, he admitted. But, he declared, we haven't accepted . . . yet. But, if the war goes on and on and we have no help from the West . . . he shrugged his shoulders. "If I'm drowning," he said grimly, "and even my worst enemy hands me a red-hot poker — I'll take it. I have no choice."

This is Frank Kearns, reporting from inside Algeria. Now back to CBS News, in New York.

Approximate script for separate SOF report on devastated
Algerian "Meshtas," or groups of farms:

(REPORTER)

Above all else, the Algerian soldiers are bitter over
French attacks on this country's "meshtas," or groups of
farms. War is war, they say, and they welcome combat between soldiers, even hand-to-hand combat. But war on civilians, they declare, is cowardly and little more than butchery . . . especially on the defenseless farms.

(FILM: Stock of Algiers, scenes after terrorism, or landmarks, or security checks, and the like)

The French probably rettort (sic) that Algerian underground activities — terrorism — in the towns and cities
is also war against civilians, equally cowardly butchery,
against defenseless men, woman (sic) and children. The
Algerians admit this, in part, but say the urban civilians
have protection, hordes of police, territorials and armed
civilians, what even the French call "saturation" security
measures.

(FILM: Shots of valley, and/or farms, and/or CU's of hut -
like farmhouses)

Regardless, here on the spot, it's obvious that the
farmer, his family, his home and his farm are the most defenseless of all participants or spectators in this undeclared war. An angry, or even a bored pilot — usually
flying an American B-26, or a P-38 — can wipe out an entire
farm in a matter of seconds. And, for an Algerian farmer,
this danger exists every minute of every daylight hour,
from sunup till sundown.

(REPORTER)

Even more devastating has been the razing of entire
villages, and "meshtas." Sometimes, allegedly, in savage
retaliation for Algerian ambushes or raids. Other times,
as part of a huge "Ratissage," or combing out, of an
entire area.

(FILM: LS of valley, perhaps scene showing our section going down mountainside into valley; etc.)

This valley, for example, which we passed through, was
full of thriving farms less than six months ago. It's rich
farming country, strikingly similar to parts of West
Virginia, Pennsylvania. Up till 4 months ago it was a
quiet, peaceful place with some 5,000 inhabitants, men,
women and children.

(Page 2, script for SOF report on Algerian "Meshta," or farms)

(REPORTER)

Then, suddenly, the French mounted a typical Ratissage
operation. First, heavy artillery barrages. Then, bombing
and strafing by planes. Then, thousands of troops tightening up a vast circle . . . all too many with nervous
trigger-fingers.

(FILM: LS's, MS's and CU's of gutted farm buildings, weed-
grown fields, gardens in shambles, etc.)

Within a few days it was all over. And the valley was
dead. It's still dead. The former farmhouses are only gutted ruins. The thatched roofs have gone up in flames. Only
the low stone walls remain. The rich fields are producing
nothing but weeds. And gardens have grown wild. Even in
daylight, this place has the eerie atmosphere of a graveyard at night.

(REPORTER)

Hundreds of the people who lived here, according to
the Algerians, are now in French concentration camps. ALN
records claim 374 persons were killed in the Ratissage,
scores wounded . . . mostly women and children. Out of
5,000 people, less than 1,000 are left.

(FILM: Shots of civilians climbing mountain, white-
turbaned men and boys gathering under trees, squatting on
the ground; women, at base of cliff; including human-
interest CU's.)

Once a month, civilians from each section receive a
pitifully small ration, to help them keep alive. Here, for
example, there are about 125 men, women and children, mostly the young and the aged. They gather on a mountainside,
under trees and a protecting cliff, hiding from curious
French planes scouring the skies.

(FILM: Shots of men listening to political officer, under
trees; then shots of women, children, babies huddled at
base of cliff)

The men listen impassively as a young ALN political
officer delivers a political talk, explains why we have come
to this typical area deep inside Algeria, and gives the
latest news. At the base of a nearby cliff, the women wait
patiently, trying to calm their babies, waiting for the
family name to be called for rations.

(FILM: LS, MS's, and CU's of actual ration distribution)

(Page 3, script for SOF report on Algerian "Meshta," or farms)

The woman collects the family's ration. It's not complicated. One bucket of corn. That's it. The monthly ration. Also, a piece of cash, an average of 1,000 francs for
each family . . . less than $3 a month. This is the ration.

(FILM: Shots of women receiving new dresses, some dumping
corn ration into new dress)

Every six months, the family gets a new
dress . . . usually, not for the woman, but as material for
clothes for the children. This particular distribution, I
suspect, is staged just for us. Distribution of the dresses
stops as soon as our camera stops.

(FILM: Shots of corn, money distribution. Then shots of
valley and gutted farmhouses and CU's of civilians, their
bare feet, ragged, clothes, etc., to stress poverty . . .
alternately, where appropriate.)

The rest of the ration is real, however. A bucket of
corn and less than $3 in cash — for an entire month. It's

a scene of incredible contrast. . . . Here, the bare feet,
the gaunt faces and bodies, the ragged clothes, the obvious hardship . . . and, down below, rich, fertile farming
country, a beautiful valley which only recently supported
5,000 people.

(REPORTER)

   A typical contrast of war . . . and, especially, of
this war.

   This is Frank Kearns, reporting from the mountains of
Algeria. Now back to CBS News, in New York.

Approximate script for SOF report on a mysterious Algerian leader:

(REPORTER: Tease-opening for WNR (World News Roundup), if wanted)

This is Frank Kearns, reporting from the mountains of Algeria. We've just learned that the Algerians have a single, mysterious leader for their war against the French.

(REPORTER: Reopening for WNR, or as opener for straight news report)

This is to reveal, for the first time, that a single, shadowy figure is leading the Algerians in their fight against the massive French army.

(FILM: Shots of Cairo and/or Tunis FLN offices, or general views, ours or stock, of Cairo and Tunis. And/or studio chart showing FLN organization, top to bottom)

Back at Algerian foreign headquarters in Cairo and Tunis, officials insist, as they always have, that both the FLN and the Algerian army are directed by a central committee of 34 men, 17 regular members and 17 supplementary members. Of these 34, they say, 5 form a higher, or executive, council — the top men.

(REPORTER)

Ever since starting this trip, we have questioned this setup. Anything so well organized as the FLN, both abroad and inside Algeria, we've insisted, must have a single leader. A committee, we've emphasized, is too cumbersome, too awkward for direction of such a complicated effort. And no army, we have pointed out, no army can operate by committee, without one top man, one top general.

(FILM: Various shots, in quick sequence, of Kearns, and Masraff, traveling through Algeria, interviewing soldiers and civilians and refugees and officers, etc.)

We've found the answer in the front lines, in the camps, and on the march, in mental fencing with dozens upon dozens of officers, soldiers, refugees and civilians. As usual, in the front lines there is little subtlety . . . and much honesty. A combat officer or soldier, or a refugee, has no time for subterfuge, for diplomatic double-talk. They all confirm the committee of 34, the higher council of 5. But, here and there, an officer or a soldier answers a direct question with a direct answer.

(Page 2, separate SOF report on Algerian leader)

(REPORTER)

Yes, of course we have a leader, one admits. Yes, another declares, naturally we have one man leading our army . . . every army needs a general. Every revolution must have a leader, still another agrees — and we have ours. No one seems to know who he is, however. And all agree that now is not the time for him to come forward . . . after the war, they say, but not now.

Then, a political officer chakes (sic) his head warningly, or another officer changes the subject abruptly, and the mask is replaced on this secret leader.

But, after almost six weeks with the Algerians, both here in the mountains and back in Tunisia, we are convinced that their intricate, highly organized war against the French is directed by a mysterious, shadowy, secret figure — one of the most mysterious men in the world today.

This is Frank Kearns, reporting from the mountains of Algeria.

Now back to Eric Severeid in New York.
Now back to CBS News in New York.
Now back to Douglas Edwards in New York.

(Approximate Script for separate SOF report on Communist offer
of arms to Algerians)

(REPORTER: Alternate opening, if wanted for W-N-R)

This is Frank Kearns, reporting from the mountains of
Algeria. The communists have offered arms to the Algerians.

(REPORTER: Re-opening W-N-R, after tease-opener, or opener
for regular news shows)

We can disclose, for the first time, that the communists have offered arms to the Algerians, for their war
against the French. The offer is for almost any kind of
arms, in almost any quantities, to be delivered anywhere
the Algerians name.

(FILM: Shots of Kearns and Masraff traveling with Algerian
soldiers, in camp, then looking at arms, and MS's and CU's
of various Algerian arms, especially Czech submachine gun
and drill made in Czechoslovakia)

In almost six weeks spent with the Algerians, here in
the mountains, in no-man's land along the border, and back
at camps and headquarters in Tunisia, we've seen every type
of weapon . . . everything from old-fashioned shotguns
to modern mortars. We've seen small arsenals. And we've
seen the weapons in the hands of hundreds upon hundreds of
Algerian soldiers.
Some of these weapons have come from all over the
world, everywhere from Italy to Spain. But most of them are
French or American, taken from the French. The majority are
American.
In all this time, with all this careful search-
ing, we've seen only a few arms from behind the Iron
Curtain. All submachine guns, less than a dozen, made in
Czechoslovakia. And probably from Egypt.
Also, one drill — made in Czechoslovakia.

(REPORTER)

That's it. We can't speak for other sectors of Algeria
or Tunisia, or for Morocco. We can't speak for secret arms
depots. We can't speak for any arms shipments enroute. But

we can say we've seen no real evidence of Communist arms
here in Algeria.

(FILM: Shots of Kearns interviewing soldiers, officers; living and talking with them)

The Algerians we've met swear emphatically, they have
not received any communist arms. In fact, they're indignant
at the charge, because they say, quite frankly, the communists have offered arms — and the Algerians have turned
them down. If we accept

(Page 2, SOF report on Commie offer arms to Algeria)

Communist arms, they point out, would we still have soldiers without rifles? Above all, they add, if we took
Communist arms, we'd have ack-ack against French planes,
we've (sic) have weapons against tanks and armored cars,
we'd have plenty of ammunition.

(REPORTER)

From what we've seen, they're right. In the areas
we've visited, the Algerians are well-armed, with small
arms. But there are still a lot of ancient shot-guns and
pistols, still soldiers without guns. And every soldier
here treats his weapon like his best friend, which it is.
Firing a rifle needlessly can, as we have seen, send an
Algerian soldier to an underground guardhouse for 8 days.
Even rifle cartridges are than (sic) precious.

(FILM: Stock shots of French army, stressing modern weapons
and mass)
These men are hungry for arms and ammunition to fight
the huge, modern French army here in Algeria. And they get
hungrier every day for arms to use against bombers, fighters, even jets, against tanks and armored cars. A shotgun
isn't much use against a P-38 or a Mystery jet, a lady's
handbag pistol isn't' (sic) much use against American 105
and 155 artillery.

(REPORTER)

The communist offer of arms still stand, the officers
here say. And, obviously, every day it becomes more tempting. So far, the Algerians apparently have held out. More
realistic than their Middle East brothers, they're afraid
of the hidden strings attached to any communist offer.

But, they say frankly, if this fighting drags on and
on, without any material or diplomatic help from the
West . . . eventually, they warn, the Algerians will HAVE
to accept the communist offer.

This is Frank Kearns, reporting from the mountains of
Algeria.

Now back to Eric Severeid, in New York.
Now back to Douglas Edwards, in New York.
Now back to CBS News, in New York.

PAGE 1, ENDING — Algerian report: Conclusions.

(REPORTER)

    Finally, it's time to leave. You've spent some
six weeks on this story . . . six weeks with the
Algerians . . . in Tunis, at the Tunisian border, and
inside Algeria itself.

(FILM: Short sequences of film to illustrate each phrase,
such as film of FLN office in Tunis, then shot of Algerian
refugees, then shots (of) Kearns taking cover, then drinking from canteen and then eating, etc. If absolutely necessary, this section can be eliminated, but methinks it adds
more authority and drama to the conclusion following)

    You've talked at length with FLN officials at the office
in Tunis. . . . You've seen and talked with the Algerian
refugees who pour across Tunisia's frontier. . . . You've
crossed that frontier yourself and spent long days and
nights with the Algerian army.

    You've seen and felt what it's like to hear a 105 ar-
tillery shell land 200 yards away, where you've been sleeping. You know and understand what it's like to take cover
from French bombers and fighters overhead during the day, to
march up to 40 miles in one night, up and down mountains,
through territory alive with French troops.

    You've lived the life of an Algerian soldier . . . of-
ten drinking from the same bucket or rusty tin can as 50
or 100 other men, and six mules. . . . Getting by, sometimes, on only one meal a day, even a green corncob filched
from a field. . . . You've slept on the ground, ground so
alive with insects that you've counted up to 73 bites
on one leg alone, in one night. . . . You know what it's
like to be so exhausted you can fall asleep on a bri-
ar patch. . . . You've seen what it's like to be wounded,
seriously wounded, dying, without drugs or medicine, even
aspirin.

    Above all, you've talked with the Algerians, their
officers and the soldiers. In camp, on the march, under artillery fire, taking cover from French planes, you've talked and asked questions, millions of questions, digging and
probing every waking moment for the facts.

(REPORTER)

And, heading back toward peace, toward home, you find yourself coming to certain conclusions.

First of all, you know now that no matter what you call it — rebellion, or civil war, or undeclared war — this fighting in Algeria is war, all-out war, a bloody, no-quarter war with no holds barred.

(PAGE 2, ENDING — Algerian Report: Conclusions)

Secondly, you've seen with your own eyes that this is hardly a wild, ragged band of outlaws, as the French claim. The Algerians have an army, a uniformed, armed, organized, disciplined army which fights under definite tactical and strategic direction.

And its soldiers are real soldiers, tougher than any you've ever seen, mostly veterans of the French army itself . . . and now, in this terrain, worth up to three to five soldiers of any other army, including the French. Volunteers, their esprit, their morale, is (sic) as high as that of our Marines.

Third, despite continual, relentless probing, there is no evidence here of communist leadership among the Algerians, no evidence of communist arms . . . yet.

There is, however, evidence that the communists have offered arms. So far, the Algerians insist they have turned down this offer. They say they want no part of communism, are well aware of the invisible steel strings attached to any communist offer.

But, if this war drags on and on, and there's still no material or diplomatic help from the West — America in particular — the Algerians warn frankly that they may have to accept arms, and other help, from the communist east.

Fourth, the Algerians get a lot of their help from the Arab nations. Tunisia and Morocco are bases for shipments into Algeria, actively cooperate in every way possible. And that's understatement. Other help comes from Libya, Egypt, Syria, even Southeast Asia.

Fifthly, regardless of French law and over 100 years of history, it's difficult, here on the spot, to go along with the idea that Algeria is an integral part of France, that these people are Frenchmen. Many think and speak French, but these men here are Arabs . . . make no mistake about it.

Also, they are Moslems, and this is a Moslem army, through and through. So far, there is little talk of a Holy War. But, here and there, you hear occasional fanatic talk of a Jee-had, a Holy War . . . an Arab Holy War, or a Holy War waged by a reawakening Islam.

Number Six. These people are absolutely, sincerely convinced, they are fighting for liberation and liberty; absolutely, sincerely convinced they are fighting for a just cause. Not fanatically, as you might suspect from a distance, but devoted in a quiet, determined way unknown among Arabs of the Middle East.

Point Number Seven: The reasons for the fighting are deep-rooted. And the Algerians say quite bluntly, after the price they've paid already — between two and four hundred-thousand civilian deaths alone — they're not prepared to accept any Tunisian or Moroccan-style independence. Bitterness and distrust is so deep now, they declare, that they will not even accept full independence, if it comes from French hands. They insist on full independence recognized by the United Nations, guaranteed by the United Nations.

(PAGE 3, ENDING — Algerian Report: Conclusions)

Point Number Eight: here on the spot, it sounds rather ridiculous to hear Washington statements the United States cannot interfere in this fighting. Every day, the Algerian sees America interfering — in the form of American bullets from American guns, American bombs, including napalm, from American B-26's and B-29's; artillery barrages, devastating barrages, from American 105's and 155's; everything from flame-throwers to American helicopters.

Some Algerians know these arms were sent to France for use in NATO. But they say they've heard no violent protests from Washington against the French diverting these arms to Algeria. And the average Algerian knows only that these arms being used against him are American. Either war (sic), he laughs at non-interference statements out of Washington. And asks, "What is the difference between Algeria, and Hungary?"

Which leads to Point Number Nine: Despite all this, the Algerians are almost pathetically hopeful the United States will, somehow, come to their aid. Here they are, attacked daily by American guns, yet, and yet, they are unashamedly pro-American. It's a fantastic, unbelievable faith, heart against the mind, faith against facts and bullets. And it's the over-riding impression of this whole trip. But, it's being murdered slowly, day by day. Time is running out for America, here in Algeria.

A tenth, and last point: The French may claim all this is a strictly internal affair. But the bulk of her war machine is furnished by America, diverted from the international defense known as NATO. The refugees pouring into Tunisia and Morocco are fast becoming an international problem. All the countries giving aid to Algeria — Tunisia, Morocco, Libya, Egypt, Syria, part of South East Asia — give further international color to the Algerian problem.

And the communist offer of arms, more and more tempting to arms-hungry Algerians fighting Indian-style against a jet-age army, looms more and more ominous on the horizon. Communist participation in this fighting could only mean, at the least, another Korea . . . or, an Arab Holy War from the Atlantic to the Persian Gulf . . . or, at worst, the long dreaded World War III.

In short, the fighting here has been going on three years now, come November. Neither side is giving an inch, or gaining an inch. Neither side will give the other a way out, neither side will accept any kind of compromise. Yet, every day, the situation becomes more international.

To a determinedly neutral observer here on the spot, inside Algeria, it seems obvious that this is a war . . . that it's becoming more international every day . . . that it's time to recognize the Algerian problem AS an international problem, before it becomes an international war.

This is Frank Kearns, reporting from the mountains of Algeria. Now back to CBS News, in New York.

Chronology

·····································

(Compiled from various sources.)

1917   *November 28*: Frank Michael Kearns is born in Gary, Indiana, to parents Michael Joseph Kearns and Mary Ruth Semans Kearns.

1938   *June*: Kearns graduates from West Virginia University with a degree in journalism.

1941   *August 30*: Enlists in the US Army and trains with Miles Copeland for duty in counterintelligence in the European Theater of Operations.

1943   *October 5*: Marries Gwendoline Ethel Shoring in London, England.

1946   *January 12*: Leaves military service as a captain.

1948   Signs with literary agent Bertha Klausner in New York and ghostwrites the international best-seller *Eisenhower Was My Boss* by US WAC Capt. Kay Summersby.

1950   Son Michael is born.

1953   *Summer*: Kearns joins CBS News as a stringer for radio news and moves to Cairo, Egypt.

1954   *May 7*: Dien Bien Phu falls in Indochina.
        June 18: Pierre Mendes-France comes to power in France.
        November 1: All Saints' Day. FLN revolt begins. France sends reinforcements.

1955   *January 25*: Jacques Soustelle appointed governor general of Algeria.
        February 6: Mendes-France falls.
        April 18: FLN invited to Indonesia to attend the Bandung Conference of twenty-nine Third World countries from Africa and Asia.

July 21: Frank Kearns files his first TV news report from Cairo.

August 20: FLN massacres *pieds noirs* at Philippeville.

1956 *January 26*: Guy Mollet succeeds Edgar Faure as prime minister of France.

February 2: Soustelle is replaced by Robert Lacoste.

September 30: FLN bombs the Milk-Bar and Cafeteria; the Battle of Algiers begins.

October 16: A ship from Egypt bearing arms for the FLN is intercepted.

October 22: Ahmed Ben Bella is imprisoned by the French.

November 5: A French-Anglo engagement occurs at Suez.

1957 *January 28*: General solidarity strike begins in Algiers.

May 21: French Socialist Prime Minister Guy Mollet falls.

May 31: FLN massacre at Melouza.

July 2: US Sen. John F. Kennedy supports nationalist Algerians in a speech to the US Senate.

July 11: Frank Kearns and Joe Masraff arrive in Tunisia.

July 24: After many delays, Kearns and Masraff depart Tunis. Their driver tells them, "You will never return; you will die in Algeria!"

August 1: Kearns is now convinced the nationalists are a true army.

August 18: Kearns and Masraff return to Tunis with their story.

August 23: Kearns and Masraff arrive in Rome; the film is shipped to New York. Kearns begins to summarize the trip for his editors and producers.

September 24: The French win the Battle of Algiers.

October 6: CBS News airs *Algeria Aflame* to good reviews.

1958 *April 13*: Kearns's hard-hitting interview with Egypt's President Nasser airs.

April 15: Kearns and Masraff win the George Polk award.

April 29: Kearns and Masraff win the Overseas Press Club award.

September 8: Kearns is offered the staff correspondent position at CBS News with a first-year salary of $11,180.

1962 Frank Kearns is named Africa bureau chief, but is based in London. Algeria gains independence.

1966 *June*: Kearns meets Sara DeMaine, a native of Wales living in London, who also is on vacation in Bermuda. They begin a serious relationship a year later.

1970   *January 21*: Kearns makes his final report—in Nigeria—for CBS News.

1971   *August 16*: Retires from CBS News in Rome and is named one of ten distinguished Benedum professors at West Virginia University in Morgantown, West Virginia, where he teaches classes in journalism. His divorce with Gwen is finalized.

1973   *January 27*: Marries Sara in McLean, Virginia. Eric Severeid is best man.

1976   *February 10*: Frank Kearns is identified during the Church Committee hearings in Washington, DC, as one of two former CBS News employees in the 1950s who had a relationship with the CIA. He vehemently denies it.

1983   *June*: Kearns retires from academic life at West Virginia University and moves for a while to Sardinia, then later to the village of Christleton, England.

1986   *August 1*: Frank Kearns dies at Sloan-Kettering Memorial Cancer Center in New York. Anchorman Dan Rather pays tribute on *The CBS Evening News*.

Notes

....

Epigraph

....

1. Letter from President Dwight D. Eisenhower to Cecil Brown, President of the Overseas Press Club of America, Inc., on March 25, 1958, and published in *Dateline 1958*, Volume Two, Number One, an annual member publication.

Preface

....

The material about the experiences of Frank Kearns in Nigeria's separatist state of Biafra comes from a story on *The CBS Evening News with Walter Cronkite* on January 21, 1970, which I obtained from the Vanderbilt Television News Archive. Additional information came from an on-camera interview with Sara DeMaine Kearns in Morgantown, WV, in 2003.

The information about Kearns's time in Algeria was drawn from his various papers, which are owned by his widow, Sara, and his son, Michael Kearns.

1. From a videotape at the Vanderbilt Television News Archive of *The CBS Evening News with Walter Cronkite*, January 21, 1970 (via satellite).
2. Interview with Sara DeMaine Kearns in 2003 in Morgantown, WV.

1. A Small Office in Cairo

The information about the American lifestyle was drawn from several sources: Stephen J. Whitfield's *The Culture of the Cold War*, David Halberstam's *The Powers That Be*, Martin Mayer's *About Television*, and William Manchester's *The Glory and the Dream*.

For accounts about the Eisenhower Doctrine, Arab Unity, and the Algerian issue, I relied on *Nasser: A Political History* by Robert Stephens, *Nasser* by Anthony Nutting, *Containing Arab Nationalism* by Salim Yaqub, and *Ropes of Sand* by Wilbur Crane Eveland.

The Kearns-Masraff relationship was drawn from my personal recollections of conversations with Frank Kearns and from interviews with individuals who knew the two men, including Sara Kearns, Michael Kearns, George Masraff, Patricia Bernie, Kurt Hoefler, Marvin Kalb, Ralph Paskman, and Sandy Socolow.

1. "The YOU idea in car making" advertisement, p. 41.
2. Business card of Frank Kearns, Columbia Broadcasting System, courtesy of the Kearns Archive belonging to Sara Kearns.
3. "Potent Voice in the Middle East," p. 118.
4. Unsolicited and undated (2007) letter from Van Gordon Sauter to the author.
5. Telephone interviews with Michael Kearns and George Masraff in 2007 and 2006, respectively.
6. Yaqub, p. 66.

2. La Guerre d'Algérie

So much has been written about the Algerian war that it's difficult to narrow down the range of authors who can quickly provide some perspective. I happened to rely primarily on *Politics in North Africa* by Clement Henry Moore, *Journal 1955–1962* by Mouloud Feraoun, *A Savage War of Peace* by Alistair Horne, *The War Without a Name* by John Talbott, *A Diplomatic Revolution* by Matthew Connelly, and *My Battle of Algiers* by Ted Morgan. Some very interesting perspectives were provided by John Super, PhD, during an interview conducted in 2008 for the documentary *Frank Kearns: American Correspondent*.

1. The western territories of North Africa—Morocco, Algeria, and Tunisia—make up the area known as "the land of the setting sun" (Horne, p. 32).
2. Connelly, p. 22.

3. Ibid. p. 69.
4. Morgan, p. 19.
5. Talbott, p. 38.
6. "Foreign News," *Time*, November 15, 1954, p. 23.
7. Horne, p. 105.
8. Ibid.
9. Ibid.
10. Ibid. p. 106.
11. Ibid.
12. Ibid., p. 221.
13. Connelly, pp. 28–29.
14. Morgan, p. 208.
15. Horne, p. 247.

3. A Reporter's Journey to Algeria

Much of the family history and war records of Frank Kearns were drawn from the Frank Kearns Papers, which were made available separately by Sara Kearns and Michael Kearns. In addition, material also was drawn from the Edgar F. Heiskell Papers, which are owned by Heather Heiskell Jones and Family.

A book by Miles Copeland, called *The Game Player*, provided details of some of Kearns's time in the US Army during World War II. In addition, some information about his freelance career was contained in the Bertha Klausner Papers at the University of Wyoming.

1. Register of Marriages, Logan County, WV, signed and witnessed on September 9, 1916.
2. Application for Membership to the National Society of the Daughters of the American Revolution, filed by Ruth's sister Georgia Semans Wilkinson.
3. Diary of Edgar Frank Heiskell Jr., October 5, 1935, p. 23.
4. Résumé vita prepared by Frank Kearns.
5. Stewart, p. 3.
6. Biographical memorandum prepared by Capt. Frank M. Kearns in London, England, on January 2, 1945, p. 1.
7. Ibid.
8. Ibid.
9. Reply message on February 24, 1983, from Frank Kearns to Shirley M. Hartman,

retirement consultant, at the State of West Virginia Teachers Retirement Board in Charleston, WV.

10. Kearns biographical memorandum, p. 1.
11. Copeland, p. 16.
12. Ibid., p. 19.
13. Kearns biographical memorandum, p. 2.
14. Memo from Col. Sumner Waite to Officers at HQ GTWOSA on January 11, 1943.
15. Ibid., p. 2.
16. Memorandum to Headquarters by Maj. Roy F. Atwood, July 16, 1943.
17. Note from Frank Kearns's son, Michael Kearns, to the author, February 2, 2007.
18. Memo from 1st Lt. Frank M. Kearns to Commanding General, ETOUSA, August 1, 1943.
19. Memorandum from F. M. K. to All Officers, October 5, 1943.
20. Signed "Report of Individual Equipment" by 1st Lt. Frank M. Kearns, March 17, 1944 (amended on June 17, 1944).
21. Memorandum from Maj. F. B. Machol to Lt. Col. Lord Rothschild in London, March 21, 1945.
22. Memorandum from 1st Lt. Frank M. Kearns recommending specific CIC training courses, April 18, 1945.
23. Kearns biographical memorandum, p. 1.
24. Ibid., p. 2.
25. Letter to [Frank] Michael Kearns from Jean H. Huber, Trade Book Division of Prentice-Hall, July 29, 1948.
26. *Editor & Publisher*, New York, NY, September 11, 1948 (taken from Luce's Press Clipping Bureau clipping).
27. Memorandum of Agreement between Kay Summersby and Michael Kearns, signed June 18, 1948, in New York City.
28. Letter from George T. Bye to Frank Kearns, August 6, 1948.
29. Summersby.
30. Letter from Frank Kearns to Bertha Klausner, February 7, 1949.
31. Letter from Frank Kearns to Bertha Klausner, December 14, 1948.
32. Letter from Frank Kearns to Bertha Klausner, January 29, 1949.
33. Ibid.
34. In-person interview with Sara DeMaine Kearns in Morgantown, WV, in 2003.

4. "The Unrealistic or Impossible Assignment"

There is a tremendous amount of information about CBS, William S. Paley, and many of the well-known correspondents and executives from the 1950s and 1960s. A lot of the memoirs were self-centered promotions, particularly those of David Schoenbrun, Don Hewitt, Mike Wallace, and Daniel Schorr. But some respected authors weighed in with helpful information about placing the people and activities in the Kearns era. These included *Prime Time* by Alexander Kendrick, *The Decade That Shaped Television News* by Sig Mickelson, *The Image Empire* by Erik Barnouw, and *The Powers That Be* by David Halberstam.

Personal interviews about Kearns and Masraff proved to be revealing, especially those with Patricia Bernie, Tom Fenton, Sandy Gall, Marvin Kalb, Ralph Paskman, Guy Stewart, and Scotti Williston.

Of course, there were numerous documents that were helpful from the Frank Kearns Papers.

1. Interview with Patricia Bernie, formerly the office manager at the London bureau of CBS News and later the Rome bureau chief, in Beoley, England, on February 1, 2006.
2. Letter of introduction by Wells Church, director of news and public affairs at CBS Radio, on February 3, 1953.
3. Mickelson, p. 151.
4. From the CBS Newsfilm Archives, Assignment 106982.
5. Ibid., p. 164.
6. Mickelson, p. 164.
7. Sig Mickelson archives, University of Texas, Box 4Zd488, p. 41.
8. Mickelson, p. 164.
9. Einstein, p. 781.
10. Whitfield, p. 162.
11. Cloud and Olsen, p. 330.
12. Letter from Ralph Paskman to Frank Kearns, June 28, 1957, p. 1.
13. Ibid.
14. Ibid., p. 2.
15. Letter to Frank Kearns in Cairo from Jack Bush in New York, July 1, 1957, p. 2.
16. DuPont 930 film stock was a widely used, high-speed reversal film in the 1950s. It was favored for its inherently high contrast because it is printed from its own built-in negative, thus the positive output print is really a new generation, and it could withstand high heat and humid conditions.

17. Kodak Tri-X panchromatic negative reversal film was introduced in the mid-1950s. It was the industry standard at the time, providing medium-contrast, black-and-white images with more exposure latitude, meaning it can be "push processed" (up-rated a stop or two) if necessary due to shooting conditions.

18. A Zoomar is a varifocal or zoom lens that was developed in 1945 and adapted for 16-millimeter, professional television use in 1950. It was a highly desirable, breakthrough technology but, according to Rudolph Kingslake in his 1992 book, *Optics in Photography: Measurement and Analysis* (p. 156), such a lens would be "quite large."

19. The source for these paragraphs is a June 28, 1957 letter on CBS News stationary from Ralph Paskman, foreign editor, to Frank Kearns at his residence/office at Flat 44, Badrowi Building, 8 Shariah Salah Ayoub, Zamalek, Cairo, Egypt.

20. Mickelson, p. 129.

5. Algerian Diary

The *Algerian Diary* is written in Kearns's own words. Where necessary, I have provided some notes on locations, expressions, and people in order to bring some clarity for those unfamiliar with Algeria, Tunisia, and the background on the war.

1. Tunis, the capital of Tunisia, serves as a gateway to Africa and the Arab world. It is located on the western side of Lake Tunis. Like Algeria, it was once a French protectorate, but was granted independence some fifteen months before Frank Kearns and Joe Masraff arrived there to stage their clandestine entry into Algeria. Geographically and politically, it provided a safe route for arms suppliers and a sanctuary for Armée de Libération Nationale (ALN) forces, as well as a critical political linkage to France for quiet, behind-the-scenes negotiations between the Algerians and the French. The ALN was the military operational unit of the National Liberation Front (FLN).

2. Cairo, Egypt, was the birthplace of the Arab League. On a daily basis, Radio Cairo transmitted anticolonial propaganda to listeners across North Africa, creating an impression that Egypt was solidly behind the Algerian uprising. It was clear to the French as well as to the aligned countries of North Africa that the support of Egypt was crucial, despite the fact that Egyptian President Gamal Abdel Nasser "gave his word as an officer that no Algerians were receiving military training in Egypt" (Connelly, p. 102).

3. Front de Libération Nationale, or FLN, was officially organized on October 10, 1954, by the so-called "Committee of Twenty-two"—five members of the Comité Révolutionnaire d'Unité et d'Action (CRUA) and seventeen advisers—who

mistakenly believed at the time that the French army had been wiped out in Indochina. This newly formed identity was the result of a meeting over the previous summer by select members of the CRUA (Horne, p. 79).

4. Yousef Masraff, like Frank Kearns, was a part-time employee (stringer) with CBS and served as a cameraman for the network. He was fluent in seven languages and was known to be close to and trusted by Egyptian President Nasser.

5. A long robe worn by men and women in the Middle East.

6. In the last year of his career with CBS News in 1971, Frank Kearns was based in Rome, where Winston Burdett, one of the original "Murrow Boys," was the senior correspondent. Bert Quint was a correspondent there, too, as well as Tom Fenton, who had just been hired from the *Baltimore Sun*. [From interviews with Patricia Bernie and Tom Fenton.]

7. In the 1950s and 1960s, very few airlines traveled the east-to-west corridors of Africa. Nearly all point-to-point travel required connections to be made through Europe, with most African flights originating in London, Paris, and Rome. [From interviews with Patricia Bernie, John Tiffin, Johnny Peters, and Sandy Gall.]

8. The ALN ran a thousand weapons each month, plus other military resources from among the estimated 150,000 heavily armed Algerians living in Tunisia, including teams of trained combatants as large as full battalions, across the frontier between Tunisia and Algeria. So the French built a highly fortified *cordon sanitaire*, known as the Morice Line (named for the French Minister of Defense André Morice), to stop the in-flow. Significant construction was being done when Kearns and Masraff were crossing the border. Running a length of three hundred kilometers, the line of eight-foot-high electric fencing carried five kilowatts of voltage. This was surrounded on both sides by minefields, more barbed wire, intermittent watchtowers, and radar installations that could locate weapons movement and places where the fence was cut. It was completed in September 1957, after Kearns and Masraff had left Algeria. By the end of that year, some eighty thousand troops defended the line. Historian Alistair Horne called it "a remarkable and sinister triumph of military technology . . . where no one could hope to cross it undetected" (Horne, pp. 230, 248, 264).

9. The Aures Mountains, part of the Atlas Mountain Range that separates Algeria and Tunisia, is home to the Berbers of Kabylia, representing the largest Muslim population in the country. Most identify themselves as Arab Berbers, having given up identities that separated them from the rest of their countrymen. Belkacem Krim, one of the leaders of the CRUA, was a native of the region (Horne, pp. 77–78).

10. In contrast to activities surrounding the day for Kearns and Masraff in Tunis, elite French paratroopers wearing red berets and representing some of the 400,000

soldiers committed to the maintenance of Algérie Française, paraded down the Champs-Élysées. They represented, as the *Paris-Presse* reported, the new army struggling "against rebellion and to construct, with the population, a new Algeria" (Talbott, p. 65).

11. In 1955, Tunisian attorney Habib Bourguiba took control of a nationalist government when he returned from exile in Cairo. The power given to him by the French was limited, however. As leader of the Neo-Destour movement, he had been exiled several times going back to the 1930s. When Tunisia finally gained complete independence from France in 1956, Bourguiba became prime minister. A year later, he was the president. From this position, he provided logistical and diplomatic support to the FLN. Although he brought with him into office a significantly different legislative view—legal and education reform, family planning, equal rights for women, etc.— he remained politically pro-West and, surprisingly, pro-France, thus maintaining a French influence throughout the country at the same time he was harboring the Algerians (Horne, pp. 247–50).

12. An idiomatic term meaning "to walk." In this case, Kearns and Masraff spent their day walking around Tunis.

13. According to historian Matthew Connelly, "As long as the ALN avoided clashes with French troops stationed in Tunisia and respected its sovereignty, [President Habib] Bourguiba would help them transport arms from Libya to the Algerian frontier." This became "the lifeline of the ALN." In the four days of July 1957 while Kearns and Masraff were in Tunis awaiting transport into Algeria, approximately sixteen tons of munitions were being transported by the ALN (Connelly, p. 144).

14. During his years as a foreign correspondent, Kearns had become addicted to Nembutal, a barbiturate, known in street slang as "yellow submarines" because of their color and shape. According to his widow, Sara DeMaine Kearns, he started taking the sleep aid as a result of his military experience in World War II because of the many horrible things he witnessed as a counterintelligence officer. Kearns was one of the first soldiers to go inside Dachau, the second German concentration camp liberated by British and American forces. That experience along with his later work as a reporter covering wars, especially in the Congo, caused him nightmares for the rest of his life.

15. By the time Kearns and Masraff left North Africa, the official tally showed that approximately 46,000 refugees lived in camps in Tunisia, bringing to this conflict the spotlight of international attention and aid from the United Nations. Still considering them to be a French responsibility, France provided some relief, but most of it came from the International Red Cross and Algerian Red Crescent, even the Soviet Union (Connelly, p. 140).

16. From the Koran, 4:74 (Set 15, Count 38): "Therefore, let those fight in the way of Allah, who sell this world's life for the hereafter; and whoever fights in the way of Allah, then be he slain or be he victorious', We shall grant him a mighty reward" (Shakir, p. 78). In other words, those who observe jihad in the name of Allah and the belief in His word will be admitted to Paradise if he dies.

17. The American-made Thompson submachine gun—a "Chopper" or "Tommy gun"— was valued for its relatively light weight and for its rapid-fire assault capability. It used .45 caliber cartridges, which could deliver over nine hundred rounds per minute. Widely used during World War II, the US Department of Defense replaced it with newer weaponry during the Korean War. Old or excess weapons were given to NATO allies, including France. They were supposed to be used as offensive warfare weaponry, but often showed up outside of Europe, which was of continuing concern to the American government. [From various Internet reports.]

18. Television reporters often lay out stories ahead of time (or even after the fact) to help guide editors in the cutting of the film and voice-overs. This was especially true during the formative years of TV news. The Kearns archives contain several examples of direction and sound-on-film commentary with an outline of filmed shots to accompany the story.

19. The Morice Line actually was set back from the border some thirty to fifty kilometers. The space between the true border and the barricade itself was a dangerous no-man's-land (Connelly, p. 140).

20. The Phoenician city of Carthage with its stirring history was a major center of influence around the Mediterranean Sea in the ancient world. It is a day trip outside of Tunis and is situated along the eastern shore of Lake Tunis. The city was destroyed by the Romans in the Third Punic War. The destruction was so thorough that very little remains (Crowther and Finlay, p. 335).

21. Tunisia was once ruled by a line of beys, or Turkish chieftains (the equivalent in Europe of a Duke) within the Ottoman Empire (ibid., p. 296).

22. One of thirty-eight *caïdats*, or magistrates, in Tunisia when the country gained its independence from France in 1956, Souk el Arba was reorganized into one of the fourteen *wilayats*, or governorates. It is located due west of the capital in the mountains along the northwest border between Tunisia and Algeria. The 1957 edition of the *Encyclopedia Britannica World Atlas* indicates that the population of this 3,050-square-kilometer governorate was 199,270.

23. Ghardimaou is a small town in the Jendouba governorate of Tunisia, located just sixteen kilometers from Algeria. [From composite Internet reports.]

24. For some fifty years, the United States and the Soviet Union competed for political

influence around the world in a so-called Cold War, so a line of questions by Kearns regarding communist influence would be expected. Individual members of the Parti Communiste Algérien (PCA), the Algerian communists, were known to have been absorbed into the FLN but were without party affiliation since the PCA also was aligned with the French communists (Horne, pp. 128, 136). It was France, however, that invoked its defense of NATO's southern flank from the spread of communism as a reason for holding onto its North African presence (Connelly, p. 84).

25. The FLN strategy was to use its relationships with Moscow and Peking to pressure the United States into choosing sides and forcing its ally, France, to let loose its colonial hold on Algeria (Connelly, p. 84).

26. The reference here is probably to the Kabyles, the Berber region in the Aures Mountains, which was the site of early FLN attacks in Algeria.

27. This traditional Scottish song is attributed to Robert Burns and in many cultures is used to signal a passing or farewell, as these troops certainly were doing. [From various Internet reports.]

28. The twin-engine B-26 Marauder, built by the Martin Company, was known variously as the "widow-maker" or "flying coffin" because of a number of early problems with this aircraft. It carried a bomb load of three thousand pounds plus eleven 12.7-millimeter fixed machine guns as part of its armaments. The plane was used for low-level tactical support. [From various Internet reports.]

29. A 105-millimeter howitzer is a World War II–era type of heavy artillery weapon used by a number of armies throughout the world. [From various Internet reports.]

30. The Lockheed P-38 "Lightning" was a World War II fighter used in the Pacific Theater and in the China-Burma Theater for photo reconnaissance as well as bombing runs. It had a box-shaped fuselage. [From various Internet reports.]

31. The Boeing B-29, or "Superfortress," was a so-called heavy bomber and was among the largest planes used in World War II. Designed primarily for high-altitude missions, it was used by the French in Algeria for low-altitude bombings and reconnaissance. [From Internet reports.]

32. A sirocco is a desert wind, or *qibli*, blowing off the Sahara in North Africa, which can reach up to hurricane-force wind speeds.

33. The longest, most intense fighting by the French Expeditionary Corps in the Indochinese war took place in the spring of 1954 at Dien Bien Phu, resulting in a massive defeat and the collapse of French colonial expansion in Southeast Asia.

34. The French Cross of War was bestowed on foreign fighters who were allied with France during the two world wars.

35. The Lee-Enfield rifle was the standard carbine weapon used by fighting forces of the British during the two world wars. It was a bolt-action, repeating rifle that enabled users to fire off its .303 cartridges at a rate of up to fifteen rounds per minute. [From various Internet reports.]

36. Duvivier is a small valley town in the Aures Mountains not far from the Mediterranean coast. In the 1950s, it was one of many stops along a 4,375-kilometer railroad system that crossed Algeria from the Moroccan border in the west to the Tunisian border on the eastern side of the country. [From various Internet reports.]

37. In this case, the farmer's land consisted of some fifteen thousand square meters, or slightly more than thirty-seven acres. [From various Internet reports.]

38. Bernarr Mcfadden (b. Bernard McFadden) was a turn-of-the-century promoter of alternative health and wellness, which he called "kinesetherapy," and later a maverick publisher of pulp magazines and tabloid journalism. He died in New York at age eighty-seven on October 7, 1955, less than two years before Kearns and Masraff journeyed into Algeria. [From various Internet reports.]

39. Kearns is referring to the "sirocco," or intense Mediterranean winds that sweep across North Africa from the Sahara desert (Op. cit., p. 47).

40. Named for the sound it made when fired, an ack-ack gun is a light antiaircraft weapon used for defensive purposes.

41. A *dou'ar* is an encampment of Arab tents laid out along "streets," representing a small village. [From various Internet reports.]

42. During World War II, Kearns was a senior counterintelligence officer in the US Army. In this role, he had intimate knowledge of such reporting methods and documentations.

43. Internet reports, p. 47.

44. A small town located about eighty kilometers west of the border with Tunis. [From various Internet reports.]

45. Kearns would have been anxious to interview President Bourguiba because of his generally pro-West support. However, in July 1957, Bourguiba wrote in an article for *Foreign Affairs* that nationalists "might be tempted to turn, out of sheer despair, to the Communists," thus trying to force the United States into the fray (Connelly, p. 147).

46. The so-called Red Hand organization was used by the French government to hide many of its more questionable counterterrorism assaults. For example, when a known arms dealer who was doing business with the FLN had his car blown up when he started to drive it, "investigators discovered the imprint of a red hand" (Richelson, p. 255).

47. Kearns is referring the 1956 Revolution in Hungary where the United States remained neutral in order to avoid conflict with the Soviet Union (Connelly, p. 120).

6. "Evidence of Considerable Interest"

A number of helpful documents written by Frank Kearns and Ralph Paskman helped to construct this chapter, as was information from the Frank Kearns Papers owned by Michael Kearns. Especially helpful were unpublished manuscripts, including Kearns's "Facing Danger and Death."

1. Letter from Frank Kearns to his parents, written on October 4, 1957, and received by them ten days later.
2. Ibid.
3. Letter from Frank Kearns in Rome to Ralph Paskman in New York on August 23, 1957.
4. *The CBS Evening News* didn't become a thirty-minute program until Labor Day, 1963.
5. Ibid.
6. Ibid.
7. Kearns's letter to his parents.
8. Ibid.
9. Note from Ralph Paskman to Frank Kearns on October 2, 1957.
10. CBS News release, October 1, 1957.
11. Radio schedule published in the *New York Times* on October 14, 1957, n.p.
12. Telephone interview with Ralph Paskman at his home in North Carolina in 2003, shortly before his death from heart disease.
13. "Focus on Algeria," *Time*, October 21, 1957.
14. From the 1957 Peabody Award Digest of Entry submission, as provided to author/ researcher Clayton Farrington by the Grady College of Journalism and Mass Communications, University of Georgia, Athens, GA.
15. Letter from Eric Severeid to Frank Kearns on October 15, 1957.
16. From the 1957 Peabody Award citation, as provided to the author/researcher Clayton Farrington by the Grady College of Journalism and Mass Communications, University of Georgia, Athens, GA.
17. Letter from Abd-el-Kader Chanderli to Frank Kearns on April 29, 1958.
18. Letter from CBS President Frank Stanton to Frank Kearns in Cairo, July 12, 1958.
19. Letter from David Klinger, director of business affairs at CBS News in New York, to Frank Kearns in Cairo, September 25, 1958.

20. Interview on November 12, 2008, with Scotti Williston, former CBS bureau chief in Cairo.

21. Patricia Bernie interview in 2006.

22. From *CBS Cueline*, an undated, internal CBS information service, p. 1.

23. Morgan, p. 269.

24. "Facing Danger and Death: A Veteran Foreign Correspondent's Straight Answers to Uncomfortable Questions about Danger and Death . . . and Life," an unpublished manuscript written by Frank Kearns while on the faculty of West Virginia University, pp. 6–7.

25. Ibid.

26. *CBS Cueline*, p. 1.

27. Literally the term means "written" or "scripted," but it also can mean "fate," which is Kearns's intent (Feraoun, p. 335).

28. From an unpublished article prepared for *Reader's Digest* "First Person," entitled "The Story of the Southern Cross We Wear," by Frank Kearns.

29. Kearns, "Facing Danger," p. 19.

Epilogue

For information about the CIA-CBS connection and the naming of Frank Kearns as a key player, I relied on reporting by Carl Bernstein and Robert Scherr. In addition, William S. Paley and Sig Mickelson covered this ground in good detail. Further, I benefited from a professional working relationship with another author, Clayton Farrington, who shared some of his research from the Sig Michelson Papers at the University of Texas.

A surprise connection was made with Van Gordon Sauter, a former president of CBS News, who found me and shared what he knew about Yousef Masraff.

1. Copeland, p. 33.

2. Paley, p. 286.

3. Mike Livingston, "For Some Powerful People, D.C. Building A Real Alibi," *Washington Business Journal*, July 12, 2002.

4. Bernstein.

5. Transcription from Box No. 4ZD488 (Mickelson, Sig Papers), folder titled "Oral History Interview of Sig Mickelson conducted by Elizabeth Heighton, Broadcast Pioneers Library, San Diego State University, March 13, 1979" originally transcribed

April 9, 1979, at 10:35 a.m. by Clay Farrington, October 25, 2007, at the Center for American History.

6. From Box No. 4ZD489 (Mickelson, Sig Papers), an outline dated July 6, 1994, for a book of reminiscences of early television, which included the Frank Kearns story, p. 4, as provided by Clay Farrington from his research trip to the Center for American History, University of Texas Library, Austin, TX.

7. Telephone interview with Van Gordon Sauter at his home in Idaho, July 2006.

8. Index cards discovered in the Frank Kearns Papers of Sara DeMaine Kearns.

9. Response document prepared by Frank Kearns on May 27, 1977, "in answer to newspaper report Richard Salant says FMK worked with the CIA in 1965."

10. Interview with former Dean Guy Stewart in Morgantown, WV, on July 20, 2004.

11. Fullerton, p. 9.

12. Kearns, "Facing Danger," p. 4.

Glossary

....

Algérie française: The rallying call for residents of Algeria who opposed independence from France.

ALN: The Armée de Libération Nationale was the military wing of the FLN based in Tunisia.

Arab: The ethnic minority in Algeria, living mostly in the metropolitan and coastal areas.

Aures Mountains: A rugged mountain chain that rises up in eastern Algeria, in the area around Constantine.

Berber: The largest non-Arab minority in Algeria, living primarily in the rural, mostly mountainous, area.

CIA: The US Central Intelligence Agency, a centralized intelligence organization that coordinates the country's intelligence activities, grew out of the Office of Strategic Services, which was formed when the United States entered World War II.

Colon: A European settler in Algeria.

CRUA: Comité Révolutionnaire d'Unité et d'Action, or Revolutionary Committee for Unity and Action, which preceded the FLN.

Duvivier: A small valley town in the Aures Mountains near the Mediterranean coast.

emir: Also known as amir, this is the commander of the faithful for the defense of Islam.

évolués: Native Algerians who were educated in France.

FLN: The Front de Libération Nationale (National Liberation Front), which was the nationalist Algerian political movement that was created in 1954.

Fourth Republic: The French government from post–World War II in 1946 until Gen. Charles de Gaulle took over as president in 1959.

jihad: Holy war.

Kabylia: A mountainous region in eastern Algeria between Algiers and Constantine where the Kabyles, or non-Arab ethnic group with their own distinct Berber dialect, live.

mektoub: The translation of this term means "written" or "scripted." It also can mean "fate."

Muslim: Also seen in Kearns's diary as "Moslem," these are Arab Algerians of Islamic faith.

ONI: The US Office of Naval Intelligence is the longest continuously operating intelligence service in the United States.

Philippeville: A medium-sized port town along the northeastern Algerian coast, now known as Skikda, which in 1955 served as a central battle site in the Algerian war.

pied noir: "Black foot," a nickname given by the Arabs to French settlers who arrived wearing black leather shoes, many of whom returned to France after Algeria gained its independence.

Red Hand: An organization used by the French government to hide many of its more questionable counterterrorism assaults.

stringer: A part-time reporter who is paid on a retainer or only for filed reports.

White Hand: A militant, counterterrorism organization operating in Morocco.

Wilayats: A military or administrative region.

Bibliography

....

A Note on Sources

....

While undertaking research on this subject, I utilized personal archives belonging to family members, Sara DeMaine Kearns and Michael Kearns. In each case, these documents of various types were not available in any organized manner and no classification process existed.

Other works, all in English, that I relied upon to develop a contextual understanding of Frank Kearns and his influencers, include but are not limited to the following:

Algeria and North Africa

....

Abdel-Malek, Anouar. *Egypt: Military Society*. Translated by Charles Lam Marmann. New York: Random House, 1968.

Aussaresses, Gen. Paul. *The Battle of the Casbah: Terrorism and Counter-Terrorism in Algeria, 1955–1957*. New York: Enigma Books, 2002.

Connelly, Matthew. *A Diplomatic Revolution: Algeria's Fight for Independence and the Origins of the Post-Cold War Era*. New York: Oxford University Press, 2002.

Crowther, Geoff, and Hugh Finlay. *Morocco, Algeria & Tunisia: A Travel Survival Kit*. Berkeley, CA: Lonely Planet Publications, 1989.

Feraoun, Mouloud. *Journal 1955–1962: Reflections on the French-Algerian War*. Lincoln: University of Nebraska Press, 2000.

Heikal, Mohamed. *The Cairo Documents: The Inside Story of Nasser and His Relationships with World Leaders, Rebels and Statesmen.* Garden City, NY: Doubleday & Company, Inc., 1971.

Horne, Alistair. *A Savage War of Peace: Algeria 1954–1962.* New York: Penguin Books, 1977.

Lucas, W. Scott. *Divided We Stand: Britain, the US and the Suez Crisis.* London: Hodder & Stoughton, 1991.

Moore, Clement Henry. *Politics in North Africa: Algeria, Morocco, and Tunisia.* Boston: Little, Brown and Company, 1970.

Morgan, Ted. *My Battle of Algiers: A Memoir.* New York: HarperCollins, 2005.

Nutting, Anthony. *Nasser.* New York: E. P. Dutton & Co., Inc., 1972.

Schoenbrun, David. *As France Goes.* New York: Harper & Brothers, 1957.

———. *The Three Lives of Charles De Gaulle: A Biography.* New York: Atheneum, 1966.

Shakir, M. H. *Qur'an.* New York: Tahrike Tarsile Qur'an, Inc., 1983.

Stephens, Robert. *Nasser: A Political Biography.* New York: Simon and Schuster, 1971.

Talbott, John. *The War without a Name: France in Algeria 1954–1962.* New York: Alfred A. Knopf, 1980.

Wilford, Hugh. *America's Great Game: The CIA's Secret Arabists and the Shaping of the Modern Middle East.* New York: Basic Books, 2013.

Yaqub, Salim. *Containing Arab Nationalism: The Eisenhower Doctrine and the Middle East.* Chapel Hill and London: The University of North Carolina Press, 2004.

Television, CBS News, and the Cold War

Barnouw, Erik. *The Image Empire: A History of Broadcasting in the United States from 1953,* vol. 3. New York and London: Oxford University Press, 1970.

Bernhard, Nancy E. *U.S. Television News and Cold War Propaganda, 1947–1960.* Cambridge: Cambridge University Press, 1999.

Bluem, A. William. *Documentary in American Television.* New York: Hastings House, 1965.

Boyer, Peter J. *Who Killed CBS?* New York: Random House, 1988.

Cloud, Stanley, and Lynne Olson. *The Murrow Boys: Pioneers on the Front Lines of Broadcast Journalism.* Boston and New York: Mariner Press, 1996

Cronkite, Walter. *A Reporter's Life.* New York: Alfred A. Knopf, 1996.

Edwards, Bob. *Edward R. Murrow and the Birth of Broadcast Journalism.* Hoboken, NJ: John Wiley & Sons, Inc., 2004.

Einstein, Daniel. *Special Edition: A Guide to Network Television Documentary Series and Special News Reports, 1955–1979*. Netuchen, NJ, and London: The Scarecrow Press, Inc., 1987.

Friendly, Fred W. *Due to Circumstances beyond Our Control*. New York: Random House, 1967.

Goldmark, Peter C., with Lee Edson. *Maverick Inventor: My Turbulent Years at CBS*. New York: Saturday Review Press/E. P. Dutton & Co., Inc., 1973.

Halberstam, David. *The Powers That Be*. Urbana and Chicago: University of Illinois Press, 2000.

Hewitt, Don. *Tell Me a Story: Fifty Years and 60 Minutes in Television*. New York: PublicAffairs, 2001.

Kendrick, Alexander. *Prime Time: The Life of Edward R. Murrow*. Boston: Little, Brown, 1969.

Leonard, Bill. *In the Storm of the Eye: A Lifetime at CBS*. New York: G. P. Putnam's, 1987.

Mayer, Martin. *About Television: The Full Story—The People and Places; the Technology, Talent and Money—of the Spectacular Machine That Changed Everyone's Life*. New York: Harper & Row, 1972

Mickelson, Sig. *The Decade That Shaped Television News: CBS in the 1950s*. Westport, CT, and London: Praeger, 1998.

Paper, Lewis J. *Empire: William S. Paley and the Making of CBS*. New York: St. Martin's Press, 1987.

Schoenbrun, David. *On and Off the Air: An Informal History of CBS News*. New York: E. P. Dutton, 1989.

Sperber, A. M. *Murrow: His Life and Times*. New York: Freundlich Books, 1986.

Foreign Correspondence and War Reporting

Knightly, Phillip. *The First Casualty: The War Correspondent as Hero and Myth-Maker from the Crimea to Iraq*. Baltimore, MD, and London: The Johns Hopkins University Press, 2004.

Lewis, Jon E. *The Mammoth Book of War Correspondents*. New York: Carroll & Graf Publishers, Inc., 2001.

Reynolds, Quentin. *A London Diary*. New York: Random House, 1941.

Sheean, Vincent. *An American among the Riffi*. New York and London: The Century Co., 1925.

———. *Personal History*. New York: The Literary Guild, 1934.

Shirer, William L. *Berlin Diary: The Journal of a Foreign Correspondent, 1934–1941*. New York: Alfred A. Knopf, 1941.

Frank Kearns and His Circle

Copeland, Miles. *The Game Player: Confessions of the CIA's Original Political Operative*. London: Aurum Press Ltd., 1989.

Paley, William S. *As It Happened: A Memoir*. Garden City, NY: Doubleday & Company, Inc., 1979.

Smith, Sally Bedell. *In All His Glory: The Life of William S. Paley, the Legendary Tycoon and His Brilliant Circle*. New York: Simon & Schuster, 1990.

World War II, the CIA, and the Cold War

Butcher, Harry C. *My Three Years with Eisenhower: The Personal Diary of Captain Harry C. Butcher, USNR, Naval Aide to General Eisenhower 1942–1945*. New York: Simon & Schuster, 1946.

Richelson, Jeffrey T. *A Century of Spies in the Twentieth Century*. New York: Oxford University Press, 1995.

Smith, R. Harris. *OSS: The Secret History of America's First Central Intelligence Agency*. Berkeley and Los Angeles: University of California Press, 1972.

Summersby, Kay. *Eisenhower Was My Boss*. Edited by Michael Kearns. New York: Prentice-Hall, 1948.

Whitfield, Stephen J. *The Culture of the Cold War* (2nd ed.). Baltimore, MD: The Johns Hopkins University Press, 1996.

Wilford, Hugh. *The Mighty Wurlitzer: How the CIA Played America*. Cambridge, MA: Harvard University Press, 2008.

Other Publications

Kingslake, Rudolf. *Optics in Photography*. Bellingham, WA: SPIE Press, 1992.

Shakir, M. H. *The Holy Koran [Qur'an]*. Translated in 1919. EZReads.net, 2009.

Manuscript and Video Archival Collections

[Used with permission.]

Edgar F. Heiskell Jr. Papers, Heather Heiskell Jones and Family, Charleston, WV

Frank M. Kearns Papers and Archives, Michael Kearns, Rye, NY

Frank M. Kearns Papers and Archives, Sara De Maine Kearns, Warwick, NY

Bertha Klausner Papers, American Heritage Center, University of Wyoming, Laramie, WY

Sig Mickelson Papers, University of Texas Library, Austin, TX

Vanderbilt Television News Archive, Vanderbilt University Libraries, Nashville, TN

Articles

Bernstein, Carl. "The CIA and the Media: How America's Most Powerful News Media Worked Hand in Glove with the Central Intelligence Agency and Why the Church Committee Covered It Up." *Rolling Stone*, October 20, 1977, 61–62. www.carl bernstein.com/magazine_cia_and_media.php.

"Foreign News." *Time*, November 15, 1954, p. 23.

Fullerton, Robert. "A Farewell to Violence." *West Virginia University Magazine*, Fall 1971, p. 9.

Livingstone, Mike. "For Some Powerful People, D.C. Building A Real Alibi." *Washington Business Journal*, July 15, 2002, www.bizjournals.com/washington/stories/2002/07/15/focus10.html.

"Potent Voice in the Middle East." *Broadcasting*, May 5, 1958, p. 118.

Stewart, Bonnie. "The Unstoppable Perley Isaac Reed." *Perley Isaac Reed School of Journalism News Magazine* [West Virginia University, Morgantown, WV] (Summer 2007), p. 3.

"The YOU idea in car making" advertisement. *Dateline 1958*, Overseas Press Club of America annual publication, p. 41.

Selected Periodicals

Cueline (CBS News)

Dateline 1958 (Overseas Press Club of America)

Editor & Publisher
Morgantown (WV) Post
New York Times
Perley Isaac Reed School of Journalism Magazine (West Virginia University)
Rolling Stone
Time
Washington Business Journal
West Virginia University Magazine

Personal Interviews

[* Signifies telephone conversation, email, and/or other written correspondences]

Bernie, Patricia	Bernstein, Carl*
Berridge, Bennielee*	Brizzi, Norma*
Burger, Chester*	Calvert, Diana
Casola, Tony*	Copeland, Lorraine
Copeland, Miles, III*	Esper, George
Farrington, Clayton	Fenton, Thomas
Fotiades, Ann*	Gall, Sandy
Goodrich, Austin	Hawkins, J. Brent
Hoefler, Kurt	Hottelet, Richard C.*
Jenkins, Paul*	Kalb, Marvin
Kearns, Michael	Kearns, Sara DeMaine
Kercheval, Hoppy	Lucas, W. Scott
Masraff, George*	Niebruegge, Kersti*
Paskman, Ralph*	Peters, Johnny
Racies, Larry*	Sauter, Van Gordon
Saxe, Anthea*	Schorr, Daniel*
Shuman, Betty	Socolow, Sanford
Stewart, Guy	Super, John
Tedesco, Kevin*	Tiffin, John
Walls, John*	Watson, Leighton
Williston, Scotti*	

Index

ABC, documentaries on, 27

Abd-al-Qadir al-Jazairi, 7

Ackerman, Varda, 111–12

advertising, 2–3

Africa, 97, 101–2. *See also* Kearns covering stories in, 24, 30; North Africa

"African World War" (Congo), xxii

agriculture: in Algeria, 7–8, 44; French destruction of Algerian farms, 61, 67, 70, 85; French retaliating against Algerian farmers, 64, 80–81

Ahmed, Hocine Ait, 98, *first photo insert*

Ahmed, refugee grandfather, 54–56

airplanes: ALN taking cover from, 72, 80–81; ALN's lack of, 60, 63; French observation from, 58, 62, 65, 81; French shooting from, 66, 80; French using American, 47–48, 54, 62, 66, 85, *second photo insert*; incendiary shells from, 61; Kearns and Masraff hiding equipment from, 79

Algeria, 9; border with Tunisia, 47–48, 76; divided into departments, 59–60, *second photo insert*; first war of independence, 7; flag and national anthem of, 52; France considering French, 9, 73, 102; France sending NATO weapons to, 9, 53, 69–70, 85–86, *second photo insert*; French civilians in, 8, 11, 51, 97–98, 102; French history in, 5, 7–8, 10; French trying to prevent journalists entering, 47; frontier war with Morocco, 98–99; independence of, 11, 97, 102–3; Kearns and Masraff in, xxv, 47, 57–58, 80, 100; Kearns and Masraff's reports from, 88–89, 103–4

Algeria Aflame, xxix, CBS News department, documentary on Algeria by; impact of, 97, 101; Kearns and Masraff's awards for, 95; Kearns in, 94, *first photo insert*; praise for, 94–95; Severeid to anchor, 93; timing of, 93, 101

Algerian National Liberation Front, 95

Algerian war, 97; as actual war, 83, 86; CBS coverage of, 6, 88–92 (*See also Algeria Aflame*); CBS coverage of Algerians' perspective on, xxii, 5, 94; CBS desire to tell full story of, 6, 27, 93–94; difficulty of presenting story of, 89–91; France considering as treason, 9, 33–34; international response to, 13, 86, 92, 101; OAS massacre in, 97–98; US position on, 5, 97, 102–3

Algerians: civilian casualties among, 74–75, 80–81, 85; civilians collaborating with French, 69, 73; civilians supporting ALN, 11, 68–73, 90, *second photo insert*; compared to other Arabs, 45, 69, 84; desperation for independence, 70, 86; faith that US will eventually help them win independence, 69–70, 85–86; fighting

Algerians (*cont.*)
  for French in Indochina, 51, *second photo insert*; French attacks on civilian, 12, 51, 68, 80–81; French civilians and, 51; French treatment of, 72–73, 85; not bitter toward US, 54; as refugees, 37–40, 54–56, 86, 90, *second photo insert*
Algiers, 11, 30
All Saints uprising, 8–10
ALN. *See* Armée de Libéracion Nationale (ALN, National Liberation Army)
Alsace-Lorraine, lost in Franco-Prussian war, 7
Alsations, moving to Algeria, 7–8
America's Great Game: The CIA's Secret Arabists and the Shaping of the Modern Middle East (Wilford), xxiv
anticolonialism, 102
appearance, Kearns's, 17, 24; effects of weight loss, 82, 87, 92
The Arab Tide, 26
Arab unity movement, 5, 26, 102
Arabs, 53; Algerians compared to other, 45, 69, 84; helping Algerians, 84, 102
Armée de Libéracion Nationale (ALN, National Liberation Army). *See also* Front de Libération Nationale (FLN): attacks by, 11, 68, *second photo insert*; civilians and, 64, 70–71; civilians' support for, 69, 75, 90; discipline within, 52, 74; fighting and moving at night, 63, 66–67; Kearns and Masraff's assignment with, xxiv–xxv, 56–57, 81, 93; massacres by, 11–12; numbers kept secret, 60, *second photo insert*; nurses with, 45–46, 77; organization of, 59–60, 68–69, *second photo insert*; outnumbered and outequipped by French, 63–64, *second photo insert*; as real army, 52, 59, 83–84, 89, *second photo insert*; recruits for, 75, *second photo insert*; strengths of, 72, 84, *second photo insert*; tactics of, 67, 68–70, 72; taking care of Kearns and Masraff, 42, 73–74, 79–80, 88, *second photo insert*

Armée de Libéracion Nationale camps, 50, 52, 73, 80; children in, 51, 54, 61, 75, *second photo insert*; Kearns's pride in images captured, 90–91; locations of, 49, 59–61, 65; rough conditions in, 46–47, 49–50, 57, 82, *first photo insert*
Armée de Libéracion Nationale soldiers, 71, *first photo insert*; ages of, 51, 59, *second photo insert*; backgrounds of, 45, 51; casualties among, 58, 74–75, 77; commitment of, 50, 60, 77–78, 84, 89; comradely spirit among, 40, 45–46, 51–52, *second photo insert*; discipline and experience in, 52, 56; escorting Kearns and Masraff, 44, 46–47; faith of, 78, *second photo insert*; greeting Kearns and Masraff, 44–45; Kearns and Masraff talking politics with, 51–53; pay for, 45, 59, 70, *second photo insert*; rough living conditions of, 63, 89, 92; toughness of, 65, 67, 71–72, 84; training for, 40, 59, *second photo insert*; women and, 51–52, 77–78; wounded, 41, 58, 65–67, 83
arms race, Cold War, 3
army, Algerian. *See* Armée de Libéracion Nationale soldiers
Army, US, Kearns in Counterintelligence Corps of, 17–19
artillery, French, 58–62, 64–65, 67, 74, 77
As France Goes (Schoenbrun), 95
As It Happened (Paley), 104
Atlas Mountains, 90

Bandung Conference, 11
Batista y Zaldivar, Ruben Fulgencio, 102
Beirut, Lebanon, 96
Ben Bella, Ahmed, 11, 98, 100
Ben-Gurion, David, 110
Berbers, casualties among, 12
Bernie, Patricia, 96–97, 112
Bernstein, Carl, 104–5
Bey of Tunisia, 43, 46
Biasetti, Mario, 112
Blair, Jack, 15

Blum, Leon, 8
Blum-Viollette proposal (1936), 8
bombings, 11, 75, 77
Bourguiba, Habib, 46, 82–83
Britain, 11, 22
broadcast news, xxvii. *See also* CBS News; development of, xxvi, xxviii, 2–3; Kearns teaching, 111–12
Bruck, Paul, 25, 95
Burdett, Bob, 15
Burdett, Winston, xxvii
Bush, Jack, 28
Bye, George T., 21

Cairo. *See also* Egypt: CIA operations in, 103; Kearns in, xxviii, 92–93
Cairo new bureau, CBS, xxvi, 4, 23–25, 97
cameramen, 25, 96. *See also* Masraff, Archak Yousef "Joe"
"Captain," ALN, 61–62, 67; brutal march pace of, 65, 72; Kearns and Masraff talking politics with, 51–53; managing Kearns and Masraff's trek, 50, 56, 74
Carthage, Kearns and Masraff visiting, 43
Casbah, ALN bombings in, 11
Castro, Fidel, 102
Catholicism, Kearns abandoning, xxii
The CBS Evening News with Walter Cronkite, 106
CBS News department: accusation of Kearns employed by CIA and, xxi–xxii, 104–6; competing for air time, 25; documentary on Algeria by, 5–6, 92–94 (*See also Algeria Aflame*); early news programs, 2; government agencies and, xxvii–xxviii, 104–5, 109; Kearns and Masraff's Algerian assignment for, xxiv, 42, 50, 79, 89–90; Kearns and Masraff's reports for, 43, 57, 61, 88–92, 95–96; Kearns as legend at, 101, 112; Kearns's career with, xxiii, 23, 42–43, 96, 106, 109–10; ordering more in-depth programs, 26–27; overseas bureaus of, xxvii, 4, 23; reputation of, xxvi,

94–95; Saxe introducing Kearns to, xxix, 22–23; staff of, xxvii, 26, 93
CBS Radio, 26; Algerian reports on, 38, 93; Kearns with, 24–25
CBS Television, 24–25, 27
censorship, French efforts at, 12–13
Chanderli, Abd-el-Kader, 95
Charles X, King (France), 7
chemical warfare, French accused of, 41, 83
Chevalier, Jacques, 10
Child, Julia, 97
China, propaganda films from, 37
Church, Wells, 24
Church Committee. *See* US Senate Select Committee on Intelligence
CIA, 28; CBS relation with, 103–5; Kearns accused of being employed by, 104–8, *first photo insert*; Kearns's relations with, xxiii, xxviii, 103; not confirming or denying involvement with Kearns, 109; Senate Committee investigating, xxvii; use of media, 106, 107–8
"CIA perspective," network news shaped by, xxvii
Cincinnati *Enquirer*, Kearns's job at, 16
civilians. *See under* Algerians; *pied noirs* ("black feet," French settlers raised in Algeria)
Clark, Blair, 93
Claude Worthington Benedum professor, Kearns as, 111–12
Colby, Anita, 21
Cold War, 1, 102; cooperation between journalists and government in, xxvii, 104, 109; news in, xxvi, 3
Collingwood, Charles, xxvii, 4
Collo mountains, 47
The Colonel (FLN leader), 42, 57
colons (French settlers in Algeria), 8, 51, 97–98, 102
communism, xxii, 70; Algerians' lack of interest in, 46, 84, 89, *first photo insert*
Comuntzis, Gus, 15

Congo, xxii

Connelly, Matthew, 8

conservatism, of US politics, 1

consumerism, 1

Copeland, Miles, xxiv, 17, 27–28, 103

Counterintelligence Corps (CIC), Kearns
in, 17–19

Courriere, Yves, 9

Cronkite, Walter, xxvii, 4

Cuba, 102

Cyprus, Kearns's coverage of, 26, 29–30,
95–96

Dachau concentration camp, 19, 39

danger: in Kearns and Masraff's Algerian
assignment, 29–30, 89, 91; in Kearns's
experience covering rebellions, 29–30;
Kearns's weariness of assignments in,
110–11; Masraff and Kearns's close
calls, 5, 81–82, 98–99; of reporting from
Algerian war zone, xxiv–xxv

De Gaulle, Charles, 10

death, Kearns's, xxi, 112

democracy, 70; Arabs' expectations for US
as, 53, 85–86

depression, of Kearns and Masraff, 82

Deuxième Companie (2nd Company), 61

developing countries, US and, xxiii

diary, Kearns's daily, 29, 89; reproduction
of, 31–86

Digest & Review magazine, 20

dogs, 37

dopesheets, for TV film, 40, 88

Douar (mountain region), depopulation
of, 68

Douglas Edwards with the News, 2, 89

Downs, Bill, 4, 105

Dulles, Allen Welsh, 103–6

Dulles, John Foster, 5, 103

economy, US, 1–2

economy Algeria's, 62, 76, 85

editor, Kearns as, 16, 20–22

education, Kearns's, 15–16

Egypt, 53, 97, 102. *See also* Cairo; CIA
operations in, 28, 103; Kearns's contract
to write book about, 24–25; as Soviet ally,
3–4; supporting Algeria's independence,
11–12

Egyptian-Israeli war, 26

Eichelberger, James, 27–28, 103

Eisenhower, Dwight D., xxv, 5, 13; fear of
Soviet influence, 3, 103; Kearns editing
memoir of chauffeur for, 20–22

Eisenhower Doctrine, 3–4, 103

Eisenhower Was My Boss (Summersby),
20–22

El Sadat, Anwar, 109–10

entertainment programs/commercial programs, 3, 24

equipment, Kearns and Masraff's, 34, 45,
57; battery problems with, 52, 76–77,
79; damage to, 91; FLN care for, 42–43,
73–74, *second photo insert*; hand carried,
33, 87; personal luggage left in Tunis
hotel, 42, 44; quantity taken by Kearns
and Masraff, 28–32, 30

ethics, journalistic, 16

Europe, 4, 20, 102; on Algerian issue, xxv,
97

Face the Nation, 26–27, 100; Khrushchev
interviewed on, 27, 95

Fairness Doctrine, FCC's, xxvi

families: of ALN soldiers, 45, 55, 59,
second photo insert; French killing rebels',
37, 51, 55

Faure, Edgar, 10–11

FCC, Fairness Doctrine of, xxvi

Fenton, Tom, 112

5th Company, 68, 77

filming: air reconnaissance and, 79, 80, *second photo insert*; at Algerian civilians, 38,
62–63; of Algerian soldiers, 46, 63, 66–
67, 83; increasing sophistication of, 25;
Kearns writing scripts for sound-on-films,

88–89; Kearns's pride in material captured, 90–91; Masraff processing still photos, 88; Masraff's, in Algeria, 28–29, 42, 87–88; of news programs, 25

finances, Kearns's, 21–22, 24–25, 91, 96, 111

finances, of ALN soldiers, 45, 59, 70, *second photo insert*

firefight, Kearns and Masraff's close call in, 98–99

fires, French starting forest, 61–62, 64, 71, 77

FLN. *See* Front de Libération Nationale (FLN)

foreign correspondents, 104

foreign editor, 5, 87

Foreign Legion, German deserters from, 41

forests, French damage to, 85. *See also* fires, French starting forest

France, 12, 35. *See also colons* (French settlers in Algeria); military, French; on Algerian crisis, xxiv, 12, 92, 102; Algerian crisis and, xxii, 11, 41, 86, 101; CBS presenting perspective on Algerian war, xxv, 27, 90, 93; considering Algeria French, 9, 73, 84, 102; dismissing ALN as not real army, 83–84; domestic turmoil in, 11–12; granting independence to Morocco and Tunisia, 9, 44; history in Algeria, 5, 7–8, 44; losing war in Indochina, 9–10, 102; not considering Algeria struggle a war, 5, 33–34; sending NATO weapons to Algeria, 53, 69–70, 85–86; uprisings against, 8–9, 11; US and, 5, 13, 85–86

Franco-Prussian war (1871), 7

Frank Kearns: American Correspondent (documentary), xxiv, 106

free-lancer, Kearns writing as, 20, 22

French resistance, to Nazis, 8–9, 10, 73

Friendly, Fred, 25

Front de Libération Nationale (FLN), xxv, 45. *See also* Armée de Libéracion Nationale (ALN); assets of, *first photo insert*; commitment of, *first photo insert, second photo insert*; contacts in Tunis, 35–36, 83; diplomatic recognition of, 11; French and, 12–13, 41, 47, 76, 83; goals of, 8–9, 11; headquarters of, 31, 33–34, 40, 47, 82; international support for, 12, 102; Kearns and Masraff's assignment with, 28–29, 32, 46, 50, 94, *first photo insert, second photo insert*; Kearns and Masraff's frustration with delays by, 49, 56–58; Kearns and Masraff's report on, 27, 88–91 (*See also Algeria Aflame*); lack of interest in communism, 46, 84, 87; leaders of, 8–9, 11–12, 37–38, 41–42, *first photo insert*; motives of, 40, 45, *first photo insert*; propaganda by, 12–13, 84; western orientation of, *first photo insert*

Front des Forces Socialistes (FFS, Socialist Forces Front), 98, *first photo insert*

The Game Player (Copeland), 103

gender relations, 45–46, 51–52, 77–78

George Polk Memorial Award, Kearns and Masraff given, 95

Ghomem, Zakaria, 25

ghostwriting, by Kearns, 21

Ginders, Sara DeMaine (wife), 111–12

Goodrich, Austin, 106

government, US: journalists' relationship with, xxvii–xxviii, 104, 109; media's separation from, 3, 26–27; spoon-feeding news stories, xxvi–xxvii

Gross, Robert, 22

Habans, Paul, 93

Harlow, James, 111

health: effects of rough living on, 92; Kearns's illnesses, 41, 78; Masraff's illnesses, 57, 78–79, 87

Heiskell, Ed, 15, 26–27

high-tension poles, ALN sabotaging, 69

Hitchcock, Chip, xxiv

Hottelet, Richard C., 4

Hoyt, Edwin, 93
human interest, Kearns's desire for stories on, 110
Hungary, 26, 102
Hussein, Saddam, 110

imperialism, 46
indigenes (native Algerians). *See* Algerians
Indochina: Algerians fighting for French in, 51, *second photo insert*; French losing war in, 9–10, 102
"Indochine," 2nd Company commanded by, 61, 62, 67
intelligence, ALN's: civilians gathering, 72–73; effectiveness of, 47, 67, 69, *second photo insert*
Intercontinental Ballistic Missile (ICBM) systems, 3
Iraq, US in, 12
Islam, of Algerians, 8, 84, *second photo insert*
Israel, 5, 53

Johnson, Malcolm, 93
Jordan, Key to the Middle East, 26
journalism, xxv–xxvi; importance of, xxvii–xxviii; Kearns's career in, xxviii, 5–6, 15–16, 112; quality of Kearns's, 29–30, 109
journalists, 98. *See also* broadcast news; CBS News; French trying to prevent from entering Algeria, 47; relationship with government, 104–5, 109
Juan Carlos I, King (Spain), 110

Kabylia region, FLN massacres in, 12
Kabylie, FFS in, 98
Kalb, Marvin, xxvii, 97
Kearns, Frank, *first photo insert, second photo insert*
Kearns, Gwendoline Ethel Shoring (wife), 22, 57; divorce of, 110; travel of, 20, 22, 91; wedding of, 18–19

Kearns, Mary Ruth Semans (mother), 14–15, 110–11
Kearns, Michael (son), 91, 103
Kearns, Michael, Frank using as byline, 21
Kearns, Michael Joseph (father), 14–15, 110–11
Kearns, Sara DeMaine (wife), 111–12
Kendrick, Alexander, 4
Kennedy, John F., 13
Kenyatta, Jomo, 110
Khrushchev, Nikita, 27, 95
Klausner, Bertha, 20–21
Korean War, 1
Kuralt, Charles, 110
Kuwait: Middle East Oil Prize, 26

Lacoste, Robert, 11
language, 19; English speaker to accompany trek to mountains, 36, 41; French, 32, 35; Masraff's, 32, 52
"Le Main Blanche" (the White Hand), 10
"Le Main Rouge" (the Red Hand), 10, 83
LeSueur, Larry, xxvii, 4
Libya, 33
Lieutenant, ALN sabotage sections under, 68–69, 78, 81
Littell, Blaine, 93
London, Kearns stationed in, 17–18, 97
Lucas, Scott, 103

Mabrouk, Djebrane, 82
magazines, Kearns writing for, 20, 22
Mahmoud, leading Kearns and Masraff's expedition, 37–38, 44; delays in expedition under, 40–41, 43, 47
Makarios, Mihail, 110
marching: brutal pace of, 33, 48–49, 65; Kearns and Masraff hiking to prepare for, 34–36, 41, *first photo insert*; Kearns finding exhilarating, 46, 48; riding mules *vs.*, 61, 64–65, 71
Markham, George, 25, 93
marriages, Kearns's, 18–19, 110–12

Masraff, Archak Yousef "Joe," 41, *first photo insert*; career of, 96; conversation with God, 99–100; danger in assignments of, 89, 98; death of, 112; equipment issues and, 52, 76–77; FLN assignment and, 27, 28–29, 43, 52, 65, 67, 89; friendship with Kearns, 4, 100; illnesses of, 57, 78–79; Kearns and, xxvi, 4, 25, 106; languages spoken by, 32, 52; postings of, xxvi, 4, 91, 97; preparing film, 87–88; reputation of, 28, 96–97; riding mules, 46, 49; weight loss in mountains, 82, 87

McCarthy, Joseph, 3

McClure, Bill, 25, 112

media. *See also* broadcast news; journalism: CIA's use of, 105–8; FLN's propaganda movie, 33; separation from government, 3, 26–27

medicine: ALN lacking, 65–66, 79; nurses bringing drugs and, 77

Meir, Golda, 110

memoir, Kearns planning, 112

Mendes-France, Pierre, 9–10

Miami Tribune, Kearns's first journalism job at, 15

Mickelson, Sig, 26, 105; Kearns and Masraff meeting with, 95–96; on Kearns's CIA connection, xxviii, 104, 106–8

Mid East Smoke Screen, 26

Middle East, 101; Kearns covering stories in, 24, 30; struggle for influence in, xxii, 102, 103

military, French, 42, 74; accused of chemical warfare, 41, 83; Algerian civilians collaborating with, 69, 73; ALN as veterans of, 51, 59, *second photo insert*; ALN attacks on, 72, 88; ALN intelligence on, 47, 69, 72–73; ALN *vs.*, 33, 64; behavior in war, 11, 55, 85; casualties among, 58, 75; journalists in Algeria and, 47, *first photo insert*; prohibiting Algerian flag and national anthem, 52; retaliating against Algerian farmers, 61, 64, 67; strength

of, *second photo insert*; in Suez crisis, 11; tactics of, 40, 41, 67–68; treatment of Algerian civilians by, 37, 54, 68, 75, 85; troops in Algeria, 33, 60–61, *second photo insert*; in Tunisia, 40, 76; weapons of, 54, 63–64, *second photo insert*

military, US, 109

Milk-Bar and Cafeteria (Casbah), 11

Mollett, Guy, 11–12

Moose International, Kearns writing script for, 22

Morgan, Ted, 9

Morgantown, West Virginia: Kearns growing up in, 14–16; Kearns returning to, 110–12

Morgantown (WV) Post, Kearns's job at, 16

Morocco, 10; Algerian refugees in, 38, 86; Algeria's frontier war with, 98–99; helping Algerians, 12, 84; independence for, 9, 85, 102

Moscow, Kearns's temporary assignment in, 97

Murrow, Edward R., xxvi–xxvii, 4, 25

Murrow Boys, xxvi, 4

Muslims, in Algeria, 8, 12. *See also* Algerians; civilians, Algerian

napalm, French using, 61, 77

Nasser, Gamal Abdel, 4, 106, *first photo insert*; Kearns's interviews with, 25, 109–10; trying to unify Arabs, 26, 102

nationalism, of developing countries, xxiii

NATO: France in, 13, 60; France using weapons from in Algeria, 9, 53, 69–70, 85–86, *second photo insert*

Nazis: French resistance to, 8–10, 73; Kearns arresting war criminals among, 19

NBC, 2, 27

New York, Kearns's temporary assignment in, 97

New York Times, 2

news departments, xxvi, 25–27. *See also* CBS News department

news media, US, 3, 13, 17
Nigeria, xxii, 111
Nixon, Richard, 110
Normandy, Kearns going ashore at, 19
North Africa, 13, 44, 97. *See also* specific
    countries; US position in, 5, 70, 103
Northern Ireland, xxii
nurses, with ALN, 45–46, 77
Nuwar, Ali Au, 25–26

objectivity: CBS instructions for, 29, 42;
    mixed with patriotism, 109
Office of Naval Intelligence (ONI), rumors
    of Kearns's employment by, 105, 107
oil, 26
Ojukwu, Chukwuemeka Odumegwu, 110
Oran, deaths in uprising in, 9
Organisation de 'Armée Secrète (OAS),
    97–98
Overseas Press Club of America, 5, 29–30,
    95

Palestine, refugees from, 38
Paley, William S., 105; CBS relations with
    government under, xxvii–xxviii, 104, 109
Paris, 19, 97
Paskman, Ralph, 5; on *Algiers Aflame*,
    27, 93–94; instructions to Kearns and
    Masraff for Algerian assignment, 28–29;
    Kearns typing up report for, 88–92
Peabody Award for News, CBS given,
    94–95
personality, Kearns's, 16, 24
Peters, Johnny, 25
Philippeville, ALN massacre at, 11
pied noirs ("black feet," French settlers
    raised in Algeria), 8, 11
Pierpont, Robert, 4
political science, Kearns's minor in, 16
politics: conservatism of US, 1; political
    officer giving lecture on FLN, 68
Polk, George, 95
Positano, Kearns family relaxing in, 92

Post-Gazette (Pittsburgh), Kearns's job
    at, 16
Prentice-Hall, 21, 24–25, 105
propaganda, 37; FLN, 12–13, 33, 68
public affairs programming, xxvi, 3
publicity, Kearns's jobs in, 16, 22

Quint, Bert, 112

radio, CBS Radio; broadcast news on, xxvi;
    Kearns writing scripts for, 40
Radio Cairo, *Voice of the Arabs* service
    of, 12
railroads, sabotage of, 47–48, 69
rapes, by French, 55
Rather, Dan, xxi, 101, 112
Ratissage (French encircling operation), 68,
    70, 77, 82
rebellions, Kearns's experience covering,
    29–30
Red Crescent, Algerian, 39
Reed, Perley Isaac, 16
refugees: Algerian, 86, 90, *second photo in-
    sert*; camps in Tunisia, 37–40, *second photo
    insert*; Kearns and Masraff interviewing,
    54–56, 90; Palestinian, 38
religion. *See also* Islam: coexisting in Tunis,
    36; Kearns and Masraff's, xxii, 99–100
Rendezvous magazine, Kearns writing for,
    16–17
Rice, Tim, 111
Rome, 31–32, 87
Rushdi, ALN English speaker, 44, 49
Russia. *See* Soviet Union

sabotage, 19, 47–48, 68–69
Sahara Desert, Kearns and Masraff lost in,
    98–99, *first photo insert*
Salant, Richard, 105, 108
Sardinia, Kearns and wife in, 112
satellites, xxiii, xxviii, 3
Sauter, Van Gordon, 4, 106
Saxe, Edward L.: introducing Kearns to

CBS, xxix, 22–23; at Kearns's wedding, 19; recommending Kearns as editor, 20

Scheer, Robert, 108

Schoenbrun, David, 4, 95; presenting French perspective, xxv, 90, 93

Schorr, Daniel, xxvii, 106

Schwartzkopf, Gerhard, 25

security, Kearns assessing for Counterintelligence Corps, 17–18, 30

See It Now, 20th Century, 95

Seko, Mobutu Sese, 110

Selassie, Haile, 110

Semans (Kearns's grandparents), 14

Semans, Aunt Georgia, 14–15

Sergeant, FLN, 49–50

Severeid, Eric, xxi–xxii, xxvii, 4; anchoring *Algiers Aflame*, 93–94

Shirer, William L., xxvii, 4

Shoring, Elizabeth (mother-in-law), 18

Shoring, Harry (father-in-law), 18

Shuman, Bob, 15

Sinai, Kearns covering fighting in, 30

60 Minutes, 108

Smith, Howard K., xxvii, 4

Smith, Ian Douglas, 110

Souk el Arba, 44

Soustelle, Jacques, 10–11

Southern Cross, importance to Kearns and Masraff, 99–100

Soviet Union: FLN not puppet of, 87; growing influence of, 2–3, 102–3; Kearns's temporary assignment in, 97; offering FLN weapons, 46, 86; staying out of Algerian conflict, 12; US to balance influence of, 3–4

speeches, Kearns writing, 22

spirituality, Kearns's, xxii

spying, Kearns accused of, xxi–xxiii. *See also* CIA

staff correspondent, Kearns promoted to, 96

Stahl, Leslie, 112

Stanton, Frank, 27, 96

Star (Miami Beach), Kearns writing for, 20

Stewart, Guy, 111

storyteller: Kearns as, xxii; Masraff as, 4

strafings, by French, 75, 80–81

strike, in Algiers, 11

stringers: Kearns as, 23, 104; Paskman assignments to, 5, 28–29; pay as, 24–25; working with CIA, 104, 106

Suez crisis, 5, 11, 102, *first photo insert*

Summersby, Kay, 20–22

Sun-Tropics (Miami Beach), Kearns writing for, 16

Swayze, John Cameron, 2

Tagerouine, refugee camp in, 38–40

technology, broadcast news changed by, xxviii

television: becoming national *vs.* local, 2–3; Kearns writing for, 25–26, 40; programming content on, 2–3, 27

This Is New York, 95

Tiffin, John, 25

torture, by French, 11–12, 55

Tripoli, Libya, 33

Trout, Robert, xxvii

truth, CBS instructions for, 42

Tunis: FLN in, 35–36, 83; Kearns and Masraff hiking around to get in shape, 34–36, *first photo insert*; Kearns and Masraff's delays in leaving, 33, 36, 40–41, 43; Kearns and Masraff's leaving for mountains from, 31, 44, 57; Kearns and Masraff's return to, 56–57, 80, 82; weddings outside hotel in, 33–36, 41

Tunisia, 44; Algerian refugees in, 37–40, 86, *second photo insert*; ALN hospitals in, 58, 83; children from ALN camps sent to, 61, *second photo insert*; declared a republic, 46; FLN and, 58, 84, *first photo insert, second photo insert*; French in, 40, 76; independence for, 9, 44, 85, 102; Kearns and Masraff's reports from, 103–4; Kearns and Masraff's return to,

56, 81; no-man's-land between Algeria
and, 47–48

"Underground Press Conference," Masraff
and Kearns covering, 25
unemployment, in Algeria, 10
uniforms: ALN, 40, *second photo insert*;
Arab civilian clothes *vs.*, 44, 62; Kearns
and Masraff agreeing to wear, 33, 94
United Nations, 11; Algerians' expectation
of independence through, xxv, 70, 85;
Emergency Force at Suez Canal, *first photo
insert*; taking up Algerian question, 92, 97
United States, 101–2. *See also* government,
US; Arabs' high expectations for, 53,
69–70, 85–86; developing countries'
relationship with, xxiii, 54; FLN soldiers
questioning policies of, 52–53; ignoring
French use of NATO weapons in Algeria,
9, 85–86, *second photo insert*; point of
view, xxii–xxiii; position on Algeria, 5, 97,
102–3; reluctance to pressure France to
negotiate with Algerians, 5, 53–54; staying out of Algerian conflict, 12, 13, 70
US Senate Select Committee on
Intelligence (Church Committee), xxvii,
106–7

Vafiados, Markos, 95
villages, Algerian, 75, 85, *second photo
insert*
Viollettee, Maurice, 8
Voice of Algeria (for FLN propaganda), 12
Voice of the Arabs (service of Egyptian State
Broadcasting), 12

Wallace, Mike, 108
war criminals, Kearns apprehending, 19
Warren, Earl, 22
Washington, DC, Kearns stationed in, 17
weapons: ALN vastly outequipped by
French, 60, 63–64; ALN's, 9, 34, 54,
58, *second photo insert*; ALN's sources
of, 9–10, 33, 46, 54, 68, 86, 102, *first
photo insert*; ammo captured from
French, 44–45; France using NATO, 9,
53, 85–86; French using American, 48,
53–54, 59, 85–86; Kearns and Masraff
and, 32–34, 94
weather: cold nights, 49, 50, 58; heat from
forest fires, 64, 73; heat of Sirocco winds,
48, 73
West Virginia, Kearns growing up in, 1
West Virginia University, Kearns at, 15–16,
110–12
Wilford, Hugh, xxiv
Williston, Scotti, 96
Wilson, Edward, 110
WMAL-AM, Kearns as news editor at, 20
World War II: broadcast news in, xxvi;
Kearns in, xxii, 17, 30
Wyler, William, 21

Yazid, 66

Zellmer, David, 93

About the Authors

....

GERALD DAVIS is the producer, writer, and director of *Frank Kearns: American Correspondent*, a one-hour documentary film developed by Greenbriar Group Films in association with West Virginia Public Broadcasting. A native of Elkins, West Virginia, Davis earned undergraduate and graduate degrees from the P.I. Reed School of Journalism at West Virginia University, where he was a student of Frank Kearns.

TOM FENTON reported nearly every major European and Middle Eastern story of the day, from the Islamic Revolution in Iran to the collapse of the Soviet Union and the wars in Afghanistan and Iraq, during his career as Senior European Correspondent for CBS News. He is the author of *Bad News: The Decline of Reporting, the Business of News, and the Danger to Us All* and *Junk News: The Failure of the Media in the 21st Century.*